A Practical Guide to Teaching Physical Education in the Secondary School

The new edition of *A Practical Guide to Teaching Physical Education in the Secondary School* provides a wealth of practical activities and materials, underpinned by relevant evidence and theory, designed to support your teaching and learning.

Fully updated with the most recent research and developments in the field, this second edition includes chapters on:

- reflective teaching
- developing your own curriculum
- the use of ICT
- PE in cross-curricular learning
- applying learning theories to your teaching
- managing and promoting behaviour for learning.

Annotated reference and resources sections provide advice about selecting the best resources on the web and elsewhere, and photocopiable resources and materials, also available to download from the Routledge website, offer easy assistance in lesson planning and preparation.

Illustrated throughout with case studies and examples of existing good practice, *A Practical Guide to Teaching Physical Education in the Secondary School* provides a range of tried and tested strategies that will support all student teachers in their development.

A Practical Guide to Teaching Physical Education in the Secondary School, 2nd edition complements *Learning to Teach Physical Education in the Secondary School: A Companion to School Experience*, 3rd edition (edited by Susan Capel and Margaret Whitehead), and can be used to reinforce some of the basic teaching skills covered in that textbook. However, the book can also be used equally successfully on its own, and will be particularly useful for NQTs and students taking school-based initial teacher education routes.

Susan Capel is Professor and Head of the School of Sport and Education at Brunel University, UK.

Peter Breckon is Senior Lecturer in Physical Education at Brunel University, UK.

Routledge Teaching Guides
Series Editors: Susan Capel and Marilyn Leask

These Practical Guides have been designed as companions to **Learning to Teach X Subject in the Secondary School**. For information on the Routledge Teaching Guides series please visit our website at www.routledge.com/education.

A Practical Guide to Teaching Physical Education in the Secondary School

Second edition

Edited by Susan Capel and Peter Breckon

Routledge
Taylor & Francis Group

LONDON AND NEW YORK

Second edition published 2014
by Routledge
2 Park Square, Milton Park, Abingdon, Oxon OX14 4RN

and by Routledge
711 Third Avenue, New York, NY 10017

Routledge is an imprint of the Taylor & Francis Group, an informa business

First edition published by Routledge 2006

British Library Cataloguing in Publication Data
A catalogue record for this book is available from the British Library

Library of Congress Cataloging in Publication Data
A practical guide to teaching physical education in the secondary school / edited by Susan Capel and Peter Breckon. – Second edition.
pages cm
1. Physical education and training–Study and teaching (Secondary) 2. Physical education and training–Curricula. I. Capel, Susan Anne, 1953- II. Breckon, Peter, 1948-
GV361.P58 2013
613.70712--dc23
2013004273

ISBN: 978-0-415-81482-9 (pbk)
ISBN: 978-0-203-06679-9 (ebk)

Typeset in Palatino and Frutiger
by Saxon Graphics Ltd, Derby

Printed in Great Britain by Bell & Bain Ltd, Glasgow

Contents

CONTENTS

Figures

Tables

Contributors

Jackie Arthur is a senior lecturer in physical and coach education in the Faculty of Sport, Media and Creative Arts at the University of St Mark and St John. For further details, please visit: http://www.marjon.ac.uk/aboutmarjon/stafflistandprofiles/name_1569_en.html.

Lerverne Barber is a principal lecturer in physical education in the Institute of Sport and Exercise Science at the University of Worcester. For further details please visit: http://www.worcester.ac.uk/discover/lerverne-barber.html.

Phil Barrett is the physical education coordinator at Bodmin College. He specialises in ICT and emerging technologies that enhance the learning experience for pupils, delivering training for both the YTS and afPE. For further details, please visit: www.handheldlearninginpe.com.

Sophy Bassett is a senior lecturer in physical education at the University of Bedfordshire. For further details, please visit: http://www.beds.ac.uk/howtoapply/departments/physical/staff/sophy-bassett.

Richard Blair is a lecturer in physical education and sports coaching in the School of Sport and Education, Brunel University, London. For further details, please visit: http://www.brunel.ac.uk/sse/education/staff/dr-richard-blair.

Mark Bowler is a senior lecturer in physical education and leads the BA (Hons) Secondary Physical Education (QTS) degree at the University of Bedfordshire. For further details, please visit: http://www.beds.ac.uk/howtoapply/departments/physical/staff/mark-bowler.

Peter Breckon is part-time senior lecturer in physical education at Brunel University. For further details, please visit: http://www.brunel.ac.uk/sse/education/staff/mr-peter-breckon.

Susan Capel is Professor (Physical Education) and Head of School of Sport and Education at Brunel University. For further details, please visit: http://www.brunel.ac.uk/sse/sport-sciences/people/professor-susan-capel.

Anne Chappell is a lecturer in education and physical education, and leads the secondary PGCert physical education course at Brunel University. For further details, please visit http://www.brunel.ac.uk/sse/education/staff/mrs-anne-chappell.

Suzanne Everley co-ordinates the PGCE secondary physical education at the University of Chichester. For further details, please visit http://www.chi.ac.uk/staff/dr-suzanne-everley-0.

Gill Golder is Head of Department (Physical Education and Coaching) in the Faculty of Sport, Media and Creative Arts at the University of St Mark and St John. For further details, please visit: http://www.marjon.ac.uk/aboutmarjon/stafflistandprofiles/name_1571_en.html.

Vanessa Jones is Associate Head of the Institute of Sport and Exercise Science at the University of Worcester. For further details, please visit: http://www.worcester.ac.uk/discover/vanessa-jones.html.

Julia Lawrence is a principal lecturer and staff lead for Initial Teacher Education and Continuing Professional Development at Leeds Metropolitan University. For further details, please visit: http://mediacentre.leedsmet.ac.uk/author/dr-julia-lawrence.

Julia Longville is a senior lecturer in physical education and Programme Director for the MSc Physical Education and Sport Course leader at Cardiff Metropolitan University.

Julie Money is the Deputy Centre Leader for the Centre for Sport, Dance and Outdoor Education at Liverpool John Moores University. For further details, please visit: http://www.ljmu.ac.uk/ECL/122512.htm.

Angela Newton is a principal lecturer in physical education at the University of Bedfordshire. For further details, please visit: http://www.beds.ac.uk/howtoapply/departments/physical/staff/angela-newton.

Andy Theodoulides is a principal lecturer and programme leader for PE and Dance at the University of Brighton. For further details, please visit: http://www.brighton.ac.uk/sasm/about-us/contacting-staff/academic-staff/at129/.

Barbara Walsh is a National Teaching Fellow and Centre Leader for Sport, Dance, Coaching and Outdoor Education at Liverpool John Moores University. For further details, please visit: http://www.ljmu.ac.uk/ECL/122567.htm.

Margaret Whitehead is a physical education consultant and a visiting professor at the University of Bedfordshire. For further details, please visit: www.physical-literacy.org.uk.

Kerry Whitehouse is a senior lecturer and Secondary Subject leader PGCE physical education in the Institute of Sport and Exercise Science at the University of Worcester. For further details, please visit: http://www.worcester.ac.uk/discover/kerry-whitehouse.html.

Andy Wild is currently Head of Continuing Professional Development (CPD) at the University of Chichester, where he manages the Teaching and Learning Academy; the masters level provision within the Education Department; and international CPD. For further details, please visit http://www.chi.ac.uk/staff/andy-wild.

Paula Zwozdiak-Myers is a lecturer in education at Brunel University. For further details, please visit http://www.brunel.ac.uk/sse/education/staff/dr-paula-myers.

Series editors' introduction

This practical work book is part of a series of textbooks for student teachers called the *Routledge Teaching Guides*. It complements and extends the popular generic book entitled *Learning to Teach in the Secondary School: A Companion to School Experience*, as well as the subject-specific book *Learning to Teach Physical Education in the Secondary School*. We anticipate that you will want to use this book in conjunction with these other books.

Teaching is rapidly becoming a more research- and evidence-informed profession. Research and professional evidence about good practice underpins the *Learning to Teach in the Secondary School* series and these practical work books. Both the generic and subject-specific books in the *Learning to Teach in the Secondary School* series provide theoretical, research and professional evidence-based advice and guidance to support you as you focus on developing aspects of your teaching or your pupils' learning as you progress through your initial teacher education course and beyond. Although the generic and subject-specific books include some case studies and tasks to help you consider the issues, the practical application of material is not their major focus. That is the role of this book.

This book aims to reinforce your understanding of aspects of your teaching, support you in aspects of your development as a teacher and your teaching and enable you to analyse your success as a teacher in maximising pupils' learning by focusing on practical applications. The practical activities in this book can be used in a number of ways. Some activities are designed to be undertaken by you individually, others as a joint task in pairs and yet others as group work working with, for example, other student teachers or a school or university-based tutor. Your tutor may use the activities with a group of student teachers. The book has been designed so that you can write directly into it.

In England, you have a range of colleagues to support in your classroom. They also provide an additional resource on which you can draw. In any case, you will, of course, need to draw on additional resources to support your development. Other resources are available on a range of websites, including that for *Learning to Teach in the Secondary School: A Companion to School Experience*, 6th edition (www.routledge.com/cw/Capel), which lists key websites for Scotland, Wales, Northern Ireland and England.

We do hope that this practical work book is useful in supporting your development as a teacher. We welcome feedback which can be incorporated into future editions.

Susan Capel
Marilyn Leask
Series Editors

Introduction

SUSAN CAPEL AND PETER BRECKON

This workbook covers the practical application of a range of topics particularly relevant to teaching physical education. It has been specifically written to be used alongside the textbook, *Learning to Teach Physical Education in the Secondary School: A Companion to School Experience* (3rd edn, 2010) but could equally be used on its own. It is written primarily for student teachers, but should also be valuable to teachers in their early years of teaching. The pattern of teacher education and the context in which it takes place have undergone considerable change in recent years. Today the wide variety of initial teacher education (ITE) opportunities means that some student teachers may be attached to a university with considerable input from university tutors whereas others will be predominately working in a school with most learning being supported by specialist and non-specialist teachers. Further variations in patterns of ITE operate in other countries. This book is designed to prepare physical education teachers working in all these contexts.

The book is divided into four parts:

- Part I 'Knowing your subject', including the nature of the subject, aims and knowing your own views of the subject.
- Part II 'Planning for pupil learning', including long-, medium- and short-term planning, planning for broader aspects of pupils' learning, the use of information and communications technology, the contribution of physical education to cross-curricular learning and health and safety.
- Part III 'Teaching for pupil learning', including theories of learning, creating an effective learning environment, enabling pupils to meet intended learning outcomes, promoting positive pupil behaviour, maximising pupil achievement, assessment of pupils, working with others to support pupil learning and viewing physical education from a different perspective.
- Part IV 'Your own professional learning', including being a reflective practitioner and undertaking action research.

Each chapter includes:

- an introduction setting out the aims and rationale of the chapter;
- objectives which set out what you should know, understand, be able to do after working through the chapter;

- some background information about the specific topic, the research base or professional insights from classroom observations and experience;
- this is supported by a range of practical activities, including some of the following:
  - case studies or scenarios;
  - lesson plans/evaluations;
  - worksheets;
  - reflections on hypothetical, observed or taught lessons;
  - planning how to use material in your teaching;
  - setting a learning activity for pupils;
  - reflective questions;
  - personal audit;
  - further readings and/or links which provide an in-depth reading to supplement the material in this text.

Although the material is divided into Parts and chapters; some similar content is covered in a number of chapters (e.g. intended learning outcomes are covered in a number of chapters). In such cases the content is generally considered from different perspectives and hence the material reinforces that in other chapters. Where similar content is covered in a number of chapters, there is cross-referencing to relevant content in another chapter.

Different terminology is adopted on different ITE courses. The terminology used in this book might not be the same as that used in your ITE situation. In this book, we call school children *pupils* to avoid confusion with *students*, by which we mean people in further and higher education. We refer to those learning to teach as *student teachers*. The important staff in your life are those in school and higher education institution; we have called all these people *tutors*. Another area in which terminology may differ is the use of terms 'objectives' and 'learning outcomes'. In Chapters 1 and 2 you are asked to consider the two terms. On some courses the term 'objectives' is used to identify what pupils will know, understand, be able to do both at the end of the unit of work and lesson plan; on other courses the term 'objectives' is used to identify what pupils will know, understand, be able to do at the end of the unit of work, and the term 'learning outcomes' (sometimes with a word such as intended added) is used to identify what pupils will know, understand, be able to do at the end of a lesson; on other courses the term 'learning outcomes' is used to identify what pupils will know, understand, be able to do at both the end of a unit of work and a lesson. (Sometimes both terms are used in units of work and lesson plan, e.g. the Qualifications and Curriculum Authority (QCA) units use both learning objectives and learning outcomes in their units of work.) In this book, the term 'objective' refers to the intentions that guide the planning of units of work. Intended learning outcomes refer to the steps to achieve objectives and describe what pupils are able to demonstrate at the end of a lesson. You should use the terminology used on your course.

Likewise, different practices are adopted on different ITE courses, including different formats for unit of work and lesson plans. These might be different ways of presenting the same information, but might also require slightly different information. For example, in some plans (and on some courses) lesson learning outcomes are written for the whole class, and achievement of pupils against the learning outcomes forms part of the formative and summative assessment. However, on other plans (and on some courses), it is the learning outcomes themselves that are differentiated to cater for the range of pupils in the class. For example, learning outcomes can be divided into three bands: those that can be achieved by most of the pupils in the class, with different learning outcomes for pupils who cannot achieve those, and additional outcomes for those pupils who need to be extended further. The examples used in this book, and on the accompanying website (www.routledge.com/9780415814829), may be different to the formats you use on your ITE course. We suggest you use these as examples of different ways in which similar information may be presented, then use the format required on your course or select the format most appropriate for your needs.

As this is a workbook designed to support your development as a teacher, it includes many activities which you are asked to complete. These include a number of different approaches, some of which involve you in activities that impinge on other people, for example, observing a teacher in the classroom, or asking for information. In addition, some information may be personal or sensitive, and you need to consider issues of confidentiality and professional behaviour in your inquiries and reporting. If a task requires you to undertake activities that involve others and/or is likely to generate sensitive information, *you must first of all seek permission of the person concerned.* Remember that you are a guest in school(s); you cannot walk into any teacher's classroom to observe.

You can complete most activities individually. The activities can also be used for collaborative work with other student teachers or your tutors. Most of the activities benefit from wider discussion, which we encourage you to do whenever possible. Once you have completed an activity we suggest that you compare your outcomes with those of other student teachers and discuss them both with other student teachers and with your tutor. This way you can reflect on your own responses and identify other potential responses and others' views.

The book has been designed so that you can write directly into it and therefore keep it as a record of your work. However, if an activity asks you to complete a table or figure, a copy of the proforma, table or figure is also included on the website which accompanies the book (www.routledge.com/9780415814829).

We suggest you keep a professional development portfolio (PDP). You can store the tables and figures in your PDP as part of a selective record of your development as a teacher, your strengths as well as areas for further development, hopes for the future, and elements of your emerging personal philosophy of teaching and learning. It is likely that your institution has a set format for a PDP. If not, you should develop your own. You can use any format and include any evidence you think appropriate. However, to be truly beneficial, it should contain evidence beyond the minimum required for your course. This further evidence could include, for example, work of value to you, a response to significant events, extracts from a diary of reflective practice, good lesson plans, evaluations of lessons, teaching reports, observations on you made by teachers, outcomes of activities undertaken, assessed and non-assessed course work. It could also include teaching reports written by teachers, tutors and yourself.

At the end of your course you can use your PDP to evaluate your learning and achievements. It can also be used as the basis for completing applications for your first post and to take to interview. It can form the basis of a personal statement describing aspects of your development as a teacher during your course. Your PDP is something that you can continue to develop throughout your teaching career in order to identify aspects of your work in need of development and thus targets for induction and continuing professional development (CPD) in your first post, then as part of the appraisal process you will be involved with as a teacher.

The book can be used in a number of ways. You should use it alongside your course handbook, which outlines specific course requirements, agreed ways of working, roles and responsibilities and probably activities or observations for you to undertake. It is designed more for you to dip in and out of, to enable you to focus on a specific area for development or foci on your course, for example, rather than for you to read from cover to cover (although you may want to use it in both ways, of course).

This book will not suffice alone; we have attempted to provide you with guidance to further reading by two methods: first, by references to print and web-based material in the text, the details of which appear in the references; second, by further readings and relevant websites at the end of each unit.

There is much educational material on the Internet. Government and the subject association websites are useful. However, there are many others. Useful websites are listed in each chapter in the book. The website which accompanies this text, www.routledge.com/9780415814829, includes further information and links to useful websites. It also contains several chapters from other related books, which support material in this text and which you may have difficulty accessing now. We suggest you keep a record of useful websites in your PDP.

We hope that this practical workbook is useful in supporting your development as a teacher.

Part I

Knowing your subject

Chapter 1   The nature of physical education

MARGARET WHITEHEAD

INTRODUCTION

This chapter is designed to help you clarify your thinking about key aspects of the nature of physical education. It looks at the relationship between aims, objectives and learning outcomes and how aims relate to values and justifications. It also encourages you to think about the difference between physical education and related activities such as sport, as well as alert you to the way aims can be ends in themselves or means to other ends. In essence, this chapter has a philosophical flavour and rather than give you all the answers, it challenges you to reflect on your current thinking and to appreciate that there will always be different opinions about many of the important issues covered here.

By the end of this chapter you should be able to:

- employ the terms 'aim', 'objective' and 'learning outcome' accurately;
- identify the relationship between an 'aim', a 'value' and a 'justification';
- differentiate between key concepts in physical education and sport;
- recognise aims that are ends in themselves and those that are means to other ends.

AIMS, OBJECTIVES AND LEARNING OUTCOMES

It is very important to be clear about the aims underlying physical education and how these relate to units of work and lesson planning. Aims are usually defined as long-term intentions of a subject. The stepping stones to achieve an aim are usually referred to as objectives and are the intentions that guide the planning of units of work. Steps to achieve objectives are usually referred to as learning outcomes and these are written in such a way to describe specifically what pupils are able to demonstrate (see also Whitehead, 2010a; and also Chapters 4, 5 and 13 in this volume).

Activity 1.1a allows you to check that you have grasped both the relationship between these three important terms and the difference between these concepts.

Activity 1.1a

Aims, objectives and learning outcomes

From the list below, identify which is an aim, which is an objective and which is a learning outcome:

- Introduce pair work in simple sports acrobatic balances.
- Show stability in holding a pair balance.
- Develop the body management skill of balancing.

Complete the steps below by adding an objective and a learning outcome:

- Aim – develop co-operative skills.
- Objective –
- Learning outcome –

Complete the steps below by adding an aim and a learning outcome:

- Aim –
- Objective – introduce 5 vs 5 game of hockey.
- Learning outcome –

Complete the steps below by adding an aim and an objective:

- Aim –
- Objective –
- Learning outcome – be able to record the heart rate before and after activity.

AIMS, VALUE AND JUSTIFICATIONS

The previous section looked at aims and how these are broken down in stages and thus impact on the actual nature of the teaching of pupils. The other important aspect of aims is their role in justifying the place of the subject in the curriculum. Rather than putting aims under the microscope as in the section above, this consideration of aims looks outwards at how the subject relates to education as a whole and the place of physical activity in society. It is very important for all teachers of physical education to be able to articulate the value of the aims of the subject and be able to support this value claim with a justification.

Aims are statements of your intended goals. They answer the question, 'Why are you carrying out this practice?' *Values* answer the question, 'What is the point of carrying out this practice?' In other words, a value describes the benefit to be gained from a particular activity. A *justification* responds to the next question, 'Can you persuade me that the value you attribute to the practice is worthwhile?' A justification, therefore, goes a step further and explains why the claimed benefit is desirable. There is further discussion of these concepts in Whitehead (2010a).

For example, one could be asked, 'Why are you catching this train?' The answer could be 'To go to London.' The value question would be, 'What are you going to London for?' The answer could be 'To do Christmas shopping.' The justification question following this could be, 'What is the advantage of going to London if you could do all your shopping in Sheffield?' Your answer could indicate, for example, the amount of choice in London or that the prices are cheaper.

Similar questions in relation to physical education could be:

- Why are you doing physical education? Answer: to promote skilful body management.
- What is the value of promoting skilful body management? Answer: to help pupils to be co-ordinated and be able to control their body.
- Why is this a valuable thing to do? Answer: as humans we need to be able to function effectively physically not only to carry out activities in our daily life with ease but also to give us the opportunity to take part in the wide range of physical activities available in our culture.

Complete Activity 1.1b to check that you have grasped the relationship between an aim, a value and a justification and appreciate the distinctive nature of each concept.

Activity 1.1b

Aims, values and justifications

From the list below, identify which is an aim, which is a value and which is a justification:

- Competition is an integral part of our culture.
- Learn to handle competition.
- To experience and manage winning and losing.

Complete the trio below by adding the value and justification:

- Aim – to develop physical literacy.
- Value –
- Justification –

Complete the trio below by adding the aim and justification:

- Aim –
- Value – to ensure lifelong health and fitness.
- Justification –

Complete the trio below by adding the aim and value:

- Aim –
- Value –
- Justification – imagination and creativity are integral aspects of life and offer the potential to enrich many aspects of work and leisure.

DEFINING TERMS SUCH AS PHYSICAL EDUCATION AND SPORT

One complication in debating aims, values and justifications is that there could be an underlying misunderstanding about the subject under debate. For example, some people find it difficult to differentiate between physical education and sport;

others see both physical education and sport as forms of recreation. How people understand the meaning of a term influences their view of its value. For example, if people think that physical education is simply recreation, they may see no justification for it to be taught in school. If people believe that physical education is simply a vehicle for teaching competitive team games, they will question attention being given to dance in the curriculum. For these reasons, you need to be clear about the meanings of different terms. While everyone else may not agree with you, you need to know and be able to state what you understand by a particular term.

The way terms are used is often differentiated by the following:

- who is taking part;
- what activities are being undertaken;
- where the activity is occurring;
- why the participants are taking part;
- what the purpose of the activity is;
- what the participants are wearing;
- whether participants have to pay to take part.

Activities 1.2a and 1.2b are designed to enable you to answer these questions in relation to a range of terms.

Activity 1.2a

Conceptual analysis

Insert your answers to the first three questions above in relation to the terms listed in the first column of Table 1.1.

Table 1.1 Conceptual analysis

Concept	Who is taking part?	What activities are being undertaken?	Where is the activity occurring?
Physical Education			
Movement Education			
School sport			
Extra-curricular activity			
Sport			
Leisure			
Recreation			

Activity 1.2b

Conceptual analysis continued

Insert your answers to the next four questions above in relation to the terms listed in the first column of Table 1.2.

Table 1.2 Conceptual analysis continued

Concept	Why are people taking part? (optional, compulsory, cultural)	What is the purpose of the activity?	What are people wearing? Have they had to pay to take part?
Physical Education			
Movement Education			
School sport			
Extra-curricular activity			
Sport			
Leisure			
Recreation			

From your answers, create a definition for each of the terms given. As well as discussing with another student teacher or your tutor, it could also be useful to discuss your definitions with someone outside the world of physical education and sport. Having completed this exercise, look up in a range of literature how others have defined these terms and compare these with your thoughts. You can find definitions in numerous publications, such as Department for Education and Employment/Qualifications and Curriculum Authority (DfEE/QCA, 1999) and Department of Education and Science and the Welsh Office (DES/WO, 1991) (see also Chapter 3, Activity 3.1).

It is important to remember that there will never be one specific definition. However, it is critical that you know to what you are referring and can recognise if there are misunderstandings between people.

AIMS OF PHYSICAL EDUCATION: AS ENDS IN THEMSELVES OR MEANS TO OTHER ENDS?

It is important to recognise that there are two types of aims: first, those which are unique to physical education, intrinsic to the subject and see physical education as an end in itself; and, second, those which the subject shares with other aspects of the curriculum, are extrinsic to physical education and use the subject as a means to broader educational goals (see also Whitehead, 2013).

An example of performing an action as an end in itself or as a means to other ends can be given in relation to eating food. One can eat food simply to provide enough energy and nutriment to support your daily lifestyle. In this case, eating is an end in itself. However, if you eat particular foods either to build muscle or stamina or simply for pleasure, the action has an extrinsic purpose beyond enabling you to live your habitual lifestyle. Other actions could also help you to realise these ends. For example, weight training would support muscle development and watching a film could give pleasure.

In the context of physical education, we might claim that the subject promotes language development. This is clearly using physical education as a means to extrinsic ends; certainly ends that can be achieved by other subject areas.

Complete Activity 1.3a to check that you recognise which aims of physical education are ends in themselves and which are means to other ends. It will not be surprising if you are uncertain about the exact nature of each aim listed.

Activity 1.3a

Aims of physical education as ends in themselves or means to other ends

From the list below, identify which aims can be categorised clearly as *ends* for physical education itself, those which are clearly using physical education as a *means* to achieve broader educational goals and those where there might be some *debate* as to whether they are ends- or means-related.

Physical education aims to enable pupils to do the following:

- take initiative;
- develop their own ideas in a creative way;
- become skilful and intelligent performers;
- gain knowledge and understanding of fitness and health;
- refrain from anti-social behaviour;
- develop self-confidence and self-esteem;
- develop skilful body management;
- take part effectively in a range of team games;
- develop perseverance;
- develop positive attitudes to learning;
- develop a range of thinking skills;
- handle competition effectively;
- realise the potential range and scope of their bodily abilities;
- make judgements about their own ability and progress.

There is, currently, no consensus about the main aim of physical education. Some would argue that nurturing the gifted and talented in the area of physical competence is our key aim, while others would identify promoting health and fitness as our priority (Cale and Harris, 2013). The view of some in the profession is that the Sport Education model has much to offer, working towards an aim of all-round personal and social development (Kinchin *et al.*, 2001). A more recent proposal is that the nurturing of physical literacy should be our fundamental aim (Whitehead, 2010b, 2013: Chapter 3). It is valuable to consider where you stand in relation to these four aims and Activity 1.3b is designed to help you with this.

Activity 1.3b

SWOT analysis

Read about and consider where you stand in relation to the four aims identified above, then complete a Strengths, Weaknesses, Opportunities and Threats (SWOT) chart for each activity, see Table 1.3 (a separate SWOT chart for each of the four aims is included on the website (www.routledge.com/9780415814829).

Table 1.3 SWOT analysis

STRENGTHS – advantages	WEAKNESSES – difficulties
OPPORTUNITIES – possible positive outcomes	THREATS – possible negative outcomes

SUMMARY

The aim of this chapter was to help you to understand the relationship between aims, objectives and learning outcomes and between aims, values and justifications. A sound grasp of the first relationship is essential in all aspects of planning, while your ability to argue cogently in support of the values and justifications of physical education will be important throughout your career. Your ability to put the case for physical education will be enhanced if you are clear both about the nature of the terms you are using, and the difference between aims that are ends in themselves and means to other ends. While there is a broad consensus about many of these topics, there will always be a variety of opinions and it is very important that you begin to think through where you stand on these much debated issues.

FURTHER READING

Whitehead, M. (2000) Aims as an issue in physical education, in S. Capel and S. Piotrowski (eds) *Issues in Physical Education*, London: RoutledgeFalmer, pp. 7–21.
This chapter addresses a range of issues in respect of the aims of physical education including the notion of aims as ends in themselves and as means to other ends. There is a brief consideration of the debates surrounding the tensions between promoting excellence or advocating inclusion, and between seeing the process of teaching/learning in physical education as of more significance than the product. In addition, the chapter looks briefly at curricular implications of adopting certain extrinsic aims.

Whitehead, M. (2010a) Aims of PE, in S. Capel and M. Whitehead (eds) *Learning to Teach Physical Education in the Secondary School: A Companion to School Experience*, 3rd edn, London: Routledge, pp. 13–23.
This chapter discusses the aims of physical education in the broader context of the aims of education and looks at the range of aims that have been claimed for the subject. In addition, there is further discussion of aims, values and justifications and of aims as ends in themselves and as means to other ends.

Whitehead, M. (ed.) (2010b) *Physical Literacy: Throughout the Lifecourse*, London: Routledge. This book sets out the definition and philosophical roots of the concept of physical literacy and discusses the implications for physical education of adopting the concept as its fundamental aim.

For articles on physical literacy, see the website www.physical-literacy.org.uk.

Note: all proformas, tables or figures you are asked to complete to help you undertake activities in this chapter are also available on the website which accompanies the book (www.routledge.com/9780415814829).

Chapter 2 How aims and objectives influence teaching

MARGARET WHITEHEAD

INTRODUCTION

The predominant focus of Chapter 1 was to help you to be clear about the nature of aims, objectives and learning outcomes and to understand the relationship between aims, values and justifications. This chapter focuses on one very important aspect of these intentions; their relationship to planning lessons both with respect to the material to be covered and the teaching approaches you might employ (see also Chapters 5 and 13). Aims, objectives and learning outcomes are also key issues in the areas of assessment and evaluation (see Chapter 16). In discussing this relationship, this chapter looks closely at unit of work objectives, being the intentions that are founded on the aims of physical education and guide the intended learning outcomes of lessons.

It is important for you to understand that while physical education has the potential to realise a wide range of intentions, the achievement of these depends wholly on your selection of appropriate content and teaching approaches. Objectives such as developing communication skills will not be achieved automatically through learners' involvement in physical education. The selection of content and teaching approach is critical to the achievement of any objective. For example, if an objective of a physical education unit of work is to develop independence, the content and teaching approaches must be planned to give learners opportunities to be less reliant on the teacher and to take decisions themselves.

By the end of this chapter you should be able to:

- identify content appropriate to realising objectives;
- identify teaching approaches conducive to realising objectives;
- identify the qualities needed for the teacher as a professional;
- recognise personal strengths and areas to be developed in yourself.

Before you read any further, we suggest that you read Whitehead with Blair (2010) which looks broadly at the overall relationship between aims, objectives and intended learning outcomes and teaching.

OBJECTIVES AND CONTENT

Activity 2.1 lists a range of unit objectives, both of physical education as an end in itself and of physical education as a means to achieving other ends such as those related to key skills, thinking skills and the development of citizenship.

Activity 2.1

Achieving objectives

Complete the right-hand column of Table 2.1 indicating which activities/aspects of activities could provide a framework for the objective to be achieved. For example, if an objective was to help learners develop flexibility and resilience, activities such as gymnastics, dance and trampolining would be particularly appropriate, and more specific work on jumps, turns and transitions between two movements could well provide opportunities to achieve this objective.

Table 2.1 Achieving objectives

Objective	Content to achieve objective
Objectives in which physical education is an end in itself • Develop body control, co-ordination and balance • Relate effectively through movement with others, missiles and objects in the environment • Develop strength • Experience the aesthetic aspects of movement	
Personal skills • Setting personal goals • Communication • Independence, decision making • Reasoning, problem solving • Creativity	
Social skills • Contributing to group work, listening, discussing • Sharing responsibility • Taking the lead • Showing empathy towards others • Understanding other cultures	

OBJECTIVES AND TEACHING APPROACHES

Activity 2.2a lists a range of objectives for physical education, again, both those that are ends in themselves and those that are means to other ends. For each objective suggest the teaching approaches you might use to achieve each objective. The suggestions could be broad or very specific. For example, if the objective was to develop creativity, approaches should allow time for learners to explore ideas for themselves rather than be dependent on the teachers' suggestions. More specifically, the teacher should look to praise individuals for innovative ideas.

Activity 2.2a

Teaching approaches to achieve objectives

Against each objective listed identify constituents of teaching and teaching approaches, the use of which could aid learners' achievement:

- Develop physical skills.
- Become an intelligent performer.
- Select compositional ideas, e.g. set a specific task in Dance to create a group composition.
- Evaluate own performance.
- Understand fitness and health.
- Take an initiative.
- Develop positive attitudes to participation in physical activity.
- Handle competition appropriately.
- Take responsibility.
- Develop co-operative skills.
- Develop self-confidence and self-esteem.

Activity 2.2b asks you to start from the 'other end' and consider when it would be appropriate for a teacher to use certain approaches. For example, it would be appropriate for the teacher to use peer teaching if the objective is to begin to develop co-operative skills.

Activity 2.2b

Appropriate use of aspects of teaching to achieve objectives

Against each aspect of teaching/teaching approach below suggest the objective to which you might be working if you employed such an element in your teaching:

- A series of work cards of increasing challenge.
- Recall questions, e.g. at the start of a lesson to remind learners of the work of the previous lesson and to help them to understand the work you have covered.
- Use of visual aids on a work area wall.
- Feedback highlighting effort.
- Highly directed practices.
- Devolution of assessment of self to each learner.
- Peer teaching.
- Learners recording outcomes on paper.
- Grouping decided by the teacher.
- Problem-solving tasks.
- A series of short varied practices.
- Learner demonstration.

THE TEACHER AS A PROFESSIONAL

Chapters 1 and 2 have set out a range of broad principles underpinning your work as a physical education teacher, for example, the key role of aims, the need to be able to articulate the value of the subject and the relationship between aims and objectives and how you plan and structure your teaching. A grasp of these principles is very important as you develop all aspects of your teaching. The next section of the chapter asks you to reflect broadly on the nature of teaching and the skills and qualities needed by all teachers, by physical education teachers and, finally, but most importantly, to reflect on how far, to date, you have mastered these skills and acquired these qualities (see Hoyle and John, 1995; Stenhouse, 1975). Now complete Activity 2.3.

Activity 2.3

The teacher as a professional

Part (a) asks you to list the qualities needed by teachers and then specifically by physical education teachers; part (b) asks you to carry out some self-reflection on your current strengths as a teacher and challenges you to map out some goals for the future. You may want to return to this sheet on a number of occasions. Part (c) challenges you to consider where your priorities lie in relation to the aims of physical education. You may want to return to this task on a number of occasions. It will not be unusual if your priorities change during your initial teacher education.

(a) Teacher as a professional 1

- List the qualities needed in *all* teachers, e.g. patience.
- List the qualities needed in *physical education* teachers.

Compare the similarities and differences in the two lists.

(b) Teacher as a professional 2

Self-analysis. From the lists above, identify:

- aspects of your teaching that are strengths;
- aspects of your teaching that need attention.

How are you going to develop these? Identify your preferred teaching approaches and select other approaches that may need to be developed.

(c) Teacher as a professional 3

Developing your own philosophy about what is important in physical education. From the variety of aims of physical education identified in Chapter 1, select two aims where physical education is an end in itself and two aims where physical education is a means to another end. State the value of each aim selected and support the importance of each value by identifying its justification.

Aim 1 _____

Aim 2 _____

Aim 3 _____

Aim 4 _____

SUMMARY

This chapter was designed to help you to understand the relationship between objectives and the selection of content and teaching approaches used with the learners. This link between intentions and planning and teaching is absolutely critical. Unless teaching is specifically designed to achieve an intended outcome, that goal is very unlikely to be realised. The chapter also asked you to consider the nature of the teacher as a professional and the particular characteristics needed by physical education teachers. An understanding of these issues was used to form a background for you to consider your strengths as a teacher and areas in which you still need to work. The final activity challenged you to begin to formulate your own philosophy of physical education by asking you to list where your priorities lie in respect of aims for the subject.

FURTHER READING

Mosston, M. and Ashworth, S. (2002) *Teaching Physical Education*, 5th edn, San Francisco: Benjamin Cummings.
This is a valuable text looking at approaches to teaching with particular reference to the objectives that can be achieved through using these different teaching methods.

Whitehead, M. with Blair, R. (2010) Designing teaching approaches to achieve intended learning, in S. Capel and M. Whitehead (eds) *Learning to Teach Physical Education in the Secondary School: A Companion to School Experience*, 3rd edn, London: Routledge, pp. 154–67.
This chapter clarifies the concepts of teaching skill, teaching approach, teaching strategy and teaching style and sets out the elements of teaching that make up, a strategy. It also looks at the close relationship between teaching strategies and intended learning outcomes and at a range of classification of strategies.

Whitehead, M. and Woodhouse, J. (2010) Wider role of a PE teacher, in S. Capel and M. Whitehead (eds) *Learning to Teach Physical Education in the Secondary School: A Companion to School Experience*, 3rd edn, London: Routledge, pp. 217–33.
As the chapter title suggests, the focus here is on selecting teaching approaches to make a contribution to the wider aims of education. Key here is that unless the appropriate approach is used, realisation of broader goals will not be achieved.

Note: all proformas, tables or figures you are asked to complete to help you undertake activities in this chapter are also available on the website which accompanies the book (www.routledge.com/9780415814829).

Chapter 3

Understanding your views about physical education and how this impacts on your teaching and pupils' learning

SUSAN CAPEL AND RICHARD BLAIR

INTRODUCTION

As an effective physical education teacher you have a responsibility to translate your knowledge and understanding of the subject into a series of lessons designed to enhance pupils' learning which enables them to progress towards achieving unit objectives. As you learn to teach, you develop the knowledge, skills and understanding to enable you to plan for this intentional learning. However, this does not mean that you will necessarily develop into an effective physical education teacher. Being an effective physical education teacher is much more complex than having relevant knowledge, skills and understanding; it also involves judgement (see, for example, Green and Leask, 2013). Your judgement is based on your values, attitudes and beliefs which influence you in terms of your views on, for example, what pupils should be learning in physical education and how you teach the subject. (Some of these issues are considered and debated in Capel and Blair, 2013; Murdoch and Whitehead, 2013; Whitehead with Blair, 2010).

You do not enter physical education teacher education as a blank canvas (Capel, 2005). Your particular view about what teachers, specifically physical education teachers, do as well as what physical education is (Capel and Blair, 2013) has developed over a long period of time and been shaped by numerous factors. Factors include your background and previous experiences of education generally and physical education specifically, and of sport, in and out of school (generally positive experiences/enjoyment and success in physical education and sport); and who you interact with: your family and friends and their interests, your teachers and coaches, your higher education institution (HEI) and school-based tutors (see, for example, Capel, 2005; Capel and Blair, 2013). As a result, each of you comes to teaching physical education with your own understandings, preconceptions and views about the subject. In turn, these are important influences on what and how you teach in physical education, and hence what your pupils learn. Thus, it is important to recognise that what goes on in the classroom has its roots in your views and values formed both inside and outside the classroom.

This chapter is designed to help you understand your views about physical education and how this impacts on your teaching and pupils learning, with a view to you being able to develop into an effective teacher of physical education.

By the end of this chapter you should be able to:

- be clear about your views about physical education;
- understand the influence of your background on your views about physical education;
- be able to take into account your views to enable you to focus on what and how you teach the subject to enable pupils to achieve the intended learning.

Before continuing, answer the question, 'Why did I become a physical education teacher?' and consider who or what was the main influence in making this decision.

YOUR VIEWS ABOUT PHYSICAL EDUCATION

Let's start by looking at what physical education is. This might, on the surface, seem to be a simple question. After all, doesn't everyone know what physical education is? Don't we all agree? At this stage, your views of the subject might be implicit; you may have just accepted your experiences and hence not thought about or tried to write down what physical education is or indeed what physical education means to you. Activity 3.1 asks you to write down your understanding of what physical education is.

Activity 3.1

Defining physical education

What does the term 'physical education' mean to you? Without looking at any other sources of information, try to write a definition of physical education.

Once you have written your definition, compare your definition with that of other student teachers. What is similar? What is different? Do the definitions cover everything you would want to say about physical education? What does your definition tell you about what you both believe is important/valuable about physical education? Do the definitions tell you anything about the background and prior experiences of the writer of the definition? If so, what?

You might have found trying to write a definition of physical education difficult. You might have found you focused on one aspect of the subject. You might, like many people, have listed a range of activities. You might have found that your definition differed from the definition of others. It is likely that your definition is based on/linked to your different backgrounds and experiences. What is most important to recognise from this exercise is that not everyone agrees what physical education is. It means different things to different people. Chapters 1 and 2 will help you to understand why this might be.

Quite often, though, physical education teachers do not understand or are not clear about what they, or others, mean by the term. Frequently we assume both that we understand what physical education is and that others share a similar view. Activity 3.2 asks you to consider one definition of the subject and compare it to your definition.

Activity 3.2

A definition of physical education

Compare the definition of physical education you wrote for Activity 3.1 with the definition below. What are the similarities and differences? What has and has not been included? What does the definition mean in terms of the content and how physical education is taught?

> Physical Education: Develops pupils' competence and confidence to take part in a range of physical activities that become a central part of their lives both in and out of school. A high quality physical education curriculum enables all pupils to enjoy and succeed in many kinds of physical activities.
>
> They develop a wide range of skills and the ability to use tactics, strategies and compositional ideas to perform successfully. When they are performing, they think about what they are doing, analyse the situation and make decisions. They also reflect on their own and others' performance and find ways to improve them.
>
> (Qualifications and Curriculum Authority (QCA), 2007a)

If you are not explicit about or cannot, or do not, articulate clearly, what you mean by physical education, then you cannot articulate the impact of your views about the subject on your teaching and cannot plan your teaching and, hence, pupils' learning to enable pupils to achieve intended learning (see, for example, Capel and Blair, 2013; Whitehead with Blair, 2010). Thus, it is important that your views about what you mean by physical education are explicit so that you can continually question them and be aware of how they influence you and what you are trying to achieve.

UNDERSTANDING THE INFLUENCE OF YOUR BACKGROUND ON YOUR VIEWS ABOUT PHYSICAL EDUCATION

Having established your current understanding of the subject, it is important to understand how you come to hold these views. What are the factors that influence your views? First, let's return to why you might have defined physical education in the way that you did in Activity 3.1, above. Activity 3.3 is designed to enable you to look at background influences on you and your views of physical education.

Activity 3.3

Your memories of your personal experiences of physical education, physical activity and sport

Use Table 3.1 to help you articulate and explore your own experiences of physical education and sport and how you felt at various times. Respond as honestly and in as much detail as you can to the statements. Feel free to add further thoughts if you wish. Take time to think about how these experiences might have influenced you to date and, in turn, how they might influence your own teaching.

(continued)

Table 3.1 How your experiences of physical education have influenced your views of the subject

Your own experiences. Respond to the statements below.	*Personal experience, how this made you feel and the impact this had on you (e.g. enjoyment, learning)*
Your first memories of participating in physical education at school (primary?)	
Your memories of participating in physical education in secondary school	
How did you become involved in physical activity/sport outside of physical education, either in school or outside school? What activities did you participate in?	
What influence did your family have on you starting and continuing to participate?	
Why do you continue participating?	
Who or what has influenced you the most in continuing (or not) to participate and why?	
Add here any further thoughts about your personal experiences.	
Personal experience (please indicate anyone who was influential, as appropriate)	
Likely impact on views about physical education and on your teaching	
Impact of your experiences on you. Respond to the statements below.	
I was good at physical education/sport so I was encouraged	
I liked physical education at school because …	
I liked participating in sports and other physical activities outside my physical education lessons because …	
Dance and gymnastics were valued as highly as games	
My physical education teachers/lecturers enthused and inspired me	
I was encouraged and enabled to participate in a wide range of physical activities for pleasure	
I was encouraged to try different activities/join a club outside school	
I learnt how to be a confident performer	
My teachers/lecturers used a wide variety of pedagogic approaches (including peer teaching and other active approaches)	
My friends also participate in/are good at physical activity/sport	
I can see the differences between teaching in physical education and coaching of my sports teams/activities	
Add here any further thoughts about the impact of your personal experiences.	

(continued)

After completing Table 3.1 on your own, if possible work through the table with: (1) someone learning to teach another subject; and/or (2) a friend of yours who did not like physical education and/or who does not now participate in any physical activity or sport (to complete this part of the activity, we suggest you download Table 3.1 from the website). After completing the table with them, ask them what their view of physical education is and what, if anything, would have made it a better experience for them. What would encourage them to participate in physical activity/sport now/in the future? Compare their experiences of physical education and consider how their views of physical education might be taken into account in your own teaching of the subject.

Activities 3.4 and 3.5 are designed to help you more explicitly recognise the influence of your school physical education on your views about the subject.

Activity 3.4

Compartmentalisation of the subject

Your experience of physical education at school may have been organised into blocks of learning, e.g. half a term or six weeks. Such compartmentalisation encourages pupils to see learning in 'units' or 'modules' or 'packages'. Also, it may allow teachers to avoid teaching certain activities or using certain approaches. The compartmentalisation is likely to be continued outside the core physical education curriculum. Pupils taking A level choose between Physical Education and Sports Studies. At degree level, students may largely avoid the study of, for example, physical sciences or social sciences (or aspects of these). Think about how different an experience these options will give pupils.

Think back over your own experience of learning physical education. How has your knowledge been compartmentalised? What impact has this had on the content included and not included, and also on the teaching approaches used? How could you explore new connections and expand your sense of the potential of physical education?

Activity 3.5 is designed to enable you to reflect on your views on one aspect of the physical education curriculum: dance.

Activity 3.5

Personal experiences of dance

- What are your views about the position of dance in physical education?
- Make an audit of your own experience of dance.
- What do you remember of dance in the curriculum in your secondary school?
- Did you participate in dance beyond the curriculum? School productions? Theatre visits? Or ...?
- Jot down some thoughts about your own experiences of dance at school. What was it like? Exciting? Challenging? Incomprehensible? Dull?
- How did your teachers make you feel about dance? That it was approachable? That it was distant? That you were free to 'play' with it? That it was to be revered?

(continued)

- How did your teachers set about teaching you dance? Try to remember a range of the pedagogic approaches they adopted.
- What are you hoping to achieve when you teach dance?
- How does this relate to what you are trying to achieve in other areas of the physical education curriculum? How does it differ?
- What kind of dance 'training' have you experienced in preparation for your role as a teacher?
- Reflect carefully on your own teaching approaches and strategies, the ways in which your pupils learn and the range of groups you teach. Extend your reflection to encompass the pressures and demands of external assessment.

Having answered these questions, fill in Table 3.2. What kind of balance results?

Table 3.2 What do I think about teaching dance in my own lessons?

Positive/For	Negative/Against

Then repeat this activity focusing on other areas of activities included in physical education: athletics; games; gymnastics; outdoor and adventurous activities (OAA); swimming. Compare your findings for other areas of activity with those for dance. (The questions and tables are on the website: www.routledge.com/9780415814829.)

Having thought through the formative influences of your own experiences of physical education in school and sport both at school and outside, including at university, it is now important to consider how these have impacted on your views about physical education and about teaching (in general and of the subject).

TAKING INTO ACCOUNT YOUR VIEWS TO ENABLE YOU TO FOCUS ON WHAT AND HOW YOU TEACH THE SUBJECT

You might not think that your definition, your background or your views matter; after all, you are teaching physical education and particularly what is set down in the curriculum which you are following in your school. The National Curriculum is an 'entitlement' document to ensure a range and breadth of content for pupils during compulsory education to the end of Key Stage 4. To see if this is the case, complete Activity 3.6.

Activity 3.6

The curriculum document being used in your school

Obtain a copy of the curriculum document on which physical education in your placement school is based, e.g. the National Curriculum in England. Spend some time looking through the document and consider:

- What are the long-term aims of the physical education curriculum? Are they clearly stated? Do you agree with these?
- How specific is the curriculum in terms of the requirements for teachers to follow and how much are teachers able to decide for themselves both in terms of what content and how they teach?
- Is the balance between different aspects of the curriculum equitable, or do some of these appear to be more important than others?
- How effectively, in your view, do the different aspects of the curriculum relate to one another and how far do they genuinely represent progression through the secondary years?
- How is progression from Key Stage 2 to Key Stage 3 expressed, and what are some of the issues pupils face as they make the transition from primary to secondary school education in physical education?

You may well have many more questions of this type. Think carefully about how the curriculum is deliberately intended to 'shape' pupils' learning in physical education. How does this make you feel? Is it a version of physical education you are happy to teach? How does this match with the answers to the questions in Activity 3.6?

Why is it important to look at the curriculum in relation to your views of physical education? It is likely that by considering the curriculum you will identify areas in which you as a teacher have to make choices. The choices you make are likely to be influenced by your background and what your views of physical education are because these influence what and how you teach. Your personal values and beliefs about the subject have an important role in bringing to life each pupil's experience of school physical education (you may have seen some of this if you have completed Table 3.2 with a student teacher from another subject).

Whether you have worked in schools recently or not, you already have a wide range of pedagogical experience through many years as a learner in physical education at both primary and secondary school, and through sport, both in and out of school. Your personal prior experiences of learning (and perhaps teaching) physical education and sport all have a significant impact on your views about the subject and how you wish to approach the teaching of it (Capel, 2005; Lawson, 1986). They have helped you to establish what you like and dislike about the subject, how you view the relative importance of developing skills and understanding of, for example, games, the role of physical education in contributing to the broader aspects of education, as well as how comfortable you feel about teaching, for example, athletics; dance; games; gymnastics; outdoor and adventurous activities (OAA); swimming. They form a major element of your content knowledge, your pedagogy and your attitudes. In turn, your understanding and views of physical education as a subject and what you want to achieve through teaching it are important in your choice of content and how you teach the subject. In order to understand how you can most effectively work with your pupils, Activity 3.7 is designed to help you understand and clarify your own views about physical education.

Activity 3.7

Your views about teaching physical education

Write down your own views about teaching physical education: what are you trying to achieve? What should the content be? How will you teach it? What is your preferred approach or way of teaching? Why? You might want to look once again at how your background has influenced your views.

Your answers to these questions, in effect, capture the unique experience of physical education pupils will gain by being in your classroom. It is a good idea to make this a formal document to which you return at regular intervals to confirm or modify, if appropriate, in light of your developing experience, or to remind you of the reasons why you wish to teach the subject.

It is important that you adopt a critical perspective as you reflect on the influence of your own experience of being taught physical education; experiences that, in all probability, worked for you (we guess that you are physically quite able and enjoy physical activity/sport) but may not work for others, particularly those who are less physically able. Hence, similar experiences may not be appropriate for all the pupils you are teaching. It is through honest self-reflection that you are able to develop into a teacher committed to inclusive practice which enhances the learning of all your pupils in your lessons. Further, it is also important that you do not espouse one thing but that your practice prioritises another, i.e. it is important that the rhetoric of your practice is matched with the reality of your practice, what you say you do is what you actually do. For example, you espouse developing a positive attitude to physical activity which encourages all pupils to continue with physical activity outside and after they leave school, but your practice focuses on winning inter-school tournaments and competitions and supporting the development of the high ability pupils in your classes by, for example, the curriculum being dominated by games or focusing on competition at the expense of other priorities. Now complete Activities 3.8 and 3.9.

Activity 3.8

Linking your views of physical education to the needs of the pupils you teach

Activities 3.3, 3.4 and 3.7 helped you to make explicit your views about physical education and what impact these might have on your teaching of the subject. You are now asked to think carefully about: the appropriateness of your views to enhancing the learning of all pupils in your lessons; where your views might hinder the learning of all pupils; areas of your own views that may need to be challenged/changed in order to enhance pupils' learning in your lessons. Answer the following questions and add any others you feel appropriate:

- Is the content you prioritise inclusive of a broad range of activities? If not, is it satisfactory to have a view of physical education that excludes one aspect of provision, e.g. dance or OAA?
- Do you prioritise one type of pedagogy? If so, is it desirable to adopt a pedagogy that does not include a range of methods and/or is not inclusive?
- Do you focus on selecting pupils for school teams/competitions within the lesson? If so, is it appropriate to focus on teams/competitions for a few?
- Are your priorities for the subject appropriate for the majority of your pupils? Are they addressing the needs/interests of most pupils? If not, why not?

Activity 3.9

Observing a class

Ask another student teacher or your tutor if you can observe a class they are teaching. Identify two pupils to observe throughout the lesson – neither of whom are of high ability and/or who enjoy physical education. Record their responses to each task the teacher sets and how and what they learn in the lesson. What do they learn in each activity? What do they like/dislike about the lesson? The subject?

SUMMARY

This chapter was designed to help you understand the influence of your own background and experiences on your views about physical education and how these impact on choices about what and how you teach. Even when you are aware of your views, it is important that you work actively and critically to ensure that their influence is supportive and appropriate in developing high quality and inclusive physical education experiences for your pupils. Hence, the chapter also aimed to support you in challenging your views and, if appropriate, to consider changing your approach to enhance the learning of all pupils. We hope that we have supported you to consider how crucial it is that you take time to explore your own beliefs and values and hence your views about physical education in order that you can identify what biases/prejudices you may be subconsciously harbouring.

If nothing else, we hope the chapter has alerted you to the importance of questioning/thinking critically whether your background and experiences and 'what worked for you' is appropriate for all the pupils you teach. What worked for you will not work for all pupils. We strongly believe that if physical education teachers can recognise the influence of their background and experiences, they can improve the quality of their teaching and the experiences and learning of all pupils. This might help us to achieve greater success in encouraging more pupils to continue to participate in physical activity and sport outside and after school. We would therefore encourage you not to plan passively around what and how you were taught or what your tutor does; rather, to question and critically reflect on every experience you have. There is nothing passive about teaching physical education.

Finally, this is not a short-term 'fix' or a one-off consideration. The chapter only provides a brief introduction. Constant checking against your values and beliefs and the rhetoric and reality of practice will be an ongoing challenge throughout your teaching career.

FURTHER READING

The following chapters and articles all provide good background information to help you consider the issues raised in this chapter.

Capel, S. (2007) Moving beyond physical education subject knowledge to develop knowledgeable teachers of the subject, *Curriculum Journal*, 18(4): 493–507.

Capel, S. (2010) Starting out as a PE teacher, in S. Capel and M. Whitehead (eds) *Learning to Teach Physical Education in the Secondary School: A Companion to School Experience*, London: Routledge, pp. 1–12.

Capel, S. and Blair, R. (2013) Why do physical education teachers adopt a particular way of teaching? In S. Capel and M. Whitehead (eds) *Debates in Physical Education*, London: Routledge, pp. 120–39.

Capel, S. and Whitehead, M. (2013) What is physical education? In S. Capel and M. Whitehead (eds) *Debates in Physical Education*, London: Routledge, pp. 3–21.

Green, K. (2000) Exploring the everyday 'philosophies' of physical education teachers from a sociological perspective, *Sport, Education and Society*, 5(2): 109–29.

Murdoch, E. and Whitehead, M. (2013) What should pupils learn in physical education? In S. Capel and M. Whitehead (eds) *Debates in Physical Education*, London: Routledge, pp. 55–73.

Whitehead, M. (2010) Aims of PE, in S. Capel and M. Whitehead (eds) *Learning to Teach Physical Education in the Secondary School: A Companion to School Experience*, London: Routledge, pp. 13–23.

Note: all proformas, tables or figures you are asked to complete to help you undertake activities in this chapter are also available on the website which accompanies the book (www.routledge.com/9780415814829).

Part II   Planning for pupil learning

Chapter 4

Long-term planning

Schemes of work

PETER BRECKON

INTRODUCTION

All the planned experiences which contribute to pupils' learning and development within the context and ethos of the school are generally referred to as the school curriculum. To plan a physical education curriculum effectively, you need to understand the mechanics of planning at three different levels: planning in the long term (schemes of work); planning in the medium term (units of work); and planning in the short term (lesson plans). However, definitions of what constitutes in particular long- and medium-term planning differ, resulting in an interchangeable use of terminology and subsequent confusion over how the physical education experience is or should be planned.

Although it is unlikely that at this stage of your teaching career you will be involved in long-term planning, it is important that you understand how your planning fits into the overall physical education curriculum. In this chapter we consider the influences that shape a school's overall physical education curriculum. In Chapter 5, we consider medium- and short-term planning.

By the end of this chapter you should be able to:

- understand the factors which influence planning in physical education and engage in a critical review of existing planning models;
- understand the constraints on a physical education curriculum and planning issues that result;
- analyse a physical education curriculum and determine the extent to which it presents pupils with a broad and balanced experience and takes account of continuity and progression;
- undertake the long-term planning of a physical education curriculum, taking account of statutory requirements.

Each school has a physical education policy which outlines the aims (the long-term intentions of the subject) and describes the objectives (the stepping stones or means of achieving those aims) of the subject. In writing the policy, staff have considered many factors which have an influence on the physical education curriculum experienced by pupils in the school, including:

- the school's ethos, values and aims;

- the ethos, values and aims of the physical education department;
- the statutory requirement (in England, the National Curriculum for Physical Education (NCPE));
- the wider demands of the National Curriculum;
- the need to provide a broad and balanced curriculum which has both continuity and progression;
- the facilities available.

It is likely that you will bring with you certain philosophies and beliefs about your subject area which influence your views of teaching and learning in physical education (see Chapter 3). These will probably have been shaped to a large extent by the curriculum you experienced as a pupil.

The school's ethos, values and aims

Physical education, like all subjects, has to justify its place in what is seen by many to be an over-crowded curriculum. The value a school places on different subject areas is reflected in the priority and, in particular, the time, given to them.

Activity 4.1

How people in the school view physical education

Record the evidence from the various sources identified in Table 4.1 that give you insights into the value placed on physical education in your placement school and how it might influence the way in which the physical education curriculum is planned.

Table 4.1 How people in the school view physical education

Form of evidence	Summary of findings
Documents, e.g. school's prospectus, notice boards, newsletter, local paper	
Attitude of the head teacher towards physical education	
Attitude of the senior management team towards physical education	
Attitudes of the governors towards physical education	
Community links	
Extent of staff and pupil involvement in extracurricular activities	
Success of school in interschool competitions	

The ethos, values and aims of the physical education department

Another factor often considered significant is the traditions of the school and the expertise and interests of the members of staff. It is quite common for a school to recruit staff with particular expertise in an activity/area of activity in which the school is strong or wishes to develop a strength. Such factors have an influence on both the formal curriculum and the range of extracurricular activities offered. The advantage of this is that the school often develops a reputation in this activity and the enthusiasm of the members of staff has a positive effect on pupils' attitudes. The disadvantage is that there can be an imbalance and pupils miss out on experiencing a variety of contexts. Very often student physical education teachers are able to stimulate an interest in an activity while they are on placement which hopefully can be maintained when they leave the school. Now complete Activity 4.2.

Activity 4.2

Factors which influence the scheme of work in a physical education department

Ask your tutor the questions in Table 4.2 and fill in the Response column.

Table 4.2 Which factors influence the scheme of work in a physical education department?

Question	Response
How is the NCPE interpreted within the department's scheme of work?	
Do personal areas of expertise within the department determine what is included within the scheme?	
How does the scheme of work cater for the needs of different groups of pupils and individuals within those groups?	
How does the department's scheme of work respond to the Key Stage 3 strategy and Learning Across the Curriculum?	
How do available facilities and equipment influence the design of the scheme of work?	
What whole school factors influence the scheme of work?	
What government documents have been utilised to support the planning process and why and how?	
What other resources and sources of support are utilised when devising the department's scheme of work?	

The statutory requirements

Schools are guided to various degrees in what they are expected to teach. Within this context, in England, the National Curriculum and NCPE clearly defines what should underpin planning in physical education. It does this by giving weight to both the content of what pupils should learn and do (product) and how they learn it (the process).

The wider demands of the National Curriculum

Changing demands and new initiatives are influencing what we teach and how we teach it. Many of these place additional demands on the teacher, particularly the need to contribute to pupils' wider education through planned contributions to other aspects of learning (see Chapters 6, 7 and 9).

A broad and balanced curriculum which has both continuity and progression

When the National Curriculum for England was introduced in 1988, one of its explicit aims was to ensure that pupils experience 'a broad and balanced curriculum whilst demonstrating continuity and progression' (DES, 1987: 4). The application of these concepts in terms of the long-term planning in physical education is explored below.

Curriculum breadth and balance

If a school is meeting the requirements of the curriculum in terms of good practice in the range and content of activities they are offering pupils, then they should be providing a broad curriculum.

Having decided *what* to teach, it is necessary to decide *how much time* is to be devoted to each. However, as well as the amount of time devoted to each activity, balance refers to many other aspects of the curriculum, including the balance of planning how learning will take place in the broader dimensions of the curriculum (Chapters 6, 7 and 9). Areas of balance within physical education which may be considered are the balance of competitive and non-competitive/co-operative activities or the balance of individual and team activities. Balance could also be looked at in terms of the demands made upon the body, i.e. the extent to which curriculum planning ensures that over the long term there is a balanced use of the body.

Physical education departments, however, rarely have the luxury of providing totally the curriculum in which they would like to achieve balance. Facilities are one of the constraints. For example, the amount of indoor and outdoor space and availability of facilities such as a swimming pool will affect the range of activities which can be offered in the curriculum. Some facilities become unavailable at various times of the year. For example, large indoor spaces are often used for examinations and drama productions. Similarly, outdoor spaces may become unusable in the winter time. In England, the Office for Standards in Education (Ofsted, 2002: 3) noted that 'one in five schools have inadequate access to specialist accommodation; a lack of indoor work areas, and outdoor play areas with poor drainage and poor standards of maintenance inhibit the programme that schools can offer'. It is important that for long-term planning purposes these constraints are taken into account, for example, by teaching indoor activities when the weather is likely to be inappropriate for teaching outside activities, such as the first half of the spring term.

Ofsted (2002: 3) noted that, 'Although in over half of schools there is a well-planned curriculum, the time allocation still favours games more than other aspects; to some extent this reflects limitations in accommodation, but also teacher preference.' Activities 4.3 and 4.4 ask you to identify the balance of work in the physical education curriculum and then add up the time spent on each activity.

Activity 4.3

The extent of breadth and balance in the physical education curriculum

Using Table 4.3, note all the activities that are taught in the curriculum at Key Stages 3 and 4. Then complete Table 4.4, indicating the total time spent on each area of activity.

Table 4.3 Activities taught in Key Stages 3 and 4

Year	Autumn term		Spring term		Summer term	
	Activity	No. of weeks/ times	Activity	No. of weeks/ times	Activity	No. of weeks/ times
7						
8						
9						
10						
11						

Table 4.4 Total time spent on each area of activity

Area of activity	Hours: Key Stage 3	Hours: Key Stage 4
Athletics		
Dance		
Games		
Gymnastics		
Outdoor and adventurous activities		
Swimming		

Activity 4.4

Balance in the physical education curriculum

Using the data you gathered for Activity 4.3, as well as the school's schemes of work for physical education, complete Table 4.5 in relation to the various dimensions of balance identified above, and then using your findings, complete Table 4.6.

Table 4.5 Dimensions of balance

Question	Detailed answer
Is there a balance of focus on developing skills/performance; planning and applying decisions; evaluating and improving; and other outcomes over the long term?	
Do any of the activities receive a larger proportion of time than others?	
What is the balance of competitive and co-operative activities?	
Is there a balance of individual and team activities?	
Does the curriculum ensure there is a balanced use of the body?	

Table 4.6 Understanding the balance

Question	Answer
What are the reasons for the differences in curriculum balance?	
What is the rationale for choosing the activities offered?	
What are the practical constraints on offering certain areas of activity, e.g. staff expertise or lack of facilities?	

CONTINUITY AND PROGRESSION

In considering long-term planning, it is also necessary to consider curriculum continuity and progression.

Using a dictionary definition of continuity as being a 'consistent line of development without any sharp breaks' Murdoch (2004: 287) considers that learning should be 'one logical, focused, seamless, smooth state of growth or advancement'. The important point is that planning should take account of what has gone before, so that new knowledge, skills and understanding builds on previous learning in a logical sequence.

Progression, on the other hand, concerns the sequencing of the content. It is based on the structures of the subject, with pupils progressing from initial to more mature forms of knowledge, skills and understanding. The concept is, according to Murdoch (2004: 288), 'that learning should take place over an extended period in steady stages that empower the learner to achieve more complex, better things'. Planning for progression is therefore a major aspect of any curriculum development. Effective planning involves carefully and deliberately sequencing the curriculum content and experiences that teachers intend learners to have. These plans should build on previous learning and achievements to promote future learning.

Now complete Activity 4.5 to analyse whether and how much continuity and progression are found within the physical education curriculum.

Activity 4.5

Critically analyse the extent to which continuity and progression exists within the physical education curriculum

Using the school's schemes of work for a Key Stage, look critically at the continuity and progression within one area of activity and complete Table 4.7.

Table 4.7 Continuity and progression

Question	Answer
Is the activity continuous over all years within the Key Stage?	
Does planning of the area of activity over the Key Stage show progression across developing skills/performance; planning and applying decisions; evaluating and improving; and other outcomes?	
Do you feel the amount of time devoted to the activity per unit of work allows progression?	
What changes would you make to ensure better continuity and progression in this area of activity?	

SUMMARY

This chapter has looked at long-term planning in physical education. It has considered many of the factors that govern planning decisions. You have been asked to analyse, challenge and seek justifications for decisions made about the physical education curriculum. In undertaking this process you will have come to the realisation that there are many constraints on the curriculum and that a number of factors prevent us from delivering our ideal curriculum. In Chapter 5, we consider how our long-term plans can be transferred into medium-term unit of work and short-term individual lesson plans.

ACKNOWLEDGEMENT

The author would like to acknowledge the significant input of Cathy Gower to the first edition of this chapter.

FURTHER READING

Cohen, L., Manion, L. and Morrison, K. (2010) *A Guide to Teaching Practice*, 5th edn, London: Routledge.
A major text which is easy to read and considers issues in planning that student teachers need to consider during school placements.

Ellis, V. (2011) *Learning and Teaching in Secondary Schools (Achieving QTS)*, 4th edn, Exeter: Learning Matters.
Chapter 5 of this book provides a useful guide to long-term planning.

Note: all proformas, tables or figures you are asked to complete to help you undertake activities in this chapter are also available on the website which accompanies the book (www.routledge.com/9780415814829).

Chapter 5　Medium- and short-term planning

Units of work and lesson plans

PETER BRECKON

INTRODUCTION

In Chapter 4 we considered influences that shape the overall physical education curriculum of a school and hence pupils' total learning experiences. We also considered the mechanics of long-term planning in physical education. In this chapter we turn our attention to the next two levels of planning: medium and short term, or unit of work and lesson plans. As a student teacher, you have little influence on the long-term planning of the physical education curriculum. However, you are required to be able to plan sequences of lessons and individual lessons in the form of units of work and lesson plans.

By the end of this chapter you should be able to:

- articulate the relationship between medium- and short-term planning in physical education;
- identify a range of factors which need to be taken into account when planning units of work and lesson plans;
- write objectives for units of work and specific and assessable intended learning outcomes and learning activities for lesson plans;
- cater for a range of preferred learning styles in planned learning activities;
- draw on the expertise of experienced teachers to plan effective physical education lessons.

MEDIUM-TERM PLANNING

The long-term overview of learning (the scheme of work) is used to inform the writing of medium-term plans (units of work). Units of work outline expectations for learning for particular groups of pupils and possibly for a particular activity over a specified period of time. In turn, units of work are used to help shape expectations for learning in the short term (lesson plans). Before you begin to plan your unit of work, you need to find out where the sequence of lessons fits into the overall scheme of work for the Key Stage.

There are many different models for planning schemes and units of work and lesson plans in physical education. Many schools use a template similar to the one used in Activity 5.5. This outlines the planned intentions for pupil learning over a period of time, but does not specify the week-by-week content. Prior to the use of such templates, it was common for departments to adopt a unit planning model which described what pupils would learn lesson by lesson or, more realistically in terms of the way in which they were written, what pupils would actually do (e.g. for basketball it might be: week one, passing; week two, dribbling; week three, set shot, etc.). Such an approach to unit planning was criticised for outlining learning in an activity-specific way, thus focusing learning largely on performance-based learning outcomes and failing to meet a broader range of learning outcomes. For example, little attention was generally given to pupils' ability to evaluate and improve performance. Furthermore, units which specify what pupils will do lesson by lesson are not always flexible enough to adjust to learning that has/has not taken place in the previous lesson. Unit planning should take account of prior attainment in order to ensure, as much as is possible, the correct pitch for pupil learning.

Therefore, a unit of work should outline the knowledge, skills and understanding that the teacher intends the pupils to acquire over a set period of time appropriately pitched and taking account of prior attainment, but you should be flexible enough to adjust expectations as you go along in order to take account of the developing needs of the group. Now complete Activity 5.1.

Activity 5.1

Factors which need to be taken into account when planning a unit of work

Make notes on how those factors listed in Table 5.1 that you need to take into account when planning a unit of work have been used to inform planning within a unit of work taken from your placement school's scheme of work. An example has been provided.

Table 5.1 Factors to take into account when planning a unit of work

Title of unit _____	
Factors which need to be taken into account when planning a unit of work	**How does the department take these factors into account in the selected unit?**
What recognition/information is provided of prior learning?	The department holds centrally records of the level pupils have achieved in each area of activity
To what extent do the objectives relate to statutory requirements?	
Do the objectives provide clear criteria to assess pupil learning, identifying aspects of quality expected in pupils' responses?	
How much time is available to teach the unit?	
What resources are required/available to teach the unit?	
How is the work to be assessed?	
What is to be taught later?	
To what extent are broader aspects of pupil learning represented in the unit plan (e.g. language for learning, key skills)?	
Are examples provided of learning activities that could be used?	
What detail is given concerning the teaching strategies to be used, and do these take account of a range of different learning styles?	
What other information is provided that is not included above?	

Writing unit objectives

Without doubt, the most important aspect of writing a unit of work is formulating your intentions for pupils' learning. In this chapter the term objectives is used to describe these intentions. However, other terminology may be used on your initial teacher education (ITE) course. You need to check, and use, the terminology used on your ITE course.

A useful model for planning is one that ensures that objectives (and also intended learning outcomes, see below) include a *verb*, *context* and *quality* to describe what pupils will know, do and understand, the context in which it will be demonstrated, and the quality you will be looking for to assess achievement of the intended learning outcome. Figure 5.1 provides a useful *aide-mémoire* when writing verbs and includes those related to what pupils will know and understand as well as be able to do by the end of a unit (and lesson) (see Gower, 2010, for more detail).

ACQUIRE	DEVELOP	SELECT
KNOW	UNDERSTAND	LINK
CRITICISE	PRIORITISE	COPY
RECOGNISE	ADAPT	MODIFY
PLAN	RESPOND	MANIPULATE
COMPOSE	REACT	DECIDE
OBSERVE	COPY	PREPARE
EVALUATE	RELATE	IMPROVE
PERFORM	ORGANISE	ANALYSE
IDENTIFY	COMBINE	REFLECT
CREATE	NAME	APPRECIATE
EXPRESS	EXPLAIN	COORDINATE
CHANGE	USE	CONTROL
COMMUNICATE	CHOOSE	INTERPRET
APPLY	CONSOLIDATE	ANTICIPATE
EXTEND	DEFINE	JUDGE
DESCRIBE	NAME	DESIGN
REFINE	RECALL	DEVISE
EXTEND	STATE	SUGGEST
SOLVE	RELATE	SHOW
EXPRESS	JUSTIFY	COMMENT
COMPARE	DISTINGUISH	ASSESS
DISCUSS	PREDICT	RESOLVE
CATEGORISE	SUMMARISE	APPRAISE
CONTRAST	DISCRIMINATE	OUTLINE
LIST	LABEL	REPRODUCE
PRESENT	EXTRACT	RECOUNT
EXAMINE	QUESTION	DIAGNOSE

Figure 5.1 Verbs which can be used to write an intended learning outcome

Now complete Activity 5.2.

Activity 5.2

Key words in objectives

Use three different colour highlighter pens to identify the distinct elements of the *verb, context, quality* framework in each unit of work objective below, i.e. pink = verb, yellow = context, blue = quality.

Year 8: Net games unit of work – 12 hours duration

By the end of this unit of work pupils will be able to:

- Demonstrate disguise in a badminton shot using pushing, tapping and whipping type actions which vary the weight, distance, angle and trajectory of the shuttle as it travels in practice and adapted game situation.
- Play a range of different shots on both sides of the body in practice and adapted game situations showing a return to base position, side on body position, efficient use of footwork and balance in preparation, execution and follow-through phases.
- Set up an attack in adapted game situations by moving your opponent out of position, playing on their weaknesses, forcing them to the extremes of the court, limiting their recovery time and sending them the wrong way.
- Win a point in adapted game situations by choosing an appropriate opportunity by exploiting your opponent's weaknesses, placing the shuttle out of reach, reducing time available to get to the shuttle and forcing them to the limits of their technical ability.
- Defend space on your own court and defend against an attack in adapted game situations by covering weak areas on the court, recovering to base position and using shot selection to create time and regain the initiative.
- Use appropriate language from a given set of criteria to describe strengths in both technical and strategic play for a given model of performance.
- Select the best place to observe the performance of a range of shots by a partner in practice and adapted game situations based on the type of shot and the body position required to execute it.
- Analyse own or a partner's response in practices and adapted game situations using a set criteria focusing upon either setting up an attack, defending against an attack or winning the point, defending space, and provide constructive, objective and sensitive feedback using appropriate terminology.
- Explain what they need to do to improve their own fitness level to be a more effective net games player.
- Identify areas of fitness most needed in net games and explain how involvement in these games contributes to their fitness, health and well-being.
- Carry out warm-up and cool-down routines safely.
- Select and incorporate pulse raising, stretching and mobilisation exercises which are suitable for net games.

Now complete Activity 5.3.

Activity 5.3

Writing objectives for a selected unit of work using the *verb*, *context*, *quality* framework

Write the objectives for a unit of work you are going to teaching using the *verb, context, quality* framework. Ensure these objectives do not focus on performance-based outcomes but include a range of different types of outcomes (see also Chapter 16).

Planning learning activities for units of work

Once you have planned your objectives, it is important to plan a range of learning activities which promote learning, such as developing and improving skills in physical activity; planning and applying decisions; evaluating and improving; making healthy, active lifestyle choices. Although this is the approach adopted in one education system, a process model such as this is appropriate to planning in many different contexts. It is also important to ensure that when planning learning activities that learning theory is considered. Learning theory identifies preferences in terms of the way in which we learn. In recent years, accelerated learning (Rose, 1985) has emerged. This is based on theories such as Gardner's (1993) theory of multiple intelligences and Kolb's (1984) theory of experiential learning. Accelerated learning has seen a simplification of such theories to the identification of three main preferred learning styles: visual, auditory and kinaesthetic (VAK). Other learning theories are discussed further in Chapter 11. Part of your professional development involves an exploration of the relationship between theory and practice and thus the understanding of how learning theories can apply to the planning, delivery and assessment of learning experiences in physical education. Now complete Activity 5.4.

Activity 5.4

Mapping learning activities against the statutory requirements and different preferred learning styles

To establish the pitch of a unit of work you are going to teach, take account of pupils' prior learning and the expectations of them in relation to the NCPE level descriptions (QCA, 2007a). Using a range of resources such as text books, websites, DVDs, videos, etc., plan a variety of learning activities which cater for different learning styles. Complete the background information and then write your learning activities in the form provided in Table 5.2.

Table 5.2 Mapping learning activities against statutory requirements

ACTIVITY:	YEAR GROUP:

PRIOR LEARNING: _____

_____

_____

_____

THE MAJORITY OF PUPILS ARE WORKING AT NATIONAL CURRICULUM LEVEL: _____

_____

	VISUAL	AUDITORY	KINAESTHETIC
Developing and improving physical skills			
Planning and applying decisions			
Evaluating and improving			
Making healthy, active lifestyle choices			

So far, the chapter has explored factors which you need to take into account when planning a unit of work; how to construct clear objectives cross-referenced to the relevant statutory requirements and how to develop related learning activities which cater for different types of learner. Teaching strategies are considered further in Chapter 13. Now complete Activity 5.5.

Activity 5.5

Writing a unit of work

Using the unit of work proforma in Table 5.3, or one provided for your course, select a group and an activity you are required to teach and write a unit of work using this format. Further guidance can be found in Gower (2010: 31).

Table 5.3 Unit of work outline

UNIT OF WORK		
ACTIVITY:	KEY STAGE:	
YEAR GROUP:	DURATION:	
RESOURCES:	LANGUAGE FOR LEARNING:	
PRIOR LEARNING:	KEY SKILLS:	
OBJECTIVES	**LEARNING ACTIVITIES**	**TEACHING AND LEARNING STRATEGIES**
DEVELOPING AND IMPROVING PHYSICAL SKILLS		
PLANNING AND APPLYING DECISIONS		
EVALUATING AND IMPROVING		
MAKING HEALTHY, ACTIVE LIFESTYLE CHOICES		

SHORT-TERM PLANNING

The unit of work plan provides a framework for planning a series of lessons. The unit objectives are the initial focus for your short-term lesson planning and are the criteria against which pupils' progress is measured at the end of the unit. Therefore, it is important you use your unit objectives to directly inform the knowledge, skills and understanding you plan for pupils to achieve in lessons – see the example of the relationship between unit objectives and lesson intended learning outcomes in a gymnastic unit of work in Table 5.4.

When analysing the relationship between the unit objectives and lesson intended learning outcomes, you will note that the unit objectives are broader in terms of the range of possible contexts. The lesson intended learning outcomes are far more specific. This enables you to assess pupils' progress against these at the end of the lesson (see Chapter 16).

In this chapter the intended learning outcomes are written for the whole class, and achievement of the intended learning outcomes by individual pupils is assessed through formative and summative assessment. However, on other courses, it is the intended learning outcomes themselves that are differentiated to cater for the range of pupils in the class. In Chapter 16, the examples of intended learning outcomes are divided into three bands: those that can be achieved by most of the pupils in the class, with different intended learning outcomes for pupils who cannot achieve those and for those pupils who need to be extended further. On other courses you may be asked to write intended learning outcomes for different aspects of pupils' learning, e.g. in terms of the knowledge pupils will acquire, the skills they will be able to perform, and what development in their understanding will result from the unit. Whatever model is used, it is important that the intended learning outcomes are written as specific and assessable statements about what your pupils will achieve by the end of the lesson (see also Chapters 13 and 16). The Office for Standards in Education (Ofsted, 2003: 5) highlighted 'Trainees' inability to consistently define objectives for learning with precision continued to undermine their ability to judge and record progress.' Thus, the ability to write specific and assessable intended learning outcomes is a crucial area for development in your ITE.

Table 5.4 Relationship between unit of work objectives and lesson learning outcomes

Year 7 gymnastics unit of work	
Unit objectives	*Related lesson intended learning outcomes*
By the end of this unit pupils will be able to…	By the end of this lesson pupils will be able to…

Developing and improving physical skills

Demonstrate a range of body actions (e.g. jumps, rolls and weight on hands movements) and balances on the floor and apparatus showing good body tension, extension and clarity of body shape.	Perform a variety or rolls on the floor from different starting and finishing positions demonstrating good body tension and clarity of body shape.

Planning and applying decisions

Select and apply, on the floor and apparatus, a range of actions and balances to produce individual sequences in which the end of one movement becomes the beginning of the next. These should demonstrate contrasts in body shape, level, speed and pathway.	Devise and perform individually a sequence consisting of three rolls, two balances and a jump demonstrating variations in body shape and changes in speed so that the end of one movement becomes the beginning of the next.

Evaluating and improving

Identify aspects relating to the strengths and weaknesses of a partner's sequence using criteria provided by the teacher and give constructive feedback, demonstrating the ability to use appropriate terminology.	Provide verbal feedback to a partner on the quality of his/her sequence, focusing on the clarity of body shape. In providing this feedback the pupils should speak clearly and demonstrate the use of appropriate terminology. (e.g. *clear shape, tucked roll, stretched jump*).

Making healthy, active lifestyle choices

Demonstrate safe practice when lifting, supporting and manoeuvring people and equipment in skill practices and when devising sequences of movement.	Support a partner during a variety of counterbalances demonstrating a solid base and appropriate posture to prevent injury.

Now complete Activity 5.6.

Activity 5.6

Relating unit objectives to lesson intended learning outcomes

In the form in Table 5.5 in relation to an area of activity you will be teaching, write a lesson intended learning outcome from the unit objectives, as in the gymnastics example above.

Having stated clearly what you want pupils to learn in your lesson, you are now in a position to identify the sequence of learning experiences you will provide to give all pupils the opportunity to succeed.

It is generally accepted that experienced teachers do not plan lessons in the same detail as student teachers, at least not explicitly. Indeed, when looking at differences in planning between beginning teachers and experienced teachers Griffey and Housner (1999) noted that the latter planned in much less depth and were more able to deviate from their planned activities based on the process of formative assessment (see assessment for learning in Chapter 16) during the lesson. On the other hand, beginning teachers with less experience to call upon, needed to think through carefully every aspect of the lesson and lacked the experience to adapt plans during the lesson. Activity 5.7 on p. 53 is designed to help you to 'unpick' much of the implicit planning that experienced teachers develop.

Table 5.5 Lesson intended learning outcomes from unit of work objectives

Area of activity: _____	
Level at which the unit is pitched: _____	
Unit objectives	**Related lesson intended learning outcomes**
By the end of this unit pupils will be able to:	By the end of this lesson pupils will be able to:
Developing and improving physical skills	
Planning and applying decisions	
Evaluating and improving	
Making healthy, active lifestyle choices	

Activity 5.7

Observing and analysing lessons delivered by experienced teachers

Ask an experienced teacher if you can observe a lesson. Before the lesson, complete the details in Table 5.6 and discuss the intended learning outcomes with the teacher. While you are observing, complete the columns for each learning activity that takes place. An explanation of what to include in each column is written below.

Time

Time allocated gives a picture of how pace in the lesson is established. Writing down the time allocation given to each activity/part of the lesson helps you see the balance that the teacher is able to achieve for each activity/part and in particular the amount of time pupils are active.

Intended learning outcomes being addressed

By identifying the particular intended learning outcome that is being addressed with an activity/series of activities you can trace the progress of the intended learning outcomes through the lesson.

Whole class activities

The teacher's explanations of the tasks pupils are to perform provide the bulk of this section. You may need to note more than one task if the teacher is differentiating by task (see Chapter 11).

Differentiating activities for groups and individuals

Issues related to maximising the achievement of all pupils are covered in Chapter 15, in particular, inclusive teaching in which effective learning opportunities are provided for all pupils. You should note down any pupil/s for whom the task was adapted.

Learning points

Learning points are sometimes referred to as teaching points. Again, adopt the terminology used on your course. You can complete this section by listening to the points that the teacher asks the pupils to consider. The teacher may identify different learning points depending on the ability of the pupils. Note the techniques, such as demonstrations that the teacher uses to reinforce these points and also particular words the teacher uses during this interaction. Consider how the learning points are delivered to ensure that there is depth in pupil learning, i.e. the 'why' as well as the 'what' and 'how' of the particular aspect of learning.

Organisation of equipment and resources and management of pupils

If you are observing a lesson late in the term/year, the teacher will have created a number of procedures and routines in order to streamline the management of pupils and equipment. Try to identify the hidden procedures which have become implicit within the lesson. This includes how to move into and out of activities as well as the organisation of the activity itself, i.e. the organisation of transition phases in the lesson. The teacher may also use learning resources such as work cards. You should look in particular at how the teacher sets up these tasks and the instructions given to pupils for their use.

(continued)

Teaching and learning strategies

Make a note of particular identifiable teaching strategies the teacher uses. You may want to use Mosston and Ashworth's (2002) spectrum of teaching styles or one of the other classifications of teaching strategies (see also Chapters 12 and 13). The strategy may, for example, include a range of different question and answer techniques to elicit pupil response or to monitor the quality of pupils' learning or it may involve the use of a demonstration to aid performance analysis and the development of pupils' observation skills. Note how the strategies used cater for a range of different preferred learning styles (VAK). You should be able to see a relationship between the intended learning outcome the teacher is working towards and the teaching strategy considered most appropriate.

From recording what happens in the lesson, you should be able to identify the important aspects of planning which, although not specifically noted in a plan by an experienced teacher, are necessary for you as a student teacher to note in detail (see Activities 5.8 and 5.9 on p. 58).

Table 5.6 Lesson observation proforma

Date	Year group/ KS	Area of activity	Lesson in unit	Time	Working area	No. girls/ boys	Equipment used

INTENDED LEARNING OUTCOMES
By the end of this lesson pupils will be able to:

1	
2	
3	
4	

(continued)

Table 5.6 (continued)

LESSON OBSERVATION						
Time	Which intended learning outcomes are being addressed?	What whole class learning activities are taking place?	How are the activities differentiated for groups/individuals?	What learning points are being emphasised?	How are equipment and resources organised and pupils managed?	What teaching and learning strategies are being used? What types of learners do these cater for?

Activity 5.8

Important aspects of planning

Discuss the lesson with the teacher as soon as possible, focusing on the information you have collected. Examples of questions to act as prompts are detailed in Table 5.7. The important point is that you question and ask for clarification on any aspect that you feel would help develop your ability to plan a lesson.

Table 5.7 Post-lesson conversation

POST-LESSON CONVERSATION

ASPECT OF THE LESSON	SUGGESTED QUESTIONS
Time	What informed the amount of time you spent on each of the learning activities? Did you adjust the timing of any activities? Why was this?
Intended learning outcomes being addressed	How did you utilise your intended learning outcomes during the lesson to support pupil learning? Did you deliberately adapt any of your intended learning outcomes during the lesson? Would you want to revisit any of the intended learning outcomes next lesson? Why?
Whole class activities	What informed the structure of your learning activities? Were they in that order for a particular reason? If you were to teach this lesson again, would you alter the learning activities you selected? Why?
Differentiating activities for groups and individuals	How did you identify any pupils during the lesson whom you thought needed to have tasks adapted for them? What particular techniques/approaches did you use to differentiate for these pupils?
Learning points	What informed your decision to deliver your learning points at certain key phases of the lesson? Did you use certain strategies when delivering your learning points? How do you use language yourself to develop pupils' understanding?
Organisation of equipment and resources and pupil management	What informed the ways in which you organised the equipment and facilities for your lesson? Did you group the pupils in a particular way for different activities? Why? What management strategies did you use to maximise pupil activity time and learning?
Teaching and learning strategies	Did you utilise certain strategies to cater for different preferred learning styles? What were these? How did you structure your use of question and answer throughout the lesson? Why did you select certain pupils to demonstrate?

Activity 5.9

Planning a lesson for an identified area of activity and group of pupils

Choose one of the lesson plan proformas available on the website, or one used on your own course. Plan the next lesson to follow on from the one you have observed. In order to do this you need to:

- obtain a copy of the unit of work from which the lesson is taken;
- discuss with the class teacher the intended learning outcomes for the next lesson, based on the outcomes from your discussion above.

SUMMARY

Unit of work and lesson planning demands considerable time and effort. Without clear goals in terms of what you intend the pupils to know, do and understand by the end of a unit or lesson, there is a danger that crucial aspects of learning will either not take place or will result in wasted time due to lack of focus. This chapter has tried to show the importance of thinking through all the stages of the planning process. When you sit down to plan a unit and/or a lesson you will have a lot of questions floating around in your head. Some of the questions you are likely to ask when planning your lessons may include those such as: What am I trying to achieve? What activities do I include in the time I have? How will I differentiate the activities? How will I get the equipment out? etc. By writing the answers to such questions in a systematic way you will be able to 'imagine' yourself in the teaching situation and 'rehearse' the lesson in advance. By doing so, you can anticipate problems that may arise. Over time with a class, you develop routines, procedures and relationships that allow you to predict with more certainty the impact of your decisions on pupil learning.

As you progress as a teacher, you find that many aspects of planning become routine and do not need to be written in great detail. You will also find that you are able to adapt your lesson plan as a result of formative assessments you make during the lesson. This confidence in being able to respond to pupils as the lesson unfolds is something that develops gradually. It is, therefore, important that during your ITE you build strong foundations from which you can eventually develop this flexibility.

ACKNOWLEDGEMENT

The author would like to acknowledge the significant input of Cathy Gower to the first edition of this chapter.

FURTHER READING

Capel, S., Leask, M. and Turner, T. (eds) (2009) *Learning to Teach in the Secondary School: A Companion to School Experience*, 5th edn, London: Routledge.
    Section 2.2 covers many important factors which need to be taken into account when creating an effective lesson from lesson preparation to the evaluation and future planning.

Gower, C. (2010) Planning in PE, in S. Capel and M. Whitehead (eds) *Learning to Teach Physical Education in the Secondary School: A Companion to School Experience*, London: Routledge, pp. 24–45.

This chapter provides further guidance on medium- and short-term planning, with examples of useful lesson plan proformas and examples for both units and lesson plans.

Hramaik, A. and Hudson, T. (2011) *Understanding Teaching and Learning in Secondary Schools.* Harlow: Pearson Education Ltd.
This book provides guidance on how to plan to help ensure pupil learning, with some useful reflective tasks.

Note: all proformas, tables or figures you are asked to complete to help you undertake activities in this chapter are also available on the website which accompanies the book (www.routledge.com/9780415814829).

Chapter 6

Planning for pupils' learning in broader dimensions of the curriculum 1

Citizenship, social, moral, spiritual, cultural and personal development

ANDREW THEODOULIDES

INTRODUCTION

The work of physical education teachers is not just about teaching the physical education curriculum. All teachers have a responsibility to promote pupils' wider learning (see Whitehead and Woodhouse, 2010). Pupils' learning within broader dimensions of the curriculum has a curious place within the National Curriculum for Physical Education (NCPE) in England. On one hand, the Education Reform Act (DES, 1988); the Education (Schools) Act (DES, 1992); the NCPE; Qualifications and Curriculum Authority (QCA, 2007a); Citizenship Education and the Personal and Well-Being Curriculum (QCA, 2007b), all clearly identify the importance of promoting pupils' learning in broader dimensions of the curriculum. However, the content of the NCPE at a particular time tends to be the focus of teachers' work. For a detailed discussion of the content and structure of the NCPE, see Whitehead *et al.* (2010). Moreover, when assessing pupils' learning, the 'levels of attainment' reflect learning in the key processes. Given this context an assessment-driven curriculum has the potential to marginalise learning outcomes such as those in the broader dimensions of the curriculum.

If aspects of the broader curriculum are to be learned through physical education, they must be given appropriate recognition within your work. This chapter explores how you might effectively promote pupils' learning in broader dimensions of the physical education curriculum: personal, spiritual, moral, social and cultural development and citizenship.

By the end of this chapter you should be able to:

- reflect upon your responsibility in teaching broader dimensions of the physical education curriculum;
- explore specific teaching and learning strategies that could be used to effectively promote pupils' learning in these areas.

DEVELOPING A CLEAR COMMITMENT TO PROMOTE PUPILS' LEARNING IN THE BROADER DIMENSIONS OF THE CURRICULUM

The extent to which physical education meets some knowledge claims in broader dimensions of the curriculum has been questioned (Bailey, Armour, Kirk, Jess, Pickup, Sandford and the British Educational Research Association (BERA)

Physical Education Special Interest Group, 2009). However, Bailey *et al.* (2009: 16) argue, 'Evidence suggests that physical education and school sport (PESS) can have some/many benefits for some/many pupils, given the right social, contextual and pedagogical circumstances.' With respect to pedagogy, as physical education teachers you should not assume that pupils' learning in elements of the broader curriculum is *caught*. To stand a greater chance of enhancing pupils' learning, pupils should be *taught*. If you were teaching tennis, it would not be considered good practice to give your pupils a tennis racquet each, a couple of tennis balls and tell them to 'go onto the tennis courts and play tennis'; to fail to modify the game to make it easier for the pupils to learn the skills and techniques of tennis; nor to give them any feedback on how to hit shots correctly. In effect, you let the pupils just play tennis. Activity 6.1 identifies the focus for pupils' learning, while Activity 6.2 develops a reflective approach.

Activity 6.1

Developing a focus for pupils' learning in broader dimensions of the physical education curriculum

In a lesson you are going to teach, write a learning outcome in Table 6.1 that relates to one of the broader dimensions of the physical education curriculum. For example,

- Pupils learn that they have a moral responsibility towards the environment when engaging in activities of an adventurous nature.
- Pupils are able to reflect upon the sense of well-being that taking part in physical activity can bring to the quality of their lives.
- Pupils are able to consider the needs of others when making decisions while in the role of a group leader.

Learning outcome

How could you differentiate this outcome (see also Chapters 5 and 16)?
Now teach the lesson. At the end of the lesson, reflect upon how successful you were in helping the pupils to meet the learning outcomes:

- To what extent were they achieved?
- Were the learning activities appropriate?
- How easy was it to promote pupils' learning in this area?
- How did the pupils react to what you did?
- What would you do differently next time?
- Use this information to inform the planning of your next lesson.

Table 6.1 Writing intended learning outcomes

Most pupils should be able to:
Some pupils will not have made as much progress and will be able to:
A few pupils will have progressed further and will be able to:
What range of teaching and learning strategies could you use in order to meet these outcomes?

Activity 6.2

Developing a reflective approach to the teaching of broader dimensions within physical education

1   In the tennis example above where pupils were told to 'go away and play', what criticisms would you make about your 'teaching'?
2   What is the likely outcome of your 'teaching' in terms of pupils' learning of the skills and techniques of tennis?
3   Compare this with pupils' learning in the broader dimensions of the curriculum. How does pupils' learning in these areas differ from the example given above, if at all?
4   In your experience, to what extent do physical education teachers teach pupils about the broader dimensions of the curriculum or do they assume 'it just happens'?

In undertaking Activity 6.2, you may well have realised that without a range of effective teaching and learning strategies, a teacher has very little control over what pupils learn. Your pupils may well develop into excellent tennis players, who are technically very good and who know how and when to hit the right shot. But, equally, they may pick up some bad habits, resulting in poor technique. As indicated above, it would be unacceptable for a teacher to adopt a teaching approach in which pupils are given a racquet and ball and told to 'go away and play' in the hope that they will learn simply by taking part. Yet, this is how many teachers approach pupils' learning in the broader dimensions of the curriculum. The perceived validity of this *laissez-faire* teaching approach in one sense provides a means for teachers to teach with the minimum of effort. Consequently they see no reason to adopt any specific teaching and learning strategies to promote pupils' learning. However, this is not educationally sound and for teaching and *learning* to be more effective, teachers should adopt a more critically reflective approach towards the way in which they can promote pupils' learning in broader dimensions of the curriculum. If you do not take a proactive role in promoting pupils' learning in this domain, then there is no guarantee of the type and level of learning that will take place. A good starting point is to plan ahead and identify opportunities to promote pupils' learning in dimensions of the broader curriculum (see Whitehead and Woodhouse, 2010). Now complete Activity 6.3.

Activity 6.3

Matching the teacher's intentions to pupils' learning

Observe a lesson taught by an experienced teacher and answer the following questions:

* Where in the lesson do you think pupils' learning in one (or more) dimensions of the broader curriculum may have developed?
* After observing, state *specifically* what you thought the pupils learnt in dimensions of the broader curriculum.
* Ask three pupils what they think that they learned in the broader curriculum dimension. What did they say?
* Now ask the teacher what s/he thinks the pupils learned. What did s/he say?
* Do these match up?

IDENTIFYING PUPILS' LEARNING IN BROADER DIMENSIONS OF THE CURRICULUM

When opportunities to develop pupils' learning in broader dimensions of the physical education curriculum are identified, the learning outcomes must support other learning that is taking place within a sequence of lessons and not be a 'bolt-on-extra', included 'just for the sake of it'. If learning in the broader dimensions of the curriculum is not seen to be *integral* to the work within a sequence of lessons (by both teachers and pupils), its value is immediately diminished (see Activity 6.4).

Activity 6.4

Planning for pupils' learning

Look through a plan for a sequence of lessons you are going to teach. Where in this sequence is there a *specific* contribution to pupils' learning in broader dimensions of the curriculum?

Identify further opportunities to include specific learning outcomes in a sequence of lessons which relate to broader dimensions of the curriculum. Bear in mind that learning in one dimension of the broader curriculum may overlap into another. For example, being a leader (personal development) requires pupils to communicate with others (social development) and to show consideration for others (moral development). Where possible, identify teaching and learning activities to meet these outcomes. Dance is shown as an example in Table 6.1. Across a range of different sequences of lessons write at least one learning outcome in each of the following broader dimensions of the curriculum, citizenship, personal, social, moral, spiritual and cultural development.

Table 6.2 Specific learning outcomes for dance

Range and content	Learning outcome	Curriculum dimension	Teaching and learning strategies
Exploring and communicating ideas, concepts and emotions	Pupils understand the cultural context of the haka	Cultural development	Pupils watch a video of the haka and complete a component chart to identify aspects of the dance's symbolism. Teacher-led phrase which demonstrates stylistic features and inherent symbolism of the haka. Pupils devise their own phrase of movement in the style of the haka. Pupils explain the symbolism within their phrase.

DEVELOPING EFFECTIVE TEACHING AND LEARNING STRATEGIES TO PROMOTE PUPILS' LEARNING IN BROADER DIMENSIONS OF THE CURRICULUM

Having identified where within the range of content there are opportunities for promoting pupils' learning in the broader dimensions of the curriculum, the challenge facing teachers is to write learning outcomes which are clearly focused and develop a range of effective teaching and learning strategies which enable pupils to achieve them (see Whitehead with Blair, 2010). Two features are important here.

First, you should clearly explain to pupils that they are engaged in activities that promote learning in broader dimensions of the curriculum. For example, in relation to 'fair play', if your intention is for pupils 'to respect the decision of the referee' (social/moral learning), then each game ought to have a referee. However, it is also important to inform pupils of the reasons for such activities. A game may have a referee for other (practical) reasons (e.g. because you cannot referee all the games at once), which are not related to developing pupils' learning in the social and moral domain. You should not assume that pupils will be aware of your intentions if these are not made explicit. A good starting point might be for you to ask questions which engage pupils in discussion of the need for referees in games and why it is morally desirable to respect their decisions. Useful opening questions could be: 'Was the referee effective?', 'Did s/he make any mistakes?', 'Were these deliberate?', 'How should you act when a referee makes a mistake?', 'Why should we respect referees?', 'Why should we respect other people?'

Second, part of the lesson ought to include investigation, discussion, practice, or other such learning strategies, which directly promote pupils' learning in that specific area of the broader dimensions of the curriculum (see Whitehead with Blair, 2010). For example, if the intention is to promote pupils' social skills (e.g. cooperation) through discussion of compositional ideas during group work in dance, then pupils ought to receive feedback on what constitutes effective cooperation in the *social context*. Thus, feedback would be specific to social skills, not compositional ideas. So, for example, the teacher might focus on how effective pupils were in articulating their own ideas; listening to the ideas of other pupils or other such (social) interactions. Now complete Activity 6.5.

Activity 6.5

Developing effective teaching and learning strategies

List as many different tasks as you can think of that would promote pupils' understanding of 'fair play' in team games:

- How would you structure these tasks?
- What *progressions* would you use to increase pupils' learning about 'fair play'?
- What *crucial* points would you expect pupils to have learnt by the end of the last task?

REACTING TO OPPORTUNITIES WHICH PROMOTE PUPILS' LEARNING IN BROADER DIMENSIONS OF THE CURRICULUM

Although it is incumbent upon teachers to plan for pupils' learning in the broader dimensions of the curriculum, opportunities sometimes arise that are not planned for. In these situations teachers use their knowledge and professional judgement as to how and when such opportunities need to be used effectively if they are to promote pupils' learning. Now complete Activity 6.6.

Activity 6.6

Engaging pupils' learning

Consider the example below which could be typical of the kind of incident that occurs in games lessons.

> The pupils are playing a small-sided game of rugby near the end of their lesson. As the game progresses, some pupils start appealing to the referee for him to make a decision in their favour. 'Ref, our ball!' says one boy after the ball goes off the pitch. This happens with increasing frequency. The teacher stops the game and addresses the group. He says, 'In football you may shout and appeal for the ball, but in rugby we don't do that.' He restarts the game and the boys carry on playing. However, a few minutes later another pupil appeals to the teacher for a decision. As the game continues, the teacher says to the boy, 'Right, Patrick, off you go and run around the rugby pitch. I told you not to appeal!' The bemused pupil leaves the game and starts running around the rugby pitch as a punishment. A little later another pupil appeals for the ball. Again the teacher tells the pupil, 'Go on, off you go around the pitch. I told you no appealing. I told you it might be all right in some sports, but not in rugby.'

1 What do you think the teacher wanted the pupils to understand in this incident?
2 Is the strategy the teacher adopted conducive to promoting understanding and appreciation of the relevant issues? Give reasons.

Despite the teacher's good intentions, as a learning experience it is unlikely that the strategy employed has furthered pupils' understanding. Let us examine the incident. Correctly, the teacher has reacted to the way in which some pupils challenged the referee's decisions. Clearly the teacher believed that he was teaching the pupils something about the way in which rugby ought to be played; that is, the way in which players should respect the referee's decisions (a moral issue). However, it is not clear whether pupils recognised the moral implications of their behaviour and knew why their responses were wrong. Likewise it seems unlikely that any pupil, simply because s/he is sent to run around a field, or the other pupils who continued with the game, would make the desired moral connections (an example of how, if learning is left to be 'caught', there is no guarantee of what will be learned). Even if there was no more appealing to the referee for the ball, it cannot be claimed that this demonstrated an improvement in moral action, given the pupils' lack of moral reflection. Therefore, for pupils to understand the moral implications of their/other pupils' actions, the teacher should engage them briefly in some discussion (at least) and reflection about what is, or is not, acceptable behaviour within team games.

You also need to recognise that it is undesirable for teachers to give pupils a punishment (in this case running around the playing field) which is related to the type of activity pupils are engaged in as part of their lesson. If teachers are to foster pupils' enthusiasm for learning, this strategy is inappropriate. Hence, examples such as 'running around the field,' or 'doing ten press-ups' fuel pupils' dislike of physical activity rather than encourage them to take part (see Activity 6.7).

Activity 6.7

Adopting a different approach to teaching a moral dimension

1   How would you have handled the situation described in Activity 6.6?
2   What would you want the pupils to understand/learn about appealing to the referee for the ball in rugby?
3   Is the teacher right to tell pupils that appealing to the referee in football is acceptable?
4   What teaching and learning strategies would you have used to meet this learning outcome? (See your answer for question 2.)
5   What questions might you have asked pupils?
6   How would you know if your teaching of this learning outcome had been successful?

SUMMARY

This chapter has highlighted how physical education teachers can promote pupils' learning in the broader dimensions of the curriculum. It is not sufficient to claim that it 'just happens', there should be a clear commitment by teachers to promote pupils' learning in this area – as shown in their teaching of physical education itself. Therefore, clearly planned learning outcomes which relate to the broader dimensions of the curriculum should feature in all sequences of lessons and lesson plans, supported by teaching and learning strategies which engage pupils in reflecting upon and learning about their own (and others') behaviour, values and attitudes within and beyond physical education.

FURTHER READING

Beedy, J. P. (1997) *Sports Plus: Positive Learning Using Sports*, Hamilton: Project Adventure.
In this book the author highlights teaching and learning strategies you might use to promote pupils' learning in aspects of personal, social and moral development within sport. These 'teachable moments' provide ideas for engaging pupils in learning experiences that relate to broader dimensions of the curriculum.

Dyson, B. and Casey, A. (2012) *Cooperative Learning in Physical Education: A Research-Based Approach*, London: Routledge.
In this book the authors explore the value of Cooperative Learning to pupils' education in physical education. One aspect of Cooperative Learning is the extent to which it facilitates the development of interpersonal, social (and by implication moral) skills; these are skills that can be developed through the Cooperative Learning model. The book contains some useful learning and teaching strategies to enhance pupils' learning in some broader elements of the physical education curriculum.

Laker, A. (2001) *Developing Personal, Social and Moral Education Through Physical Education*, London: RoutledgeFalmer.
This book contains a detailed analysis of the wider issues surrounding the way in which learning in these broader dimensions of the curriculum is conceptualised in education and more specifically in physical education. The book also contains some practical guidance on how to approach the planning and delivery of these broader dimensions.

Note: all proformas, tables or figures you are asked to complete to help you undertake activities in this chapter are also available on the website which accompanies the book (www.routledge.com/9780415814829).

Chapter 7

Planning for pupils' learning in broader dimensions of the curriculum 2

Key skills

BARBARA WALSH AND JULIE MONEY

INTRODUCTION

As teachers we have a responsibility to ensure that pupils have the essential qualities and skills for employment, learning and life, in order to become employable. Employees value highly the skills of literacy/communication, numeracy, information (and communications) technology (IT/ICT), working with others/the ability to work in a team, being able to improve own learning and performance and being able to solve problems. Teachers also have a responsibility to ensure that pupils value and understand the importance of these skills and how they are transferable across different subject areas.

Over the past decade a variety of 'broader dimensions' have been included across the curriculum. These have included Personal Learning and Thinking Skills (PLTs), key skills, cross-curricular links and dimensions, the Every Child Matters Agenda (ECM), Social and Emotional Aspects of Learning (SEAL) and functional skills (see Table 7.1 on p. 71). Owing to changes in the curriculum over a number of years, many of these have lost their impetus in schools. However, they are still vital qualities required in future learning, employment and life skills for pupils as they enter adult life and the workplace.

There are many opportunities for you as a physical education teacher to develop in pupils these essential qualities and skills by, for example, providing problem-solving and decision-making tasks in physical education lessons through pupils making up and playing their own small-sided conditioned games. Asking pupils to act as officials, coaches, leaders and participants has the potential to help develop their key skills of communication, application of number, working with others, improving own learning and performance, problem solving and IT.

Personal Learning and Thinking Skills (PLTs) can also provide pupils with opportunities to become team workers, independent enquirers, effective participators, reflective learners, creative thinkers and self managers.

By the end of this chapter you should be able to:

- understand the broader range of skills to which physical education contributes;
- understand your responsibility regarding the development of pupils' skills and attributes in relation to the broader dimensions of the curriculum;
- plan lessons with explicit opportunities to develop the broader dimension, particularly pupils' personal, social, health and well-being.

TYPES OF SKILLS TO WHICH PHYSICAL EDUCATION CONTRIBUTES

What are key skills?

> Key skills are a range of essential skills that underpin success in education, employment, lifelong learning and personal development.
>
> (DfES, 2005)

According to the Department for Education (DFE) (www.education.gov.uk), key skills are

> [the] generic skills which individuals need in order to be effective members of a flexible, adaptable and competitive workforce and for lifelong learning. They cover communication, application of number, information technology, working with others, improving own learning and performance and problem solving.

For the purposes of this book, IT is addressed in Chapter 8.

What are functional skills?

> The term functional should be considered in the broad sense of providing learners with the skills and abilities they need to take an active and responsible role in their communities, in the workplace and in an educational setting.
>
> (QCA, 2007a: 3)

There are Functional Skills Standards in three subjects in England; English, mathematics and IT. However, these standards are technical statements to be used as the basis for qualification development which can be transferred across all subject areas.

What are Personal Learning and Thinking Skills?

These are six groups of skills that, together with the functional skills of English, mathematics and ICT, are essential to success in learning, life and work. The six distinct and coherent groups (though interconnected) are; independent enquirers; creative thinkers; reflective learners; team workers; self managers; effective participators. Now complete Activity 7.1.

Activity 7.1

What key skills and competencies do pupils need when they start work?

Think about the key skills and competencies that will be needed by each person when they start work within the sport/physical education industry and complete Table 7.1:

- Are there any similarities in the skills and competencies needed by these four people as they are about to start work or further study?
- What are they?
- Which of the skills identified in Table 7.1 are needed by each of these four people?

Table 7.1 Key skills required

Skills and competencies	A school leaver looking for work as a leisure assistant at a local leisure centre	A school leaver looking for work as a trainee sports development officer for a local authority	An 18-year-old school leaver applying to university for a sport/physical education related degree	A 22-year-old physical education graduate starting their newly qualified teacher year
Communication				
Application of number				
IT/ICT				
Working with others				
Improve own learning and performance				
Problem solving				

These skills need to be planned into the long-, medium- and short-term aspects of the physical education curriculum. The scope of each of these key skills and how they can be planned for in physical education are outlined below.

Now complete Activity 7.2 on p. 72

Activity 7.2

Planning to include broader dimensions in your lessons

Reflect on a lesson plan that you have already taught. If possible, select a lesson in which you were observed teaching.

- Did you explicitly plan to include any of the skills listed in Table 7.1 in your lesson?
- Is there any reference through your planning or the lesson assessment/evaluation of pupil learning that they have developed any of these skills?
- Where could you have included development of any of the above skills within your lesson?

Communication

The key communication skills of speaking, listening, reading and writing can be incorporated into physical education lessons, although normally speaking and listening have been the most frequently used. When talking to other pupils or the teacher, pupils should be taught to express themselves correctly and appropriately and to use the correct terminology used within the activity covered. This can be achieved by asking pupils to evaluate their own and others' work. Feedback should always take place against predetermined success criteria (intended learning outcomes) and be age-related. Pupils should be taught to deliver feedback appropriately, for example, by using positive comments first and then making one constructive comment that will improve the performance (see Zwozdiak-Myers, 2012). The success criteria are best written on cards, either developed by the teacher, pupils or commercially produced. This should also help develop reading skills. The use of mini whiteboards is also useful in terms of pupils using and writing activity-related terminology. Pupils should always be taught the specialist and technical vocabulary of physical education and how to use and spell these words correctly. There should be, where possible, word walls or other associated displays of terminology in and around the learning environment, for example, gymnastic terms such as symmetry; asymmetry; tension and extension. Pupils should also learn to listen to other people – including listening and following instructions and to feedback from the teacher or other pupils.

Application of number

In physical education the interpretation of numerical information can be achieved through the range and content. One obvious example is in athletics where pupils' skills in developing mental calculation and their ability to interpret results and present findings can be developed. Other examples include map work in orienteering or producing diagrams/patterns of work in dance, gymnastics and games. Games may also include the scoring systems and the use of different scoring systems for certain types of shot. The application of number in all activities is also aided through the use of ICT such as stopwatches, laptops, iPads, digital cameras and mobile phones (see Chapter 8).

Working with others

The nature of many physical education activities lends itself to working together in a collaborative environment with other pupils to meet a challenge. There are many opportunities for these skills to be explicitly planned for in areas of activity. For example, the area of outdoor and adventurous activities (OAA) lends itself to pupils having to work as a team, e.g. they try to make their way up a course without contacting the ground. Similarly, pupils may choreograph a group dance or a pair sequence in gymnastics, cheerleading and Zumba.

Improving own learning and performance

The key skill of improving one's own learning and performance involves pupils reflecting on and critically evaluating their work, what they have learnt and identifying ways to improve their learning and performance. Teachers should constantly provide pupils with opportunities to review their work and discuss ways of improving their learning. It is vital they are given a framework for making these improvements and provided with targets, both self-initiated and teacher-focused, as a benchmark of their improvements. For example, a group dance may be recorded and the group can identify ways of improving their performance in relation to a framework provided by the teacher.

Problem solving

The content of the National Curriculum for Physical Education in England includes 'identifying and solving problems' as part of the breadth of study. Physical education is full of potential for pupils to develop skills and strategies to solve problems in a variety of contexts. Included in this are: the skills of identifying and understanding a problem, planning ways to solve a problem, monitoring progress in tackling a problem, and reviewing solution to the problems. For example, in games, you could set up a small-sided game and state that the challenge or problem for the pupils to solve is how to get the ball to the line without making a forward pass. This involves the pupils working as a team to solve the problem. However, as with all other aspects of the broader curriculum, it is important that you plan for these specifically in both units of work and lessons.

INFORMATION TECHNOLOGY (IT)

The use of IT as a tool to analyse and record a physical performance has a powerful effect on pupils' motivation and achievement. Whether it is using a digital or video camera, flip cameras, mobile phones and iPads for physical images or a stopwatch to record times, IT can provide much-needed evidence of knowledge of performance or knowledge of results or both. See Chapter 8 for more information on IT/ICT in physical education.

Table 7.2 provides examples of how the range of key skills can be explicitly developed in the area of performing at maximum levels in relation to speed, height, distance, strength or accuracy, as in athletic activities. You should add your own examples of these from other activities.

For each of the key skills above, think of other examples (see Activity 7.3). As you can see, several key skills may be addressed at the same time.

Having identified and planned where in a unit of work and individual lessons you can include selected key skills, it is important that you plan carefully how you will create specific and assessable learning outcomes to measure pupil learning.

Table 7.2 Key skills in performing at maximum levels in relation to speed, height, distance, strength or accuracy, in athletic activities

Broader dimension	Examples	Specific activities
Communication Functional Skill: English PLTs: Self Managers	Speaking, listening, expressing an opinion, debating and discussing, giving feedback. Reading and writing Forms of non-verbal communication	In a relay, discuss and then decide on the best order for the pupils to run depending on everyone's strengths, and relating this to the strengths and weaknesses of the other teams. Peer review and feedback on partner's throwing/running/jumping action. Keeping a diary of activity. Make notes of training sessions and suggested targets for improvement.
Application of number Functional Skill: Maths	Collecting and analysing data, measuring, calculating	Times and distance in events. Percentage improvement scores. Taking on the role of an official in relation to times and distances. Ranking the order of the competition scores. Trajectory of the implement thrown. Plan how far to run in 3 seconds. What was the actual distance? What is the difference? Target activities with associated scores. Use of IT software to analyse scores in relation to personal best.
Working with others PLTs: Team Workers	Whole and small group discussion, teamwork to achieve a set challenge.	Working as team, in relay. Measuring and recording each other's times/distances. Taking on different roles as coach, leader of warm-up, official and performer. Retrieving each other's implements in throwing activities. Being aware of their own and others' safety in all activities. Working in a team in an activity such as 'beating the world record over 1500m' in a team.
Improve own learning and performance PLTs: Reflective Learners Independent Enquirers	Evaluating, making judgements, target setting, practising, persevering, recognising improvements	In sprint activities pupils are asked to give feedback to each other regarding various aspects of technique. This could include the use of cameras to observe areas for development.

(continued)

Table 7.2 (continued)

Problem solving PLTs: Creative Thinkers	Reasoning, divergent thinking	A group of six pupils are asked to run 1500 metres. The group has to decide on individual strengths in terms of the distance each member of the team runs and in what order. A minimum and maximum distance can be determined to assist the group Assess the strengths of other groups and set the order of your team accordingly, introducing the idea of tactical running
PLTs: Effective Participator		Each pupil should be able to take on the role of performer, coach and official for various athletic events; this could also include event management, media coverage, and marketing and poster preparation

Activity 7.3

Developing the broader concepts in your teaching

Using the example provided for performing at maximum levels in Table 7.2 and in the proforma on broader dimensions in Table 7.3, outline ways in which the key skills could be taught in other areas of activity e.g. gymnastics, badminton, cheerleading, ultimate frisbee (proformas for each of these are on the website for this book (www.routledge.com/9780415814829).

Table 7.3 Teaching broader dimensions

Activity		
Broader dimension	**Example**	**Specific activities**
Social skills/team workers	Co-operation, collaboration with others. Whole and small group discussions, team work and strategy to achieve a common goal/ challenge set.	
Making informed choices about healthy and active lifestyles	Have knowledge of exit routes in different activities. Understand the benefits of a healthy and balanced diet. Appreciate the benefits both physically and mentally of the activities undertaken.	
Performing at maximum levels/ motivation	Be motivated to work hard and perform at one's own maximum level, aiming to set realistic short- and long-term targets to make improvements.	
Communication and literacy	Speaking, listening, expressing an opinion, debating and discussing, reading and writing, forms of non-verbal; communication.	
Creative thinking/ problem solving	Reasoning, divergent thinking, using imagination, creativity, applying principles, breaking problems down, considering different ways of taking on a task/problem.	

It is also important to remember that you need to plan for pupils' development in broader dimensions over a longer period of time, for example, through a scheme of work or across a Key Stage. Now complete Activity 7.4.

Activity 7.4

Learning outcomes for broader dimensions

Using the information in Table 7.2, the proforma on broader dimensions (Table 7.3) and Activity 7.3, write learning outcomes and associated activities that promote the development of key skills in a selected activity. Try this in a lesson where you feel confident and then in a lesson where you have less confidence. An example for a number of areas of activity is provided.

Table 7.4 represents the various personal and social development skills which can be included in physical education planning. It can be overwhelming if you think you have to include these in every lesson! As you design your units and schemes of work, it is worth mapping out how these broader dimensions can be included and progressed in your physical education planning. Many of the broader dimensions overlap; the shaded areas give one example of where the various skills can be linked together.

Activity 7.5

Incorporating broader dimensions in your lessons

Using your own lesson plan format, plan a lesson that starts to incorporate some of the broader dimensions. Try to map these across a unit of work where you can see how these various dimensions can be continued and progressed. An example of a lesson plan where all these various elements can be included is shown here.

Table 7.4 Indicating the various personal and social development skills that can be included in physical education planning for range and content

Range and content	Key concepts	Key processes	Personal learning and thinking skills	Key skills	Cross-curricular links and dimensions	Every Child Matters Agenda (ECM)	Social and Emotional Aspects of Learning (SEAL)	Functional skills
Outwitting an opponent	Competence	Developing and improving physical skills	Independent enquirers	Communication	Identity and cultural diversity	Be healthy	Self-awareness	Literacy
Accurate replication of actions, phrases and sequences	Performance	Planning and applying decisions	Creative thinkers	Working with others	Healthy lifestyles	Stay safe	Managing feelings	Numeracy
Exploring and communicating ideas, concepts and emotions	Creativity	Developing physical and mental capacity	Reflective learners	Improving their own and others' performances	Community participation	Enjoy and achieve	Motivation	ICT
Identifying and solving problems and challenges	Healthy active lifestyles	Evaluating and improving	Team workers	Problem solving	Enterprise	Make a positive contribution	Empathy	
Performing at maximum levels		Making healthy, active lifestyle choices	Self managers	Application of numbers	Global dimension and sustainable development	Achieve economic health and well-being	Social skills	
Exercising safely and effectively to improve health and well-being			Effective participants	ICT	Technology and the media			
					Creativity and critical thinking			

Table 7.5 Learning outcomes and teaching points for broader dimensions

Broader dimension	Area of activity	Learning outcome: By the end of the lesson pupils will be able to:	Learning points
Social skills/ team workers	Athletics	Provide the relay team with feedback on the sprint relay and make suggestions of how to improve the outcome in relation to running order for the next relay race	Listen to all viewpoints Address all strengths and areas for development Consider the other teams in the competition
Making informed choices about healthy and active lifestyles	Dance	Pupils will know where the local dance club/dance schools are located and the times and costs of these activities as well as suggested public transport routes	Value of being involved in an out of school activity Lifelong participation Values of activity both physiologically and psychologically
Performing at maximum levels/ motivation	Games	Demonstrate sustained performance through small-sided conditioned games Be able to raise the heart rate, breathing rate and be able to recover from this intense exercise	Short bursts of intense game play, progressing to longer bursts Understanding the possibility of oxygen debt and lactic acid Be self-motivated and also motivate others to work hard in game activities
Communication and literacy	Gymnastics	Provide feedback to a partner on the quality of their sequence, using criteria provided by the teacher	Speak clearly Use appropriate terminology, e.g. body tension and quality of body shape

Table 7.6 Lesson plan including broader dimensions

Theme: accurate replication of skills (based on range and content)
Area of activity: hockey

Learning outcomes (based on Key Processes)

By the end of the lesson pupils will be able to:

Develop and improve physical skills
- Show control and accuracy in moving and changing direction with the ball
- Replicate the skill of hitting the ball

Plan and apply decisions
- Utilise and accurately replicate changing direction and outwitting an opponent in the small-sided games

Evaluate and improve
- Use observation to help to improve self and others in the skills circuit

Make healthy, active lifestyle choices
- Understand the health and safety aspects of circuits involving hitting and small-sided game

Develop physical and mental capacity
- Decide when and where to use the taught actions in the game

Teaching agenda	Organisation	Points to consider/ observe	Broader dimensions
1 Exchange ball	Everyone with a ball in the D moving around. On the sound of the whistle, without speaking, communicate with another player and exchange your ball with another player. *Progression* Move around and exchange the ball without the whistle. How many times in 1 minute can you do this?	Head up, scanning the area Use of space, move into space Ball: carry out in front away from the feet to the right Weighting and accuracy on the pass Pass to the open stick side each time	Effective participators being confident and competent in moving with the ball Communication
2 Scarecrow tag	2 players with bibs without a ball, still in the D area. The 2 players have to try and steal the ball (this is a recap of last week's actions). If you lose the ball the player stands with their feet apart and can be untagged by another player passing the ball between their legs. The 2 bib players have a minute to see how many balls they can steal	Head up Use and awareness of space Keep the body between the ball and the tagger How can I keep away from the taggers? How can I help other players?	Problem solving, come up with your own ideas of how to keep the ball Creativity, how to keep the ball safe Social skills Enjoy and achieve

(continued)

Table 7.6 (continued)

3 Skills circuit (accurate replication of actions)	1 reverse stick pull or zigma Progression reverse stick pull and shot on goal 2 lift over stick moving L/R/ straight	Change of hand position Right hand pulling and pushing Movement of feet Increase the speed Movement of feet Quick change of hand position Low body position Ball away from body to strike	Reflective learners who are able to evaluate their performance and those of others Creative thinkers who can solve tasks and perform in different activities Independent enquirers who can plan what they are going to do and how they can go about doing it
	Progression 1 in pairs lift over stick pass and shoot 2 hitting and shooting on the move Progression 3 in pairs passing and shooting	Angle of the stick needs to be at 45' Ball away from body Right hand doing the action of lifting What are the changes that have to happen at speed? Position of stick and ball in relation to the body Arc of the stick in striking the ball Position of hands to allow a swing? Where does the pass have to be for an effective strike? What happens when the ball is too close? What happens when the ball is too far away? Ball protection: use of body Signalling	Enjoy and achieve
4 Play 4v4 games utilising the skills accurately in the game	Both teams use all 4 goals and can pass from behind or in front of the goal to score Differentiation – make the area bigger for beginners or those struggling to control the ball	Pass away from defence Ball carrying position What areas have been covered? How does this relate to accurate replication of actions?	Team workers who can plan and evaluate in competitive activities by utilising their team strengths and weaknesses Developing physical and mental capacity
5 Plenary	Bring group round, use the National Curriculum cards and go through the learning outcomes	What went well and why? What did you learn from this? What needs to be worked on?	Reflective learners ask players to reflect on what they have learned and how it can improve

SUMMARY

Broader dimensions, however they are presented, are key aspects of pupils' learning, as they improve their learning and performance in education, employment, lifelong learning and personal development. Physical education, as we have seen, is well placed to make a valuable contribution to the development of pupils' key skills and many of them are already being met through teachers' good practice. As with other aspects of the broader curriculum, however, this should be planned specifically for progress of learning for all pupils.

FURTHER READING

DCSF (Department for Children, Schools and Families) (2010) *Functional Skills Support Programme: Developing Functional Skills in Physical Education*, available at: http://dera.ioe.ac.uk.
This National Strategies document focuses on how functional skills underpin and complement the key processes of physical education. It is an easy-to-read document that focuses on short- and medium-term planning for teachers and learners.

DfE (Department for Education) (2010) *Social and Emotional Aspects of Learning (SEAL) Programme in Secondary Schools: National Evaluation*, available at: https://www.education.gov.uk.
This freely downloadable document shows the results of a national survey of secondary schools approaches to SEAL for pupils. It focuses particularly on its impact on staff and pupils in schools who have adopted a whole school approach to the SEAL programme.

Stidder, G. and Hayes, S. (2011) Thematic learning and teaching through physical education, in G. Stidder and S. Hayes (eds) *The Really Useful Physical Education Book*. London: Routledge.
The chapter focuses on how physical education could contribute to the teaching and learning of cross-curricular themes and whole school concepts. It is a useful resource for teachers focusing on different ways of extending learning beyond focusing on physical performance.

Zwozdiak-Myers, P. (2013) Are physical education teachers reflective practitioners?, in S. Capel and M. Whitehead (eds) *Debates in Physical Education*, London: Routledge.
This chapter focuses on physical education teachers as reflective practitioners and the process of structuring and re-structuring actions and beliefs that inform future planning and development.

Note: all proformas, tables or figures you are asked to complete to help you undertake activities in this chapter are also available on the website which accompanies the book (www.routledge.com/9780415814829).

These include proformas for each activity for Activity 7.3.

Chapter 8 Using information and communication technology in physical education

PHIL BARRETT

INTRODUCTION

The learning needs of pupils are constantly changing and none more so than in the area of Information and Communication Technology (ICT). The reason is that pupils in the twenty-first century have been raised in a digital era. Electrical items such as HD TVs with interactive services, superfast broadband, social media and smart phones are commonplace in modern families. Mention a video that you have seen and pupils instantly say YouTube. Mention downloading music and they pull out their iPod. Give them a fact to look up and they use their smart phones with 3G wireless Internet. As a result of this explosion of digital media the expectation placed upon teachers is that they must keep pace with these developments and have the skills to use ICT effectively to support learning and teaching. The rationale for using ICT was provided by Hopson, Simms and Knezek (2002) who focused on pupils using a technology-enriched environment. They reported that the technology-enriched classroom differs from the traditional classroom in several significant ways: (1) the learning is more pupil-centred and less teacher/textbook-driven; (2) the environment facilitates pupil participation; and (3) the use of cooperative groups focused on application rather than knowledge acquisition.

However, the question you must ask yourself when making a decision to use ICT is whether the organisation and use of ICT in this lesson, with this group of pupils, through this area of activity, at this particular time of the day, at this stage of the unit, will support and promote the learning of the pupils. Furthermore, does it help teachers and pupils to assess work formatively and provide sufficient and specific feedback to improve pupils' performance/attainment/achievement? (See also Chapter 16 on assessment.)

By the end of this chapter you should be able to:

- know the current range of ICT available for potential use in physical education;
- understand how different forms of teaching and learning can be enhanced by the use of ICT;
- make informed decisions about the enhancement of pupil learning through the use of ICT.

Now complete Activities 8.1 and 8.2.

Activity 8.1

Observing the use of ICT in physical education lessons

Observe lessons in as many different activities as you can and answer the following questions:

- Why is ICT being used?
- What is it being used for?
- Will ICT in this context improve pupils' skills, knowledge and understanding in physical education?
- Is it developing pupils' knowledge and understanding of the activity?
- Is its use integrated into teaching and learning in the activity?
- Is it taking away too much activity time, i.e. are activity levels maintained?
- Thus, what added value does it bring to the learning experience, i.e. does the use of ICT allow the pupils to achieve something that could not be achieved without using ICT and/or learn it more effectively and efficiently?
- Does it allow teachers and pupils to assess work formatively by enabling pupils to review, evaluate and improve their own and others' performance and provide sufficient and specific feedback to improve pupils' performance/ attainment/achievement?
- Therefore, is the use of ICT appropriate for this group of pupils to achieve learning outcomes through this area of activity, at this particular time of day, and at this stage of the unit, etc.?
- Does it therefore support and promote pupils' learning?

If the answer to the above questions are 'yes', then it is likely that the use of ICT is valid in this lesson. If not, it may be that the teacher is relying on gadgets to entertain rather than enhance pupil learning.

Activity 8.2

Audit of ICT available in your placement school

Carry out an audit of the range of ICT available in your placement school to enhance learning opportunities for pupils and/or your teaching of physical education, using the list in Table 8.1. Add any you find that are not included in the list. Talk to the physical education teachers to identify ways in which they are used by the department to enhance learning and teaching in physical education and also how they might be used in future.

Table 8.1 Audit of ICT in school

	Current use within physical education lessons	**Potential future use**
Still cameras		
Mobile phone cameras		
Motion analysis software		
Film editing		
Portable media players		
Interactive whiteboards		
Voice projections systems		
Developing FUNctional skills through physical education		
Games consoles		
The Virtual Learning Environment (VLE)		
Video conferencing		
Archos		
The use of iPods/iPads		
Podcasting		
Nintendo Wii Fit		
Dance mat systems		
Pedometers		
Heart rate monitors		
Pupil response systems/ interactive learning response system		
YouTube		

ESTABLISHED USES OF ICT IN PHYSICAL EDUCATION

Many of the above include more traditional integration of ICT in physical education lessons using such things as video cameras, heart rate monitors and motion analysis software programs such as Dartfish and Kandle. Nowadays there are devices such as games consoles with fitness programs readily available and tablets including iPads and iPods that provide a more universal, multifunctional and cost effective solution for schools. Two emerging technologies available for you as teachers are web-based and handheld learning devices. It is useful to note that both of these methods place a huge emphasis on the pupils, creating a much more pupil-centred approach to your teaching. They promote many of the higher order thinking skills that Bloom created back in 1956 to develop higher forms of thinking. For a more recent guide on how Bloom's Taxonomy fits into emerging technology, visit www.schrockguide.net/bloomin-apps.html. This website shows you how hundreds of Web 2.0 and handheld resources promote higher order thinking.

Web-based learning

Websites that use technology beyond static pages are called Web 2.0. They allow for collaboration, interaction and stimulation that traditional websites or ICT programs do not offer.

As an example, under the umbrella of Web 2.0, *blogging sites* are becoming popular where teachers set up a class blog and where pictures and videos can be uploaded during lessons. Each pupil can have a log in and can control what content is placed on the blog site, which then can be monitored by you, the teacher. This can be two-fold: first, for you to create your own educational or class-based resource hub; and, second, to allow the pupils to create and edit their own. Some examples of sites that you can do this on include Wordpress, Weebly, Wix and Wiki Spaces. In Activity 8.3 you are asked to create a blog.

Activity 8.3

Creating your own blog site

Create your own blog site using Wordpress, Weebly, Wix or Wiki Spaces and use it as a teaching resource or to blog about your teaching experiences. Additionally, consider setting up a collaborative class blog for your pupils. For examples of class blogs from teachers and schools, visit www.edublog.com for the best new blogs, sites and innovative collaborations.

Social media and Twitter

These media contain a wealth of resources of use in schools. Traditionally websites such as the Times Educational Supplement (TES) were used to find resources to use in your lessons. However, the # symbol, called a hash tag, has become extremely popular in the world of education. It is used to mark keywords or topic in a Tweet and any Twitter user can categorise or follow topics with hash tags. The most popular hash tags you can use to search for resources include: #edtech; #edchat; #schools; #teaching; #ukedchat; #mlearning; #edapp; #gbl; #vitalcpd; and #slide2learn. Beyond using Twitter as a tool for finding resources, there has been an explosion of teachers using Twitter in their classroom as a learning tool. While there is a grey area regarding social media used at school, there is no doubt that it is a powerful tool. However, before you consider using Twitter in your classroom, we advise that you seek guidance from both your initial teacher education provider and your placement school. Now complete Activity 8.4.

Activity 8.4

Creating a Twitter account

Create a Twitter account and search the hash tags above to find resources for yourself.

The 'Ultimate Twitter Guidebook for Teachers' can be found at: http://edudemic.com/2010/06/the-ultimate-twitter-guidebook/.

Virtual Learning Environments (VLEs: Moodle, Frog or Merlin)

Many schools have a virtual learning environment (VLE) on which you can effectively go paperless. The variety of tasks you can perform on the VLE includes uploading lesson notes and resources, creating quizzes, placing assignments to complete or even embed web links and videos. For courses such as General Certificate of Secondary Education (GCSE) physical education or Advanced ('A') Level, this is especially useful because pupils can access and upload resources at home. A coursework-based subject such as Business and Technician Education Council (BTEC) Sport can be run entirely online. Pupils can upload assignments and they are instantly emailed when the teacher marks their work, thus reducing the time taken to mark and feedback work. Now complete Activity 8.5.

Activity 8.5

Using a VLE

Upon commencement of your placement, find out if the school uses a VLE. If they do, find out what you are able to do on the VLE, then set up a section for a chosen lesson you teach and encourage pupils to access work and complete homework tasks from there.

Collaboration websites

There are many other collaboration websites sites you could use, including Prezi, Glogster, Edmodo, Wordle or Qwiki. These allow pupils to collaborate together without the need to be in the same room. This is particularly useful as a homework task but can also form a great basis for a starter where you could refer to a collaborative piece of class work the pupils have made.

Handheld learning

In 2007, Apple released its first touch screen iPod called the iPod touch. Such a device allows you, for example, to store downloadable applications (apps); capture and edit video; undertake video analysis; watch videos; and read or create books.

There are many advantages to using such a device, including increased pupil engagement, cost effectiveness and mobility, which is, of course, ideal for physical education. Bringing the technology to pupils allows for greater freedom in any environment. Since Apple introduced the iPhone and App store in 2008, the number of mobile apps available to consumers has grown considerably and has currently reached over a million. In a mobile technology-based generation there are apps for pretty much everything you do in life from checking your bank account to games. The education area of the app store is ever growing and there are numerous free or low cost apps available for schools to purchase and synchronise to many devices. If you have access to a handheld device such as an iPod or iPad, the following are some suggested strategies for their use within physical education.

Apps

By searching the app store or on educational websites you can find apps that are suitable to support most aspects of the physical education curriculum. See, for example, Dartfish Express and EasyTag for analysis, GCSE physical education App and iMuscle for theory, Fitness Pro for circuit training or QR readers where you can create and scan codes that link to a variety of resources. Visit www.handheldlearninginpe.com for a list of physical education specific apps and the ways to use them in the classroom.

Create your own content in the form of podcasts

Using a Mac computer you can make simple podcasts from existing PowerPoints by simply converting them into movies and adding a voice-over. For a simple tutorial on this, go to www.youtube.com/handheldlearninginpe.

Use productivity apps to create work

For subjects such as physical education where there is a need to generate evidence for coursework or practical assessments, you can add another dimension and level of creativity to your pupils' work by getting them to produce a photo or video project. Apps such as pages, keynote, dragon dictate, simple mindX, Evernote, Explain Everything, Skitch, Show Me, Educreations, Fotobabble, iMovie and iPhoto allow for such a plethora of creativity ideas to engage pupils.

Now complete Activity 8.6.

Activity 8.6

Apps

If you have access to a smart phone, tablet or handheld device, research and download apps from places such as iTunes or the Android store. Choose three to five to try in your lessons, and measure the impact on learning.

E-SAFETY

Remaining safe online and always considering e-safety or safeguarding should be of utmost importance when using ICT in schools. Every institution varies in terms of how technologically advanced they are but you must remember always to refer to the school's ICT policies on safety. Check with any network administrators or senior managers that you have permission to use any of the tools discussed in this chapter or indeed any other ICT tools or devices. The Office for Standards in Education (Ofsted) publication, *Safe Use of New Technologies* (2010), emphasises the importance of e-safety in schools. Schools should be encouraged to rewrite their policies to reflect both Web 2.0 and handheld learning, as both are becoming more prevalent in education. Now complete Activity 8.7.

Activity 8.7

E-safety

Download a copy of Ofsted's (2010) *Safe Use of New Technologies* and obtain a copy of your school's 'E-safety Policy'. Make a note of the main considerations and note any discrepancies between the two.

SUMMARY

Throughout the chapter you have been presented with a number of ways that you could use ICT and particularly emerging technologies to enhance your teaching of physical education. When you are qualified, it will be your professional judgement as to the extent of ICT you use. It is, however, evident that in a carefully planned lesson with clear learning outcomes, IT can motivate pupils and enhance their learning. However, it is important to remember that you should only use ICT if it enhances pupils' learning.

It is evident that there is a place for using ICT to enhance learning and teaching in physical education. However, it is important to remember that physical education is essentially a 'practical' subject and the use of ICT should be considered alongside the quest to increase pupils' activity time.

As technology evolves, newer and more innovative tools will be introduced and the resources currently used will probably become obsolete. One thing is certain, though, that technology will continue to move at a fast pace and no matter how little or much ICT you plan into your teaching to enhance pupils' learning, you will be presented with more potential opportunities.

FURTHER READING AND WEB LINKS

http://www.education.gov.uk/schools/teachingandlearning/curriculum/a00199693/use-of-ict.
    Outline of the current National Curriculum guidelines on the use of ICT.

http://www.edudemic.com.
    A website that shares tips and resources on the latest technology within education.

http://www.handheldlearninginpe.com.
    The author of this chapter has his own website that contains blogs, links, resources and posts on the successful integration of ICT and emerging technology within physical education.

http://www.ted.com/talks/ken_robinson_says_schools_kill_creativity.html.
    Sir Ken Robinson makes an entertaining case for the use of ICT. He expresses the view that today's young people are living in the most intensely stimulating period in the

history of the Earth. They are being besieged by information from many different platforms, including computers, iPhones, advertisements and television channels. This information draws their attention but we are penalising them for becoming distracted. It is for that reason that schools should look at the ways that they are implementing ICT in schools.

www.ofsted.gov.uk/resources/safe-use-of-new-technologies.
Evaluates the extent to which the schools in a small-scale report taught pupils to adopt safe and responsible practices in using new technologies and how they achieved this. It also assesses the extent and quality of the training the schools provided for their staff.

Note: all proformas, tables or figures you are asked to complete to help you undertake activities in this chapter are also available on the website which accompanies the book (www.routledge.com/9780415814829).

Chapter 9 Planning for the contribution of physical education to cross-curricular activity

SUZANNE EVERLEY AND ANDY WILD

INTRODUCTION

During your initial teacher education (ITE) to become a physical education teacher you consider the nature of physical education as a subject and the unique contribution that it makes to a pupil's education. No doubt, you have already begun that process. When you teach, it is very likely that you have considered learning outcomes for a lesson that are specific to an activity; in turn, those outcomes contribute to the objectives of the unit of work and aims of the subject in the school. Pupil learning outcomes for specific activities also enhance and enrich their knowledge, skills and understanding in other settings, e.g. sports clubs.

However, physical education also contributes to pupils' broader learning. The purpose of this chapter is to identify the contribution that our subject makes to the curriculum as a whole and to prompt you to reflect on cross-curricular experiences and possibilities within your placement school. Its aim is not to justify the place of physical education in these terms, but rather to highlight the vast scope of educational opportunities that the subject provides and the value it has in the broader learning of pupils and in whole school learning. A good way to think about this is to use the analogy of cogs working together to facilitate the functioning of the whole. Each type of learning is a cog; each has its separate role but none can (or should) operate effectively without influencing the other (see Figure 9.1).

By the end of this chapter you should be able to:

- understand what is meant by cross-curricular teaching;
- identify and be able to reflect on the contribution that physical education makes to the curriculum as a whole;
- understand the vast scope of educational opportunities that the subject provides and the value it has in the broader learning of pupils and in whole school learning.

CROSS-CURRICULAR TEACHING

The concept of cross-curricular teaching, also referred to as linked learning (Kellam and Whewell, 2009), addresses pupils' education within three interrelated domains: direct subject links, metacognition, and application of theory (Figure 9.2). At its most simplistic, cross-curricular learning takes place where there is

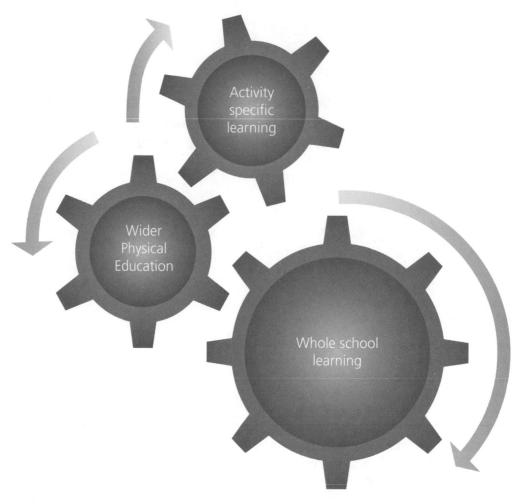

Figure 9.1 Integrating learning in physical education across the curriculum

immediate evidence of a subject existing as part of another. For example, if you ask the class to count their pulse for 15 seconds and multiply by four to calculate their heart rate per minute, it is very straightforward to identify that pupils are using a mathematical process in order to do this. However, if you ask them to consider the best strategy to throw an implement, to do so effectively, they need to think about how to achieve an optimal outcome. In order to achieve this, they also have to think mathematically and scientifically. For instance, they have to consider body position, movement and angle of release. It is realistic to expect that your class have learnt these principles in other areas of the school curriculum, which provides you with opportunity to apply these in a practical context. Thus, it is reasonable to assert that the pupil's learning experience is enriched by the practical application of theoretical concepts. It is essential therefore that your planning takes account of learning experiences in other areas of the curriculum. This requires you to have subject knowledge beyond your subject area (Fautley and Savage, 2011).

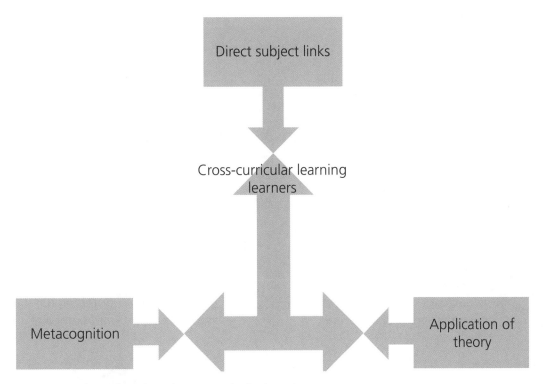

Figure 9.2 Three domains of cross-curricular learning

THE PLANNING PROCESS

Ultimately, teaching in a cross-curricular way should be a conscious process. This can be arrived at in a number of ways but perhaps the continuous cycle in Figure 9.3 can provide a guide to achieving deliberate consideration of pupil's cross-curricular learning.

Essentially, Figure 9.3 represents the cycle that you need to engage in as you integrate cross-curricular work into your teaching. While your starting point is most likely to be to identify any cross-curricular concepts that already exist in your teaching and learning, you may find yourself entering the cycle at any of the steps identified.

This should be a continual process as the nature and educational needs of pupils change and you develop in your sophistication as a teacher. To begin engaging in the process above, it is first necessary to consider what cross-curricular content and concepts actually look like. Activity 9.1 is designed to help you consider practice that you have seen in school to date.

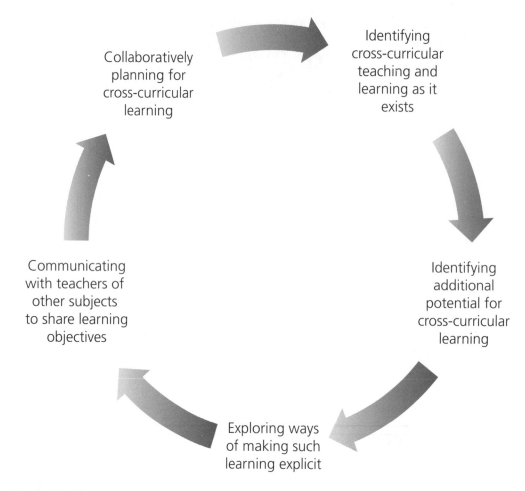

Figure 9.3 Five steps to cross-curricular learning

Activity 9.1

Identifying existing cross-curricular teaching and learning

Reflect on your school experience to date and identify where you have observed cross-curricular practice/learning. Did this form part of the tasks that were set and/or the thinking processes that pupils were being asked to engage in? What impact did the application of cross-curricular approaches to teaching have on pupil learning?

In many situations it is possible to readily identify cross-curricular opportunities occurring. In other situations it may be less apparent, as shown in the following case study.

Case study 1

Student teacher Carrie planned an athletics lesson that was designed to explore techniques of throwing. The pupils were set a task in which they experimented with different starting positions; different foot, shoulder and hip movements; and different points of release. Throughout this process, pupils achieved a number of things that related directly to the physical nature of the activity and the improvement of performance. They also needed to think scientifically, i.e. it was not possible to answer the physical education task without consideration of concepts of forces, momentum and trajectory. This provided a context for the application of theoretical knowledge developed in science lessons. Carrie had discussed this with the Science department who were able to cross-reference the pupils' experience in physical education to the theoretical knowledge they taught in the science classroom.

Extending understanding of concepts such as trajectory and forces when throwing and catching, pupils may be encouraged to consider, for example:

- flight (trajectory) of a forehand in tennis;
- rebound action of a basketball – from the backboard – in a lay up;
- decision-making and judgements when releasing a pass, e.g. from the base of a scrum (ruck or maul) by the scrum half in rugby or centre pass in netball.

Similar principles can be applied to other areas of cross-curricular potential, as shown in Activity 9.2.

Activity 9.2

Identifying opportunities

Returning to the observations you made in Activity 9.1, ask yourself the following questions:

- Could the teachers have further exploited any cross-curricular opportunities that arose during the teaching episode?
- Where did these opportunities exist?
- How could they have been made more explicit to the pupils?
- How might this have enhanced pupil learning?

Going through a process of identifying possibilities for cross-curricular learning establishes an innovative orientation towards teaching. Much of what can be considered good teaching is creative in approach. Part of being creative lies in the ability of the teacher to embed cross-curricular concepts in their work. Further, creative teaching can lead to creative learning and develop in pupils the ability to link disparate concepts and recognise the interrelationships that exist between subjects, thereby enhancing the potential for understanding meaning in learning. For example, Fautley and Savage (2011: 2) remind us that any synthesis that sets out to consider cross-curricular approaches 'should not be done in a way that destroys the cherished ideas and ways of thinking that every subject contains'. The paradox that emerges from this may present a challenge for you as you prepare to teach. It will be necessary to explore the possibilities and practicalities of developing a genuinely cross-curricular approach to your teaching. It is likely that you will particularly value the guidance from your tutor(s) in school as to what might be realistically attempted and achieved in your setting. Now complete Activity 9.3.

Activity 9.3

Embedding opportunities

Discuss with your subject tutor how to assess how pupils' learning experience can be enriched by the cross-curricular opportunities you have identified in Activity 9.2. Agree a way to embed these into the lesson planning process. Consider how task, content and assessment can serve to meet the learning outcomes that you set.

Lowrie (2011) has suggested that pupils need to be encouraged to engage in more diverse and flexible thinking through engaging in problem-solving situations. An example of this might be in netball where pupils are set the task of identifying the best technique of shooting; they then experiment with different techniques and identify which works most effectively. Setting an investigative task encourages exploration in the first instance and then requires (a potentially scientific) justification of the solution in the last. In addition, the need to study *real* situations to make learning meaningful is crucial to pupils' development. For example, the explorative task described above provides a real situation for pupils to explore the application of scientific principles. Establishing a cross-curricular approach to your teaching enables you to achieve this kind of contextual learning. Two key questions may help you to fully exploit the possibilities:

- Do all teachers know what is happening in physical education, and could their lessons take account of the application of content from their subject that is occurring in physical education lessons?
- Could you, as a physical education teacher, better liaise with colleagues in other departments to make the pupils' learning experience richer, relevant and more real by including cross-curricular learning?

Engaging in the actions required to engage in the five steps of the cycle in Figure 9.3 enables you to identify where you are already linking pupils' learning to other subject areas and how best to exploit this. These considerations should also enable you to consider how you might extend your approach to very consciously maximise the cross-curricular potential. In Case study 2, student teacher David was teaching a dance lesson to two Year 8 classes. As an introductory lesson with similar groups, he introduced a new scheme of work to one of them in the following way:

Case study 2

Part one

The pupils began to arrive in the class and the teacher immediately sets a task to engage them … music is playing and he asks them to sit, close their eyes and imagine the kind of dancing that they might see people doing to this kind of music; the pupils then begin to physically explore these movements to form the basis of their introduction to the day's focus …

This lesson worked perfectly well, but following discussions in the post-lesson debrief and a subsequent discussion with the Head of Department of English, David made some changes to his approach.

Part two

The teacher ushered the pupils towards him; as each came in, they sat with heads down, eyes closed, listening to the music. The teacher asked the pupils to engage their imaginative senses. What images were being evoked by the music … the young people described flashing lights within a darkened room; glitter balls, shapes of other dancers surrounding them … what sounds could they hear…what the environment feels like … the pupils described the heat of the environment and the heavy atmosphere … the pupils then wrote down, on sheets of A4 paper, some of the key adjectives that they felt described the environment that the music represented …

Following this, the pupils identified key adjectives that described how they wanted to move within this environment; these were written on cards and scattered around the room. The pupils considered how to express such adjectives through creative movement.

David then passed the cards to the English teacher who was working with the pupils on creating descriptive poetry; in this instance focusing on describing a party with friends.

The essential premise for David's lesson remained unchanged although the learning in which the pupils engaged was significantly enhanced by the second approach. This occurred not only in terms of becoming more reflective about the way in which they moved as a result of being required to articulate how they were doing so but also by assisting in the completion of a task in English. Pupils extended their movement vocabulary in a physical sense and enhanced the vocabulary that they could use in a literary sense to describe movement.

What was significant in the enrichment of pupils' learning in this case study was not only the reflection that David had engaged in, but the fact that he had collaborated with another member of teaching staff to communicate his ideas and listen to the learning outcomes the teachers were currently targeting with their groups. Cross-curricular approaches clearly have most impact where links are made for pupils in more than one subject area. Verma and Pumfey (1993) discuss the collective responsibility that teachers have when considering cross-curricular elements, highlighting the point that your communication with teachers in other subject areas is crucial. Now complete Activity 9.4.

Activity 9.4

Sharing with peers

Discuss and identify with another student teacher learning to teach another subject area within your placement school aspects of learning that derive from and are integral to both subject areas, e.g. map reading in geography and orienteering. Identify how you could integrate some of the learning that is taking place so that there is synergy between the different subjects.

Very often, thinking about making cross-curricular links is dominated by concepts of literacy and numeracy. However, cross-curricular learning within physical education can also impact on other subject areas. Activity 9.5 looks at cross-curricular learning with arts subjects.

Activity 9.5

Identifying cross-curricular activities

Use Table 9.1 to identify ways in which you might explore possibilities for cross-curricular learning in physical education that relates to arts education: the first column identifies the subject area; the second column provides an exemplar activity which identifies the direct link of other subjects to physical education; and the third column invites you to consider ways in which physical education can be used to introduce concepts and links with other subjects in the curriculum. You might also want to complete Table 9.1 in relation to other subjects.

Table 9.1 Identifying cross-curricular activities

Subject area	Exemplar activities	Personal suggestion for exploration
Music	Create own stimulus for dance and gymnastic activities Sports equipment can be used to create rhythm for dance, e.g. the bouncing of a basketball	
Art	Reflect and represent physical movement through an art medium (painting, drawing, clay) Consider using techniques employed in observational analysis to explore angles and perspective	
Drama	Draw on the expression demonstrated in portraying character; consider ways in which these translate to the interpretation of music within dance Focus upon contemporary events (e.g. Olympic torch relay; the controversy of racial violence in sport)	

The secondary school day has historically been structured through a subject/time model and that fragmentation in itself can cause difficulties for learners as different areas of the curriculum appear to lack meaningful connection (Eyre and Marjoram, 1990). To effect any form of cross-curricular dimension, a number of key questions are fundamentally important when planning your lessons:

- What types of problem/task are you setting for the pupils?
- How do pupils have to think in order to respond to the tasks you are setting?
- Where is the evidence of pupil learning?
- What is the full content of the topic that you are teaching?
- How might you support learning in other areas of the curriculum through this?
- How can you seek collaboration from other subject areas to support learning in physical education?

As with all of your teaching, your consideration of and approach to cross-curricular learning will develop as you gain more experience. It is, however, an aspect of teaching that, we would argue, receives rather less attention than it should, bearing in mind the enrichment it can provide to pupils' learning and creativity in the curriculum. When you begin your first teaching post, it is an area perhaps, on which you can specifically focus and thus make a difference, not just to your own professional development, but also to the department/faculty/school in which you are working. Now complete Activity 9.6.

Activity 9.6

Extending cross-curricular approaches

During your ITE year, identify ways in which cross-curricular planning could be integrated into a whole school policy to develop cross-curricular learning. How can coherent school policies be developed and successfully implemented to the benefit of both pupils and teachers?

SUMMARY

It is acknowledged that developing cross-curricular approaches to teaching is perceived as inherently problematic. For instance, Verma and Pumfrey (1993) observed that the demands of a teacher are compounded by the additional teacher duties and whole school responsibilities that form part of normal school life. It is suggested that as a subject physical education could 'have a greater involvement in the promotion and development of cross-curricular learning and work to dispel the perceived difficulties with linking the teaching of physical education to other parts of the curriculum' (Kellam and Whewell, 2009: 28). Good physical education provides pupils with the opportunity to experience:

- *Situated learning*: Learning in situations that are realistic for the task (for example, in science, pupils learn about the trajectory of flight of a ball; in physical education they learn about how to release the ball at the optimum point to create greatest distance, i.e. the science is taught in physical education where it actually happens).
- *Dialectically constructed learning*: Where pupils share ideas through discussion and build on these as they identify solutions to problems.
- *Meaning making opportunities*: Where pupils identify how the learning that they have engaged in will affect them outside the classroom.

Together these form the essential foundation of profound learning that permeates pupils' wider education as a result of cross-curricular planning and form a crucial part of what should underpin our approach to teaching.

Your ITE is a time for you to observe and consider current cross-curricular practice in school(s). You will face hurdles and difficulties; some may present as more challenging – some may even seem insurmountable. You may wish to return to this chapter and consider further the principles that you have explored through the activities herein. Take the time to reflect and discuss with others and see for yourself that change is possible. Siraj-Blatchford and Siraj-Blatchford (1998) highlight the importance of stepping back and planning – both in the short term and longer. They cite the value of reviewing the curriculum and discuss the usefulness of involving pupils in that process.

When the obstacles appear too prohibitive, then the sentiments expressed by Verma and Pumfrey (1993: 11) may be applicable: 'No person ever made a greater mistake than one who did nothing merely because to do everything was impossible.'

FURTHER READING

Eyre, D. and Marjoram, T. (1990) *Enriching and Extending the National Curriculum*, London: Kogan Page.
   This book pursues issues pertaining to enriching and extending the curriculum and suggests that teaching and learning approaches have to be varied. It further considers why, when and how enrichment and extension activities should be applied.

Fautley, M. and Savage, J. (2011) *Cross Curricular Teaching and Learning in the Secondary School in the Arts*, London: Routledge.
   This book argues for the development of a new, skilful pedagogy which embeds an authentic, cross-curricular approach to teaching and learning. It focuses on the powerful nature of cross-curricular thinking to produce a joined-up model of teaching and learning where teachers are empowered to think beyond creative pedagogies and pupils are able to engage in deep learning as a result.

Kellam, K. and Whewell, E. (2009) Linked Learning and its place within the teaching of physical education in the primary school, *Physical Education Matters*, 4, 2: 24–8.
   This article outlines a study that investigated how cross-curricular learning is used within primary school physical education. Results of the study suggest that physical education is the hardest subject in which to incorporate cross-curriculum learning.

Siraj-Blatchford, J. and Siraj-Blatchford, I. (eds) (1998) *Educating the Whole Child: Cross Curricular Skills: Themes and Dimensions*, Buckingham: Open University Press.
   The authors argue that the teaching of skills, attitudes, concepts and knowledge should not be seen as separate or alternative objectives, but rather as complementary and essential elements of the education process.

Verma, G. and Pumfrey, P. (1993) *Cross Curricular Contexts, Themes and Dimensions in Secondary Schools*, London: Falmer Press.
   Much remains undecided concerning the structure, content, pedagogy and assessment of many components of the secondary curriculum. This book considers some of the challenges and describes promising practices in the school setting.

Note: all proformas, tables or figures you are asked to complete to help you undertake activities in this chapter are also available on the website which accompanies the book (www.routledge.com/9780415814829).

Chapter 10   Teaching safely and safety in physical education

ANNE CHAPPELL

INTRODUCTION

> Good practice is safe practice.
>
> (Severs *et al.*, 2003: 7)

In a culture of accountability and liability, teachers, along with other professionals, are increasingly at risk of facing litigation when things go wrong (Raymond, 1999). The fact that all physical activity contains inherent risks, and that physical education has unique risks in relation to other subjects in the National Curriculum, demands that you have specialist knowledge and understanding to ensure that all practice is safe (Chappell and Katene, 2010). It is essential that you stay up to date in light of the regularity with which issues and advice relating to safety and safe practice develop.

As a teacher of physical education you have a legal, professional and moral responsibility to 'teach safely and safety' (Chappell and Katene, 2010: 134). Once you qualify as a teacher, you have responsibility for the safety and well-being of your pupils, in both the formal learning environment of the lesson, and as part of your extra-curricular commitment. Until then, the class teachers with whom you work retain the duty of care for the pupils, allowing you to develop your knowledge, understanding and implementation of safe practice in a supported environment with a qualified teacher present. It is also important that you teach safety to pupils and this should be integral to the planning of all lessons.

Issues relating to safety in physical education are numerous and complex, and although most rely on the application of common sense (Whitlam, 2003), it is vital that you make sure that you have a good understanding of the requirements.

By the end of this chapter you should be able to:

- understand the law and documentation about safe practice;
- implement safe practice in the learning environment recognising the direct link with good practice;
- undertake risk assessment and risk management;
- know where to go for support to ensure safe practice.

The activities in this chapter are written in such a way that you can revisit them at various points in your career, particularly as the context for your work as a physical educator develops; your levels of responsibility for safe practice increase, and when you move schools.

As you undertake the activities in this chapter you need to read relevant sources listed in the further readings.

THE LAW AND DOCUMENTATION FOR SAFE PRACTICE

The School Teachers' Pay and Conditions Act published annually sets out the legal requirements for teachers; it is vital that you understand these and how they impact on your work in the delivery of physical education. Further information on the legal responsibilities of teacher is also available via the Professional Associations and the teaching unions. It is also crucial during this time of change in the structure and organisation of educational institutions that you check the local arrangements for pay and conditions in your school as requirements may differ. There are several key legal terms which you must know. Activity 10.1 is designed to help you learn these.

> ### Activity 10.1
>
> **Legal terms**
>
> Research the definitions of the terms in Table 10.1 and complete the table.

There is an increasing amount of documentation about safety that impacts on teachers' work. The Department for Education (DfE) guides schools and departments to produce and regularly update policies outlining expectations for safe practice which take account of current legal requirements. There may also be guidance via your Local Authority (LA). These policies include information about onsite and offsite activities and provide clear guidance to support you in your practice. There are also other sources which comprehensively address issues relating to safety across the school and specifically in physical education (see, for example, afPE, 2012).

In order for the policies to have any value, for you to ensure that you fully understand your responsibilities, and to protect yourself against accusations of negligence and claims for liability, it is essential that you familiarise yourself with them. Now complete Activity 10.2.

> ### Activity 10.2
>
> **Finding documentation**
>
> Locate the documents, listed in Table 10.2, in your school and identify the key information that each contains, as the table demonstrates.

Table 10.1 Key legal terms

Term	Definition
In loco parentis	
Duty of care	
Negligence	
Liability	
Vicarious liability	

Table 10.2 Key documents related to safety

Document	Location	Key information
The Head's Legal Guide (Croner, 2010)	Head teacher's office	Detailed guidelines on all legal aspects of the school including teacher's pay and conditions and health and safety.
Safe Practice in Physical Education and Sport (afPE, 2012)		
LA Guidelines for Physical Education and School Sport		
LA Guidelines for Educational Visits		
School Health and Safety Policy		
First aid policy and accident record		
Department of Health and Safety Policy		
Department Risk Assessment Record		
Add any others		

SAFE PRACTICE IN THE LEARNING ENVIRONMENT

The Teachers' Standards require teachers to establish a safe environment for learning (DfE, 2012b). The National Curriculum for Physical Education (NCPE) offers statutory requirements for what pupils are taught explicitly about safety in relation to leading healthy, active lifestyles, as well as the implicit requirements for safe participation in the physical activities which underpin the curriculum.

A teacher requires sound knowledge and understanding of the key principles for safe exercise that apply across physical education (afPE, 2012; Norris, 1999) in order to support the development of a safe learning environment. Observing teachers provides a wealth of valuable information about safe practice in lessons, including how it is planned, established and maintained. It would also be valuable for you to look at long-term planning in schemes of work; medium-term planning in units of work; and short-term planning in lesson plans. Now complete Activities 10.3 and 10.4.

Activity 10.3

Procedures and routines in physical education

Observe a complete physical education lesson – starting as pupils arrive at the changing room. Make a note of all the procedures and routines in Table 10.3 (adding any that are not included) and identify the safety implications for each.

Activity 10.4

Providing a safe environment

Identify an area of activity which you need to target for development in relation to understanding appropriate safety issues. Observe a lesson and respond to the questions in Table 10.4 in order to develop a better awareness of the type of factors teachers need to take into account when planning for a safe environment.

Table 10.3 Procedures and routines in physical education

Routine	Observation	Safety implications
Have pupils removed all jewellery? How is this managed?		
Have any medical conditions been taken into account? What about the wearing of glasses? How are 'excuse' notes handled?		
Is pupils' clothing appropriate and do they have appropriate footwear? How is this managed? How is the wearing of headscarves managed?		
What instructions does the teacher give the pupils prior to leaving the changing room?		
What is the routine for taking equipment to the working area?		
How is equipment, such as cones, laid out?		
How does the teacher distribute bats, balls, sticks, etc.?		
How does the teacher gain the attention of the class in the teaching area?		
What strategy does the teacher use to place the pupils into groups?		
How does the teacher organise teams for games?		
What routines are used for the start and finish of an activity, e.g. are the pupils called in?		
What routines are used for the removal and dismantling of large apparatus during the lesson, e.g. gymnastics?		
Others		

© 2014, *A Practical Guide to Teaching Physical Education in the Secondary School, 2e*
Susan Capel and Peter Breckon

Table 10.4 Providing a safe environment

In what ways *could* the lesson be hazardous?
What measures has the teacher taken to minimise the risk to safety?
Write a list of questions to ask the teacher on any aspect of safety within the lesson:
Write a summary of your discussions with the teacher after the lesson:

It is very important that pupils are involved in supporting a safe learning environment via expectations, procedures and routines, and that they have ownership of knowledge and understanding about safety: their full involvement is significant in ensuring safe practice. Having looked at the teacher's role in developing the environment for learning, it is then important for you to begin your own planning by finding out what the pupils you will be teaching already know. Now complete Activity 10.5.

Activity 10.5

What do the pupils know about safety?

Speak to pupils and note what they know about safety using the following questions and ones that you devise based on your research into safety. You may wish to use these types of questions with pupils when you first work with them, and at the end of a unit of work to assess their learning.

1   What is safety?

_____

2   What is risk?

_____

3   Why is safety important?

_____

4   What do you do to make sure you and the pupils around you are safe?

_____

5   What would put you and the pupils around you at risk?

_____

6   What does the teacher do to make sure that you are safe?

_____

7   What advice would you give pupils about staying safe during physical education or in sporting activities?

_____

Based on the information collected in the first five activities in this chapter you can begin to list 'ground rules' that you will negotiate with pupils, and begin to reflect on the ways that you might include these within your own scheme of work, units of work and lesson plans. Now complete Activity 10.6.

Activity 10.6

Setting ground rules to support safe practice

Following observations of lessons, conversations with pupils and research into safe practice, write a list of general ground rules that you will develop with the pupils that you teach and reinforce in every lesson.

1 All jewellery and adornment to be completely removed for every lesson.

2 _____

3 _____

4 _____

5 _____

6 _____

7 _____

8 _____

9 _____

10 _____

As well as understanding the organisational implications for safety, you also need current knowledge and understanding of safe exercise, including contraindications in physical activity, based on current scientific research. Further, pupils need to understand safe exercise. For example, in teaching pupils about preparation of the body for physical activity, it is important that you can explain clearly the elements of a warm-up and the correct way to stretch, much of which you can also apply to the process of preparing the body for rest or cooling down (Elbourn, 2008; afPE, 2012). Now complete Activity 10.7.

Activity 10.7

Effective preparation for exercise

Elements of a warm-up

Research and make notes in Table 10.5 about the purpose of the elements of an effective warm-up for a physical education lesson.

Types of stretching

Research and compare the types of stretching in Table 10.5, taking into account the potential risk factors for pupils.
    Repeat this for mobilising and pulse raising activities.

Table 10.5 Effective preparation for exercise

Elements of a warm-up			
Element	**Purpose**	**Examples**	**Contraindications**
Mobilising activities			
Pulse raising activities			
Stretching			

(continued)

Table 10.5 (continued)

Types of stretching			
Type	**Definition**	**Value for pupils**	**Contraindications**
Static stretching			
Dynamic stretching			
Ballistic stretching			

Pupils need to know and understand why there are some activities that have more risks than benefits and so you, as the teacher, must be clear about these (Elbourn, 2008; afPE, 2012; Donovan *et al.*, 1988). Now complete Activity 10.8.

Activity 10.8

Contraindications and safe exercise

Investigate the potential dangers in the exercises in Table 10.6 which have been identified as being contraindicated. Find out what the safe alternatives are.

It is also essential that you are fully aware of how to manage the potentially dangerous issues which arise on a lesson-by-lesson basis (afPE, 2012). These issues can be procedural (e.g. what pupils are wearing) or based on lesson content. Some of these issues relate to the cultural background of pupils that you work with and so it is key for you to handle them with understanding and sensitivity. See Activity 10.9.

Activity 10.9

Safety considerations

Find out from literature and colleagues about the following factors in physical education and consider how you should manage them to ensure minimal risk.

Procedural

1 Removal of jewellery
2 Appropriate clothing
3 Appropriate footwear
4 Medical conditions
5 Wearing of glasses
6 Wearing of headscarves
7 Management of excuse notes

Lesson content

Listed in Table 10.7.

Table 10.6 Contraindications and safe exercise

Exercise	Potential risk	Safe alternative
V-sits		
Straight leg sit-ups		
Straight leg toe touches		
Straight leg side bends		
Burpees		
Full head circles		
Hurdle stretch		
Sit and reach		
Deep knee bends		
Hyperextension of the back (standing and lying)		
Ballistic stretching		

Table 10.7 Managing activities to ensure minimal risk

Activity	Managing the activity to ensure minimal risk
Order of activities	Ensure the order of activities allows the body to be appropriately prepared, e.g. mobilise shoulders before the cervical vertebrae, and lumbar vertebrae before performing lateral flexion to reduce the risk of injury
Contraindicated exercises	
Rest	
Progression	
Joint alignment	
Use of momentum	
High impact exercises	
Lack of stability	

There are different safety implications for different learning environments. As well as the procedures in place for safe practice in relation to physical activity, there is also the requirement of knowledge and understanding of policy and procedure relating to those activities which take place onsite and offsite outside of timetabled lesson time. Now complete Activity 10.10.

Activity 10.10

Extra-curricular activities

This activity is one that may take place over a period of time as you look at each element as the opportunity arises. For the activities below, identify which school staff you need support from, the guidance documentation you need and any paperwork that you need to complete and indicate these in Table 10.8:

- an evening competition off-site at another school (e.g. gymnastics competition or volleyball match);
- involvement in an offsite afternoon event (e.g. borough athletics meeting);
- an offsite educational trip during the day (e.g. to a theatre to watch a dance performance or a university laboratory for examination coursework);
- residential trips (e.g. an outdoor and adventurous activities week).

RISK ASSESSMENT AND MANAGEMENT

As a physical education teacher you are expected to identify foreseeable risks that may result in injury (risk assessment), and take reasonable practicable steps to reduce the risk to an acceptable level (risk management) (afPE, 2012). The Health and Safety Executive (HSE, 1999: 2) identify that a risk assessment is 'nothing more than a careful examination of what, in your work, could cause harm to people', and that this is done 'so that you can weigh up whether you have taken enough precautions to prevent harm'. They outline five clear steps that need to be taken in risk assessment and management (1999: 3):

1 Look for the hazards.
2 Decide who might be harmed, and how.
3 Evaluate the risks and decide whether precautions are adequate or more needs to be done.
4 Record your findings.
5 Review your assessment and revise it as necessary.

Safe Practice in Physical Education and Sport (afPE, 2012) clearly identifies the information needed to support effective risk assessment and management. This document is increasingly used in the legal environment to guide decisions about negligence and liability. The areas which you need to consider initially are those of pupils; facilities; the range and content which includes the six areas of activity in the NCPE; and environmental conditions which directly impact upon your work. In identifying the potential risks, problems or issues you are more informed; thus, making risk management more effective (see Activities 10.11, 10.12, 10.13 and 10.14).

Table 10.8 Extra-curricular activities

Activity	Staff support required	Guidance document	Completed document
An onsite lunchtime club for pupils (e.g. swimming club in the school pool)	Head of department and lifeguard	*Safe Practice in Physical Education and Sport* (afPE, 2012) Department health and safety policy, including risk assessment	None
An evening competition offsite at another school (e.g. gymnastics competition or volleyball match)			
Involvement in an offsite afternoon event (e.g. borough athletics meeting)			
An offsite educational trip during the day (e.g. to a theatre to watch a dance performance or a university laboratory for examination coursework)			
Residential trips (e.g. an outdoor and adventurous activities week)			

Activity 10.11

Accidents

Use Table 10.9 to review accidents that could happen in the physical education setting, identifying the potential outcomes for accusations of negligence by the teacher – depending on the circumstances, and possible measures for risk control.

Activity 10.12

Facilities and risk assessment

Using the example in Table 10.10, for each of the other facilities used for physical education (plus any others you can identify), note any potential hazards for which you need to plan; and the measures you could take to manage and reduce the risk. Do the risks vary depending upon the activity taking place in the facility? You can also use the school and departmental risk assessment documents to help you.

Activity 10.13

Areas of activity

Identify the important safety considerations unique to the range and content of the NCPE in Table 10.11.

Activity 10.14

Environmental considerations

Using Table 10.12, list your responsibilities to pupils in various weather conditions. Check the department and school policies to see what guidance has been given on risk management for each.

Also consider the environmental considerations for you as the teacher and the steps you can take to minimise the risks, e.g. prolonged exposure to the sun.

Table 10.9 Accidents

Incident	Issue of responsibility	Risk control
Stud earring ripped out of a pupil's ear during a netball lesson leaving a wound requiring stitches	Teacher accountable for pupils being appropriately dressed for the activity (afPE guidelines, online)	All jewellery to be removed in the changing rooms at the start of the lesson
Discus fatally hitting a pupil on the back of the head		
Pupil broke a wrist having run into a wall in the sports hall using hands to break the run during a wet weather activity		
Pupil sustained severe concussion and a cut requiring stitches when a trampoline fell while the pupil was assisting the teacher in wheeling it to the side of the gym		

Table 10.10 Facilities and risk assessment

Facility	Potential hazard	Activity	Risk management
Gymnasium	Trampolines round the edges of the room	Pose a significant hazard for games activities	Mark/cone off the area and ensure that pupils are fully aware of the area which is off limits
Sports hall			
Dance studio			
Hard courts			
Field			
Swimming pool			
Others			

Table 10.11 Safety considerations for a range of areas of activity

Area of activity	Unique safety issues
Athletic activities	
Dance activities	
Games	
Gymnastics	
Outdoor and adventurous activities	
Swimming	

Table 10.12 Environmental considerations

Weather conditions	Potential problems	Solution
Hot sunshine	Sun burn Dehydration Concentration difficulties Fatigue	Pupils to bring sunscreen and water to all lessons Shade areas to be used at appropriate intervals in the lesson High intensity activity to be avoided Pupils to wear lightweight, light-coloured clothing Indoor facilities to be used if necessary
Rain		
Thunder and lightning		
Hail		
Wind		
Low temperatures		
Frost		
Snow		

SUPPORT TO ENSURE SAFE PRACTICE

You are expected to have the necessary knowledge and skills to undertake your work safely and it is your responsibility to seek advice and support if you are in doubt about any aspect of your work (Severs *et al.*, 2003). It is important that you have an understanding of the key requirements for your professional responsibilities to facilitate a better understanding of your learning needs. It is essential that you discuss particular areas of identified need with your mentor and focus on them as part of your learning. Having referred to *Safe Practice in Physical Education and Sport* (afPE, 2012), list the professional responsibilities and key requirements of you as a teacher, in order to reflect upon all the vital factors to ensure that your practice throughout physical education is safe (Activity 10.15).

Activity 10.15

Appropriate challenge versus acceptable risk

Using Table 10.13, identify the professional responsibilities inherent in physical education and sport, highlighting the key requirements for each.

It is important to recognise that seeking support is both professional and prudent. There are many sources of support available. It is good practice to discuss issues with colleagues in your department, as well as other colleagues in the school. If you need to seek wider support, then you can make contact with the following: your union; the local authority (LA); and your professional association (e.g. Association for Physical Education).

Table 10.13 Professional responsibilities in physical education and sport

Professional responsibility		Key requirements
People	Teachers	
	Pupils	
Context	Procedures	
	Physical education equipment	
	Physical education facilities	
Organisation	Preparation	
	Teaching style and class organisation	

Susan Capel and Peter Breckon

IN CONCLUSION

A newly qualified teacher, following a particularly unpleasant accident during her first term in school, stated: 'It is horrible to learn the hard way.' The most distressing thing for her was that she recognised, in hindsight, that the circumstances prior to the accident could have been managed in a more appropriate way. Fortunately, no legal action was taken but, had it been, the teacher would have been put in a very difficult situation and the potential outcome could have been detrimental to her career. At some stage in your teaching career, there may be an accident involving a pupil. If this happens, you must be in a position to demonstrate that you have effectively managed risk, should there be any claim of negligence against you. One way would be to undertake a detailed audit of health and safety practice in the department in which you are working and familiarise yourself with every aspect of your professional environment. This information will support your planning for safety. Now complete Activity 10.16.

Activity 10.16

Health and safety audit

Complete the audit in Raymond (1999: 157–60), seeking advice where necessary.

Another way you can start to do this is to consider examples of things that have gone wrong in physical education and the detailed legal analysis and final outcome (e.g. Raymond, 1999; Whitlam 2005; Chappell and Katene, 2010; afPE, 2012). These case studies provide a valuable stimulus for critical thought and reflection about your knowledge and practice. They are also a useful tool for discussion.

Finally, Chappell and Katene (2010) and afPE (2012) identify elements of good practice that minimise the risks of harm to the pupils and negligence on your part. These provide you with a guide to enable you to reflect on what you do in a proactive, effective, professional manner and include the following principles:

- Staff have appropriate and up-to-date qualifications.
- Appropriate steps are taken to guarantee safety.
- Pupils are fully aware.
- Pupils are fully prepared.
- Visits are organised using clear procedures supported by policy.
- Records are kept (registers, lesson plans).
- Teachers are kept up to date on Health and Safety.
- Regular risk assessments are undertaken and recorded.
- Activities are undertaken in line with 'good regular and approved practice'.

SUMMARY

As you can see from this chapter, there is a lot to consider in teaching 'safely and safety' (Chappell and Katene, 2010: 134). It would be unrealistic to expect you to know everything about every element of safe practice and risk assessment in physical education when you start in your first teaching post. It is, however, imperative that you keep the development of knowledge and understanding at the top of your professional agenda and practice from the outset of your Initial Teacher Education. It is also important that you know where to get advice and seek advice and support whenever you feel it is needed. Further, it is also important that you teach pupils about safety in your lessons.

FURTHER READING

In the list of further reading are texts which have been specifically identified to support you in completing the activities included in this chapter. Those which do not relate to specific activities provide background reading to support your understanding of this complex area.

afPE (2012) *Safe Practice in Physical Education and Sport*, Leeds: Coachwise Ltd.
Activities 10.1 to 10.16.

Chappell, A. and Katene, W. (2010) Teaching safely and safety in physical education, in S. Capel and M. Whitehead (eds) *Learning to Teach Physical Education in the Secondary School: A Companion to School Experience*, London: Routledge, pp. 134–53.
Activity 10.1.

Donovan, G., McNamara, J. and Gianoli, P. (1988) *Exercise Danger*, Floreat Park: Wellness Australia.
Activities 10.7 and 10.8.

Elbourn, J. (2008) *Aerobics and Circuits for Secondary Schools*, Leeds: Coachwise Ltd.
Activities 10.7 to 10.9.

Harris, J. and Elbourn, J. (2002) *Warming Up and Cooling Down*, Leeds: Human Kinetics.
Activities 10.7 and 10.8.

HSE (Health and Safety Executive) (1999) *Five Steps to Risk Assessment*, Sudbury: Health and Safety Executive.

Hopper, B., Grey, J. and Maude, P. (2003) *Teaching Physical Education in the Primary School*, London: RoutledgeFalmer.
Activities 10.6 and 10.13.

Norris, C.M. (1999) *The Complete Guide to Stretching*, London: A and C Black.
Activities 10.7 and 10.8.

Parker, L. (2012) *The Early Years Health and Safety Handbook*, London: Routledge.

QCA (Qualifications and Curriculum Authority) (2007) *Physical Education Programme of Study for Key Stage 3 and Attainment Target*, London: Crown/QCA.
Activities 10.5 and 10.13.

Raymond, C. (ed.) (1999) *Safety Across the Curriculum*, London: RoutledgeFalmer.
Activities 10.1 and 10.15.

Severs, J., Whitlam, P. and Woodhouse, J. (2003) *Safety and Risk in Primary School Physical Education: A Guide for Teachers*, London: Routledge.
Activities 10.1, 10.9, 10.13 and 10.15.

Whitlam, P. (2003) Risk management principles, in J. Severs, P. Whitlam, and J. Woodhouse (2003) *Safety and Risk in Primary School Physical Education: A Guide for Teachers*, London: Routledge.
Activities 10.1, 10.3 and 10.4.

Whitlam, P. (2005) *Case Law in Physical Education and School Sport*, Leeds: Coachwise Ltd.
Activities 10.3, 10.4, 10.10 to 10.14.

Note: all proformas, tables or figures you are asked to complete to help you undertake activities in this chapter are also available on the website which accompanies the book (www.routledge.com/9780415814829).

Part III   Teaching for pupil learning

Chapter 11 Applying theories of learning to your practice

VANESSA JONES AND LERVERNE BARBER

INTRODUCTION: UNDERSTANDING THEORIES OF LEARNING

In order to enhance pupils' learning it is important to understand how theory underpins learning and how an understanding of learning theories is essential for the planning of creative and engaging units of work and lessons. As Rink (2009: 162) states: 'There is no single theory of learning that explains learning or lack of it in all situations, and therefore there can be no single approach to instruction.' Theories of learning can be used to support an approach to teaching. This chapter explores the link between learning theory and teaching strategies and how they underpin and facilitate the learning process.

Learning theories are essentially conceptual frameworks that explain the way in which information can be absorbed, processed and retained. The link between these three elements is explored and examples of practice presented. We focus on moving from a concern about activity and content to a concern about the learner and learning. The greater your understanding of how learning theory underpins the learning process, the easier it is to plan appropriately for the range of pupils and activities you will encounter. This chapter aims to help you to develop a 'toolbox' of ideas for your teaching which you can apply in different contexts to enhance pupils' learning. Understanding the fundamentals of learning theory should give you the scope to develop as a creative and effective teacher; one who is aware of the complexities of teaching a range of different activities to a wide range of different learners. The ability to create interesting lessons through relevant and engaging tasks should, in theory, lead to stimulating and effective learning environments.

There are a number of theories of learning, but they essentially fall into three categories: Behaviourism; Constructivism; and Information Processing (cognitivism). Each of these categories is addressed briefly in this chapter (for more information you might start with Burton (2009)). Demonstrating how these theories can be applied by matching them to appropriate teaching strategies will hopefully inspire you to develop your understanding further and experiment using the basic philosophy we present. We like to call it 'Pick n Mix' as we believe that being able to draw on a range of theories, sometimes within the same lesson, provides a comprehensive and appropriately targeted approach to teaching.

By the end of this chapter you should be able to:

- understand categories of learning theory;

- demonstrate an understanding of how learning theory underpins the utilisation of effective teaching strategies;
- apply a range of appropriate teaching strategies to plan for differentiation and pupils' preferred learning styles.

CATEGORIES OF LEARNING THEORIES

Three categories of learning theory, along with specific theories in each category, are outlined below:

- Behaviourist theories (e.g. Pavlov 1849–1936; Thorndike 1874–1949; Skinner 1904–1990);
- Constructivist theories (e.g. Dewey 1858–1952; Piaget 1896–1980; Vygotsky 1896–1934; Bruner 1915–);
- Information Processing theory (Wertheimer, 1923).

Behaviourist theories

The key characteristics of behaviourist theories are that:

- The external environment shapes behaviours.
- Learning is a result of conditioning; classical and instrumental, or operant, with a focus on praise and punishment.
- There is a tendency to concentrate on objective and observable behaviours with little account taken of thought processes and activities or context.
- The focus is on the acquisition of new behaviour through modelling; the teacher is the 'font of all knowledge'.
- A skill-based teacher-centred direct instruction is aligned with command and practice teaching strategies (see Mosston and Ashworth, 2002).

Constructivist theories

> Constructivist approaches emphasise that learning is an active process in which the individual seeks out information in relation to the task at hand and the environmental conditions prevailing at any given time, and tests out her or his own capabilities within the context formed by the task and the environment.
>
> (Kirk and Macdonald, 2009: 124)

The key characteristics of constructivist theories are that:

- Context is important; knowledge is internalised by learners, individuals construct new knowledge from experiences.
- Learning is pupil-centred.
- Critical thinking and problem-solving are important.
- Learning is an active process controlled by the learner.
- Learning is a search for meaning; the pupil constructs his/her own understanding of the world – there is not one 'right' answer or someone else's (teacher's) answer. Therefore learning must start with issues around which the pupil is trying to construct meaning.
- Learning is holistic, i.e. understanding of wholes, with parts to be understood in the context of the whole.

In addition, there are other constructivist theories:

- *Social constructivist theory* views the learner as a unique individual with unique needs and backgrounds – socialisation and education. As a result, the key features of constructivist teaching focus on problem-solving, interpretation, teaching strategies tailored to pupil interpretation; open-ended questions; analysis and evaluation with teacher and other pupils.

Specific learning theories which are based or have developed from a constructivist approach include:

- *Communal constructivism* (see Holmes *et al.*, 2001): 'An approach to learning in which pupils not only construct their own knowledge (constructivism) as a result of interacting with their environment (social constructivism), but are also actively engaged in the process of constructing knowledge for their learning community' (Holmes *et al.*, 2001: 1, cited by Leask and Younie, 2001).
- *Bruner's Scaffolding theory* (1983): This was based on a combination of the work of Vygotsky and Bruner and revolves around structured intervention within communicative learning models. The learner constructs new ideas or concepts based upon current or past knowledge. The teacher provides focused questions, appropriate resources and progressive steps to aid the learner. There is gradual adult withdrawal of control and support as the learner increases mastery of a task.
- *Situated Learning:* Learning normally occurs as a function of the activity, context and culture in which it occurs, i.e., it is situated (Lave and Wenger, 1991).

Information processing theory

Information processing can be compared to a 'simple' computer program in relation to the processing of information. Short-term memory is where information is analysed and then is stored with existing information in the long-term memory.
Key characteristics of information processing theory are that:

- The presentation, recognition, storage and selection of information to the learner, and comparison with existing knowledge, are paramount.
- Learning is explained in terms of perceptions and memory process.
- The emphasis is on finding patterns in things that allow the mind to make sense out of 'nonsense'.

Now complete Activity 11.1.

Activity 11.1

Which statement matches which theory?

Test your understanding by matching the statements to the correct theory (see Table 11.1).

Table 11.1 Learning theories

Statements	Behaviourist	Constructivist	Information Processing
1. Strengthens a certain kind of behaviour through positive reinforcement (rewards)			
2. The pupil constructs his/her own understanding of the world – not the 'right' answer – someone else's (teachers) answer			
3. An active process controlled by the learner			
4. Refers to complete structures rather than parts			
5. Knowledge internalised by learners; individuals construct new knowledge from experiences			
6. Building new knowledge structures			
7. Direct instruction (e.g. command/practice)			

(continued)

Table 11.1 (continued)

8. Cognition as a 'simple' computer program			
9. Concentrates on objective and observable behaviours			
10. Study of the presentation, recognition, storage and selection of information to the learner and comparison with existing knowledge			
11. Learning is a search for meaning, therefore must start with issues around which the pupil is trying to construct meaning. A holistic model			
12. Emphasis on finding patterns in things, that allows the mind to make sense out of 'nonsense'			
13. The acquisition of new behaviour through modelling of the 'font of all knowledge'			
14. Does not take account of thought processes and activities, or context			

LEARNING THEORIES AND TEACHING STRATEGIES

In recent decades there has been a shift from a more traditional teacher-directed approach to teaching to a learner-centred approach, with a focus on personalised learning. Different terminology is used to describe teaching approaches, methods, strategies, styles, etc. (see Whitehead with Blair, 2010: 154–6 for further information on different terminology). In this chapter, the term teaching strategy is used to describe a specific teaching approach.

The links between the underpinning learning theory and teaching strategies employed are a fundamental part of effective planning. In order to achieve a high quality learning and teaching environment, consideration needs to be given to the alignment of the different elements.

Figures 11.1 and 11.2 demonstrate how the underpinning learning theory may influence the selected teaching strategy for two different activities.

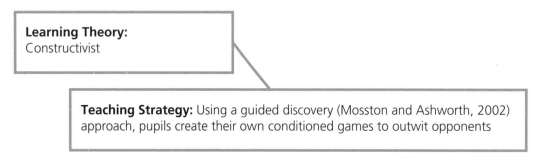

Figure 11.1 An example of a framework for learning from a constructivist approach

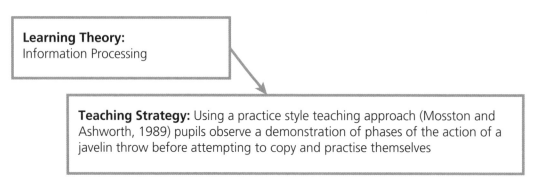

Figure 11.2 An example of a framework for learning from an information processing approach

Activity 11.2

Making connections between learning theory and teaching strategies

Looking at the boxes in Figure 11.3, can you link learning theory to an appropriate teaching strategy and provide a specific example in relation to a particular teaching activity (as shown in Figures 11.1 and 11.2).

Learning Theories	Teaching Strategies

• Behavioural
 	
• Constructivist
 	
   ○ Social Constructivist
 	
   ○ 'Scaffolding'
 	
   ○ Experiential
 	
• Information Processing
	• Teaching styles – Mosston and Ashworth (2002)
	
	• Questioning – Bloom's Taxonomy (1956), etc.
	
	• Assessment for learning
	
	• ICT
	
	• Critical Thinking/Problem-based learning

Figure 11.3 Building a framework for teaching

Activity 11.3 is designed to help you reflect on the link between theories of learning and your own teaching

Activity 11.3

Reflection on teaching

Reflect on your own teaching and answer the following questions:

- Which learning theories most frequently underpin your teaching strategies?
- Does the learning theory underpinning your teaching change according to the activity? For example, do you use a social constructivist perspective when teaching outdoor and adventurous activities and rely more on a behaviourist approach when teaching athletics?

Having completed Activities 11.2 and 11.3, you may have come to the conclusion that your teaching is not wholly underpinned by one theory of learning, that your actual practice is based on a number of theories rather than just one particular theory. However, you may have identified that you do have a preference for one theory more than the others. Activity 11.4 is designed to help you reflect further.

Activity 11.4

Identifying learning theories and teaching strategies

Look at the basic lesson plan in the Appendix to this chapter which provides an example of how different learning theories and teaching strategies might be combined in a particular lesson. Use an example of a lesson plan that you have written to help you identify and reflect on specific teaching strategies you may have used. Answer the following questions:

- How many learning theories have you used in the lesson? Is there an overriding theory which is reflected in your use of specific teaching strategies?
- Is it clear how these teaching strategies relate to a particular theory of learning?

You can repeat this exercise with a number of lesson plans that you have written.

LEARNING PREFERENCES

There has been a considerable amount of literature regarding the categorisation of learners into particular groups and types, e.g. some teachers will identify learners as having an auditory, visual and/or kinaesthetic preference. However, learning is multifaceted and generally context-dependent, resulting in different pupil responses in different settings. As learners progress, the strategies they use to cope with certain situations or tasks will change and develop (Burton, 2009). Therefore, it is important to encourage pupils to find a way to learn that is most valuable for them at any given time or situation. A well-planned lesson will provide opportunities to meet a range of learning preferences allowing pupils to work in their favoured domain, while developing their ability to learn through a variety of different approaches. Kolb and Fry (1975: 35–6) argue that effective learning involves the possession of four different learning abilities: concrete experience, reflective observation, abstract conceptualisation and active experimentation, as indicated on each pole of their model in Figure 11.4. In order to highlight that learners are likely to have developed a preference in one of the poles of each dimension, the development of a learning style inventory (Kolb, 1976) was designed to place people on a line between concrete experience and abstract conceptualisation; and active experimentation and reflective observation. Understanding the characteristics of the four types of learner identified by Kolb (1976) enables the teacher to effectively plan to differentiate learning to meet a range of learning preferences.

The information outlined in Table 11.2 (p. 138) provides a starting point for considering different learners and their preferred learning styles. This information provides a valuable tool for you as teachers to help plan appropriate teaching strategies to meet the varying needs of individual learners.

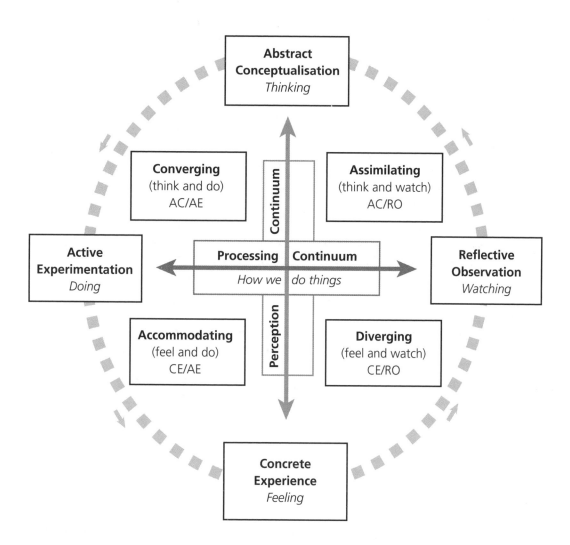

Figure 11.4 Kolb's Cycle of Experiential Learning

Source: Adapted from Kolb's (1984) learning styles.

Table 11.2 Description of different types of learning preferences

Descriptions of Kolb's (1984) learning styles

Converging (thinking and doing)	*Assimilating* (watching/listening and thinking)
Dominant learning abilities are: Abstract Conceptualisation (AC) and Active Experimentation (AE) • Finding practical uses for ideas and theories • Solving problems and making decisions • Technical tasks and problems rather than social issues and interpersonal issues • Experimenting with new ideas, simulations, practical applications	Dominant learning abilities are: Abstract Conceptualisation (AC) and Reflective Observation (RO) • Understanding a wide range of information and putting into concise, logical form • Less focused on people and more interested in ideas and abstract concepts • Prefers logical soundness to practical value • Enjoys reading, lectures, exploring analytical models, and having time to think things through
Diverging (feeling and watching/ listening)	*Accommodating* (feeling and doing)
Dominant learning abilities are: Concrete Experience (CE) and Reflective Observation (RO) • Best at viewing concrete situations from different perspectives • Good in situations that call for generation of ideas, e.g. 'brainstorming' • Enjoys gathering information • Is imaginative and emotional • Has a preference for working in groups • Tends to keep an open mind when listening	Dominant learning abilities are: Concrete Experience (CE) and Active Experimentation (AE) • Enjoys learning primarily from 'hands-on' experience • Likes carrying out plans and involving themselves in new and challenging experiences • Tends to act on 'gut' feelings rather than on logical analysis • When solving problems, relies more heavily on others for information than on their own technical analysis • Prefers to work with others on tasks and projects

Source: Adapted from Kolb (1984).

Activity 11.5

Understanding your pupils

Read the narratives of the following four pupils whom you might meet in your physical education lessons (Figure 11.5). Using the information in Table 11.1, decide which description is most suited to each of the four learners, e.g. is Dora Drew's preferred learning style at this stage in her development converging, assimilating, diverging or accommodating?

How might this information about the four different pupils in your physical education lesson impact on your planning for a particular activity?

Dora Drew	David Makepeace
A quiet girl who tends to stay on the periphery of the group. She observes and listens carefully and likes time to consolidate her ideas. She can sometimes ask challenging questions of the teacher but does not always share her thoughts or ideas with her peers.	Has a limited concentration span and is constantly fidgeting. He is often engaged in conversation with peers. He has quite good motor skills but finds it difficult to stay on task unless he is active. He finds it difficult to follow instructions but likes to experiment. He enjoys working with others but tends to rely on them to do his thinking.
Bronwyn Evans	**Mosi Osoba**
Likes to have a go at things and then watch and refine movements and ideas. She is quite good at evaluating and using feedback. She has the confidence to ask questions of teachers and the people she works with in groups. She is good at generating ideas and gathering information. She is quite creative but can also be sensitive at times.	Is very good practically, but lacks a little confidence. He finds it hard to follow instructions but is very good at copying others. He likes experimenting and prefers to take time to work out and plan what he is going to do before tackling problems. He likes to get on with things in his own way rather than working with others.

Figure 11.5 Narratives describing different types of learners and some of their learning characteristics

PLANNING TO MEET DIFFERENT LEARNING PREFERENCES

Once you have identified the needs and learning preferences of your learners, how do you plan effectively to ensure that your lessons meet individual learning preferences? The statements in Figure 11.6 provide examples of how you might structure a task, pose a question or initiate an activity to meet a specific learning preference, e.g. accommodators learn most effectively through a combination of doing and feeling which the example statements are designed to illustrate.

The example in Figure 11.7 attempts to demonstrate the range of different starting points that could be used to introduce the focus for the Year 7 lesson. Each task relates to a particular learning preference (Kolb, 1984) as identified in Figure 11.5. When planning a lesson you could use the examples in Figure 11.7 as a menu to select different starting points in order to meet the range of learning preferences in any class. For example, in week 1 you might use a DVD at the start of the lesson to introduce the idea of travelling over obstacles (Divergers) and follow this with a task which involves pupils planning in groups their own route through a series of selected equipment (Accommodators).

Accommodators – mix of feeling and doing		
Go with what you feel about it and see if it works	Will it work or not? Why do you think that?	Take a lead on …
Use the next few minutes to experiment with …	Make your own version of …	Discuss … as a group
Make a plan with your group to …	Find out from others …	Identify what you want to achieve by doing

Divergers – mix of feeling and watching/listening		
Identify what others would do in this situation	Go through the example given	Use the model to …
Having watched this, give a view on …	Brainstorm different approaches to …	Say what the consequences might be of …
What is the unique nature of …?	Gather some views on …	Imagine an alternative to …

Assimilators – mix of watching/listening and thinking		
What's your theory about …?	Analyse why …	What are the reasons for …?
Use x and y to explain z	Make a list of …	Come up with a logical argument for …
Evaluate the strengths of…	Reorder these into …	What's your judgement on …?

Convergers – mix of thinking and doing		
Practise the following and think about how …	Can you consider an alternative method when you do it next time?	What's the answer to?
Try it again and see if you can change …	Carry out an experiment to find out how …	Have a go at repeating that but with a different starting point.
Decide on how you might solve …	Come up with practical ways to …	Try out some ways of …

Figure 11.6 Examples of task openers or question starters, which relate to Kolb's (1984) identified learning styles

Learning outcome for a Year 7 parkour lesson:
To create a sequence that incorporates an inverted balance, a change of speed and the use of apparatus.

Having watched this give a view on … *(Divergers)*	*Use a video of a previous performance as an example*
Make a plan with your group to … *(Accommodators)*	*Ask the groups to plan what they are going to do before they begin to try out ideas*
Try out some ways of … *(Convergers)*	*Practise some ideas in the space first*
Evaluate the strengths of … *(Assimilators)*	*Identify what strengths individuals have and how they can contribute to the task*

Figure 11.7 Activity-specific examples of task openers

The lesson could be structured in such a way that all four tasks are available as a menu of starting points for pupils to choose from. In this way they are able to select the task that is most suited to their style of learning and therefore should be able to make more rapid progress. Alternatively, the lesson might be organised in a way which covers all four tasks at some point in the lesson and in doing so is more applicable to different learning preferences at different stages of the lesson or lessons. Activity 11.6 is designed to help you with this.

Activity 11.6

Matching tasks to learning preferences

Refer to the example lesson plan in the Appendix and adapt some of the learning activities to ensure that you meet the four learning preferences outlined above (Kolb, 1984).

Using the same process, write a lesson plan addressing the following:

Year 8
Focus '4x100m relay – it is the baton that wins the race!'
Learning approach Problem-solving
Previous learning The class have already covered principles of running – speed (sprinting), sustained running, stride patterns.

- Decide how you would engage pupils in working out the fastest way to get the baton around a 400 metre track. You want them to discover some of the fundamental skills of relay running, e.g. fast and secure handovers; receiving the baton when running to maintain its speed; rules of the event, etc.
- Create some learning tasks using the statements in Figure 11.5 demonstrating an understanding of the different ways individual pupils in your athletics class may prefer to learn, e.g. Doris Drew who is an Assimilator, will prefer to watch, listen and think and therefore the following task may support her learning experience more effectively:

Assimilator task opener

After observing the way another group has solved the baton problem and listening to their reflections, plan an approach for your group.

SUMMARY

Creating an interesting and effective teaching and learning environment for pupils involves utilising a number of different approaches to ensure that all are engaged. The greater your understanding of learning, the more likely you are to be able to select the appropriate teaching strategy to facilitate the underpinning theory/ theories you are using.

There is no one single learning theory that explains learning or can be used to plan for learning in all situations, so we would suggest that there can be no single approach to teaching; each learning theory can be used to support differing aspects of planning and teaching. It is important that you develop your own understanding of learning theories and teaching strategies so that you can draw on what is appropriate for the lessons you plan and to meet individual learning preferences.

FURTHER READING

Grout, H. and Long, G. (2009) *Improving Teaching and Learning in Physical Education*, Maidenhead: Open University Press.
This book explores a wide range of issues you need to consider to help you plan effectively to create successful learning environments.

Newton, D. (2012) *Teaching for Understanding: What It Is and How To Do It*, 2nd edn, London: Routledge.
    Understanding how the connections between teacher and pupil experiences of learning are important to develop high quality learning. This book explores the context for deeper learning.

Stidder, G. and Hayes, S. (2011) *The Really Useful Physical Education Book: Learning and Teaching across the 7–14 Age Range*, London: Routledge.
    Lots of ideas and guidance on how to teach physical education creatively.

Zwozdiak-Myers, P. (2012) *The Teacher's Reflective Practice Handbook: Becoming an Extended Professional Through Capturing Evidence-Informed Practice*, London: Routledge.
    This book provides a guide to help you reflect and further develop your teaching through evaluation of your lessons and pupil learning.

Note: all proformas, tables or figures you are asked to complete to help you undertake activities in this chapter are also available on the website which accompanies the book (www.routledge.com/9780415814829).

APPENDIX: LESSON PLAN EXAMPLE

Year:	7	Activity:	Gymnastics	Number of lesson in series:	7/10	Date:	3/3/12

By the end of the lesson pupils should be able to:
Plan (LO1), perform (LO2) and evaluate (LO3) a gymnastic sequence incorporating both floor and apparatus, using the theme of over and under.

Resources:
Task cards
Mats, benches, boxes

Learning outcomes:	Method of assessment and success criteria:	Learning activities – including adapted tasks appropriate to pupil need:	Learning strategy and links to learning theory
Pupils will be able to: LO1 Link a minimum of 5 movements to form a sequence which clearly interprets the theme	Teacher observation: 5 or more fluently linked movements using apparatus and floor work	**Warm-up** – 5 mins of simple, dynamic, content-related activity, e.g. over and under. Follow the teacher's instructions, copying actions when asked. (A) **Introductory activities** Working in a pair link together 3 travelling skills and 1 balance, e.g. forward roll, full turn, cartwheel, bridge – pupils watch another group and identify any under/over movements. (B) Pupils reflect on their own and others performance and adapt their ideas to incorporate an over or under movement using their partner. Distribute Task Card 1 to help with ideas. (B)	Command style – Behaviourist (A) Problem solving – Social Constructivist Theory (B)
LO2 Effectively incorporate floor and apparatus in the sequence demonstrating fluency		**Skill development** Revisit cartwheel – can you demonstrate and explain the key technical points? (B) (D) Practise the skill learned in previous lessons. (C) How can you progress this to travel over an object/partner? If you have not mastered the skill, what other ways can you take weight on hands as you travel? (B)	Practice – Information Processing (C)
LO3 Engage in peer assessment to evaluate others performance giving clear guidance for improvement	Questioning during task and post task Pupils record key weaknesses and suggest ways to improve Improved performance	**Sequence development** Pupils combine floor and apparatus to compose a short sequence around the theme of over and under. Minimum of 5 movements with linking actions. (B) **Conclusion** Refine and perform for another group. Pupils to use evaluation sheet which provides evaluation criteria. (D) They must use this as a prompt to give clear feedback and constructive advice about improving performance, e.g. clarity of shape well, holding balance needs improving through greater extension.	Assessment for Learning – Constructivist (D)

Chapter 12 Creating an effective learning environment

JULIA LAWRENCE

INTRODUCTION

Research suggests that the development of an effective learning environment is paramount in the promotion of learning (e.g., Cubukcu, 2012; Malie and Akir, 2012; see also Breckon *et al.*, 2010). The nature of physical education is such that the potential for your lesson to be ruined through poor organisation and management is high. This may not only impact on the learning opportunities you create and consequently the pupils' experience, but also on your own confidence and self-efficacy (Bandura, 1989). A positive learning environment/lesson climate provides the most effective learning environment. It allows you to maximise the time you spend promoting learning and is both consistent with, and supports, a positive or preventative approach to behaviour management (see Chapter 14) where pupils have a central role to play. It also reflects an inclusive schooling approach (see Chapter 15).

Your ability to organise, manage and develop a positive learning environment will develop over a period of time as you gain experience across a range of situations and opportunities. Do not expect to have 'perfected' your skills during your initial teacher education (ITE). Take time to reflect on your experiences and draw out your strengths and identify areas that require further development.

By the end of this chapter you should be able to:

* identify the characteristics of an effective learning environment;
* organise and manage your lesson to maximise the time you spend promoting learning;
* develop a positive learning environment/lesson climate.

WHAT IS AN EFFECTIVE LEARNING ENVIRONMENT?

A positive lesson climate provides the most effective learning environment (Breckon *et al.*, 2010; Lawrence and Whitehead, 2010). Further, Cockburn and Handscomb (2012: 169) suggest that

> Learning is more effective when … children understand what, why and how they are learning. In this way children are encouraged to take ownership of their own learning rather than simply carry out activities because they have been told to do so.

We can therefore start to identify a range of factors that might contribute to the effectiveness of the learning environment. You should aspire to create positive interactions and relationships between yourself and the pupils as well as between pupils (Breckon *et al.*, 2010). The adoption of pupil-centred (Lawrence, 2012) or progressive (Whitehead with Blair, 2010) teaching approaches motivates pupils to learn and develop positive self-esteem. Pupils should be expected to learn and remain on task, supported by a committed and enthusiastic teacher who is confident, authoritative and clearly in control of the situation, but also demonstrates understanding and sensitivity. The working space should be clean and tidy and convey care and attention to pupils and their learning.

Establishing an effective learning environment with a positive lesson climate is something that is within your control, so you should take some time to consider the factors that contribute to this as an explicit part of your lesson planning.

Now complete Activity 12.1.

Activity 12.1

An effective learning environment

Observe a lesson and note in column 2 of Table 12.1 evidence of each aspect of an effective learning environment listed in column 1. In column 3, note how you will develop this in your own teaching. The last aspect provides an example of how to complete columns 2 and 3.

MAXIMISING LEARNING TIME

Our aspiration should always be to create an environment where learning is maximised. This can be measured by the amount of time pupils spend on task within the lesson, this is often referred to as academic learning time. Activity 12.2 provides you with an opportunity to reflect on the amount of learning time in which pupils are engaged in lessons.

Activity 12.2

Academic Learning Time-Physical Education (ALT-PE)

Complete the ALT-PE (in the Appendix of this chapter). You may consider looking at it in relation to your own or a colleague's teaching (although be sure to seek permission before you collect any data and ensure that it is completed in line with any ethical requirements).

Table 12.1 An effective learning environment

Aspects of an effective learning environment	Evidence of this aspect	How will you develop this in your own teaching?
Positive interaction between teacher and pupils		
Effective interpersonal relationships between teacher and pupils		
Positive relationships between pupils		
Positive teaching style – feedback is given for appropriate work		
Pupils' self-esteem is enhanced		
Pupils are motivated		
Pupils are placed at the centre of lesson planning and delivery		
Lesson has relaxed, but purposeful atmosphere		
Pupils are expected to learn and to be on task		
Committed and enthusiastic teacher		
Confident and authoritative teacher		
Teacher clearly in control of the situation		
Caring, understanding and sensitive teacher		
Working space conveys care and attention to pupils and their learning	Floor clean, apparatus put away, posters on wall are recent, relevant, laminated and not hanging off the wall	Ensure that space is tidy before starting the lesson and that equipment is put away after it has been used (during and after the lesson)

ORGANISING AND MANAGING A LESSON

Research (Derri *et al.*, 2007) suggests that a key factor in maximising learning time is effective organisation and management. Organisation and management of lessons can be daunting and are likely to be one of your major foci early in your school placement, although this will develop over time. As with all other aspects of your teaching and the promotion of pupil learning, it is essential that organisation and management are integral to any planning process (see Chapter 5 and Lawrence and Whitehead, 2010). While there are a number of ways of viewing organisation and management, it is perhaps most helpful to view it from a pupil perspective. This will help you to clarify the message you wish to give, which you must then deliver consistently and reflective of the learning needs of the pupils (Vickerman, 2010). Activity 12.3 provides you with the opportunity to reflect upon possible strategies that can be employed. Now complete Activity 12.3.

Activity 12.3

Planning the organisation and management of lessons

In column 2 of Table 12.2 list strategies that may be employed to ensure that each of the organisation and management tasks in column 1 is completed effectively and efficiently to maximise the time available for pupil learning. You may also complete column 2 in relation to your own teaching by identifying the strategy in column 2 and asking someone to record in column 3 the time the strategies you use take. How does this impact on pupils' learning time? Adapt/change the strategies in light of your own evaluations/observations, feedback from pupils' responses in the lesson and from the observer.

You may want to repeat this activity using other organisation and management activities, before, during and after the lesson. See, for example, Lawrence and Whitehead (2010: 80–100), and Activity 14.2 on p. 168.

Thus, in creating an effective learning environment/lesson climate, it can be argued (Breckon *et al.*, 2010) that consideration needs to be given to the following features:

- you as the teacher;
- the learning environment;
- the pupils being taught.

You the teacher

In any teaching situation, you as the teacher are pivotal to the learning experience. You need to consider what you bring to the learning situation. This might include the way you present yourself, your confidence, competence and pedagogical approach as well as your attitude.

The environment

In Activity 12.3 you were asked to look at aspects of organising and managing the learning environment. This required you to think about and plan appropriate and clear rules and routines (see Chapter 5). It also requires you to take account of principles of safe practice (see Chapter 10). You also need to think about the impression created by the environment/spaces you are using. Breckon *et al.* (2010) and Whitehead and Lawrence (2010) explore these in greater depth.

Table 12.2 Planning the organisation and management of lessons

Task	Possible strategies	Time strategy takes in the lesson
How are pupils let into the changing rooms?		
When and how are valuables and jewellery collected?		
When and how is the register taken?		
When are the lesson outcomes outlined to the pupils (e.g. in the changing room, or gym, field, etc.)?		
Equipment/resources, e.g. Where is equipment going to be located during the lesson? Who is responsible for getting it out/putting it away? How is this going to be organised?		
Organisation of activities and movement between them, e.g. how is the first activity arranged and how is the change from one activity to the next managed?		
Organisation of groupings, e.g. how are pupils assigned to groups? Do groups change during the lesson? If so how is this managed?		

The pupils

An effective learning environment must reflect the needs of those who are accessing the learning. In essence, where possible, it should reflect the individual needs of the pupils. Consideration therefore needs to be given to the cognitive (Bloom *et al.*, 1956), affective (Krathwohl *et al.*, 1964) and psychomotor (Simpson, 1971) domains of learning as well as any differentiation needed (see Chapter 5). If you refer back to the start of the chapter we identified that pupils need to understand the what, why and how of what they are being asked to do (Cockburn and Handscomb, 2012). Thus as well as considering the needs of pupils, you also need to think about how you are going to share the learning outcomes of the lesson with pupils so they are aware of:

- What they are doing.
- Why they are doing it.
- How they will know if they have been successful.

To achieve a positive learning environment/lesson climate you must establish positive relationships with your pupils and also aim to enhance self-esteem and motivation to participate. Now complete Activity 12.4.

Activity 12.4

Promoting a positive learning environment

For each of the suggested outcomes regarding the appropriateness/effectiveness of the action in your lessons, listed below, identify in column 2 of Table 12.3 how the appropriateness/effectiveness of the action has been/could be demonstrated in a lesson. You can do this by selecting a few actions on which to focus (in evaluating your lessons or from observation by a teacher) in any one lesson. If you complete this activity for a lesson you teach, note in the third column what you would change next time and any development activities that would help you to be more effective. One outcome has been completed to provide an example.

Table 12.3 Promoting a positive learning environment

Teacher action	How its appropriateness/ effectiveness was OR would be demonstrated in your lesson	What you would change next time and any development activities that would help you to be more effective?
Lesson planning was appropriate		
The lesson built on the previous lesson and on pupils' prior knowledge	For example: Pupils were provided with activities that demonstrated continuity and progression Pupils were encouraged to reflect on their prior learning through the use of questioning and also the opportunity to select and apply skills they had performed during the previous lesson in different situations	Evaluations of lessons need to be more specific to the learning that had taken place Plan peer and self-review opportunities in order that pupils can look to target, set and reflect upon their own and others' performances
Pupils knew what was going to happen in the lesson		
Pupils were clear at the start of the lesson what they were learning, why and how it fitted with what they already knew/could do		
The intended learning outcomes of the lesson were clearly stated at the start		
Pupils knew at the end of the lesson whether or not they had achieved the intended learning outcomes		
Expectations of pupils' achievement was high		
The teacher had the knowledge to be able to move beyond telling pupils 'how to' do something to helping them to understand 'why'		
Pupils were actively engaged in and made sense of their learning rather than just 'did it'		

(continued)

Table 12.3 (continued)

Pupils were helped to develop their own learning skills		
At the start of the lesson and before each new activity pupils were clear what behaviours were needed for the learning to be successful		
The learning needs of all pupils were understood and met		
Assessment for learning was used effectively to help pupils reflect on what they knew/could do, reinforce the learning and set targets		
There were high expectations of what pupils could achieve		
Communication between teacher and pupils was good		
The lesson had a purposeful atmosphere		
The lesson was lively and well paced		
The lesson activities were stimulating		
The organisation and management enabled pupils to spend maximum time on learning activities		
Lesson transitions were efficient and effective		
Rules were applied firmly and consistently		
There were established routines		
Positive reinforcement was used		
Appropriate feedback and positive correction were used		
Pupils were listened to and their answers and opinions respected		
Expectations of pupils' behaviour was high		
Inappropriate behaviour was pre-empted		

SUMMARY

Effective learning takes place when a pupil-centred approach is adopted with consideration given to the content, delivery and assessment of lessons. Central to this are the planning, organisation and management of the lesson. While each teacher has their own approach, they have to take account of, and fit in with, school policies and practices. These vary between schools and therefore it is important that you look to develop your own strategies based on the observation you make and the reflections you undertake. This will allow you to modify your practice according to the expectations of the school in which you work.

However, good organisation and management do not in themselves promote pupil learning; rather, they create the time for learning to occur. The effectiveness of learning is maximised by developing and maintaining positive relationships with your pupils and developing a positive learning environment/lesson climate.

FURTHER READING

Fautley, M. and Savage, J. (2010) Developing your classroom practice, in M. Fautley and J. Savage (eds) *Secondary Education: Reflective Reader*, Exeter: Learning Matters, pp. 47–66. This chapter allows you to explore in more detail how learning environments are affected by the pedagogical approaches adopted, as well as how groupings can impact on the effectiveness of the learning environment.

Lawrence, J. (2012) How pupils learn and develop, in J. Lawrence, *Teaching Primary Physical Education*, London: Sage, pp. 11–24
This chapter provides an overview of domains and theories of learning allowing the student teacher the opportunity to reflect upon the characteristics of effective learning environments within a physical education context.

Lawrence, J. (2012) Approaches to teaching physical education, in J. Lawrence, *Teaching Primary Physical Education*, London: Sage, pp. 25–38.
This chapter provides an overview of pedagogical approaches to support the teaching of physical education, allowing the reader the opportunity to develop a deeper understanding of how pupils learning can be influenced by the approaches to teaching adopted.

Note: all proformas, tables or figures you are asked to complete to help you undertake activities in this chapter are also available on the website which accompanies the book (www.routledge.com/9780415814829).

APPENDIX: ACADEMIC LEARNING TIME-PHYSICAL EDUCATION (ALT-PE)

Source: Siedentop, Tousignant and Parker (1982)

PURPOSE

This instrument is often used to judge teaching effectiveness in PE. Specifically, its purpose is to describe the amount of time pupils are engaged in motor activity at an appropriate level of difficulty. This is based on the assumption that the longer pupils are engaged in motor activity at an appropriate level of difficulty, the more they learn.

DEFINITIONS OF CATEGORIES

Four categories of activity are identified:

1 **Motor appropriate (MA)**. The pupil is engaged in a motor activity related to the subject matter in such a way as to produce a high degree of success.
2 **Motor inappropriate (MI)**. The pupil is engaged in a motor activity related to the subject matter, but the task or activity is either too difficult or too easy for the pupil's capabilities, therefore practising it does not contribute to the achievement of lesson objectives.
3 **Motor supporting (MS)**. The pupil is engaged in a motor activity related to the subject matter with the purpose of helping others to learn or perform the activity (for example, holding equipment, sending balls to others or spotting the trampoline).
4 **Not motor engaged (NM)**. The pupil is not involved in a motor activity related to the subject matter.

RECORDING PROCEDURES

There are four different methods of observation available to collect ALT-PE data about the categories above. These methods use:

- **Interval recording**. This involves alternating observing and recording at short intervals. One pupil or an alternating sample of pupils is used. The observer watches one pupil during the **observing interval**. During the **recording interval**, the observer records the observation as **MA, MI, MS** or **NM**. Data can be presented as a percentage of each category. This is the most common observation method used.
- **Group time sampling**. This involves the observer scanning the group for 15 seconds every 2 minutes, and counting the number of pupils engaged at an appropriate level of motor activity **(MA)**. Data can be presented as an average for the class.
- **Duration recording**. This involves the observer using a time line to categorise into one of the four categories **(MA, MI, MS** or **NM)**, what one pupil is doing the entire period. Alternatively, the observer can measure **MA** time only. A stopwatch is started when the pupil is appropriately engaged and stopped when the engagement stops. Total **MA** time for the lesson can be presented as a percentage of total lesson time.
- **Event recording**. This involves the observer counting the number of **MA** practice trials at an appropriate level of difficulty (the practice must include discrete trials). Trials are measured (and data presented) per minute or over longer units of time.

EXAMPLE OF ALT-PE USING THE INTERVAL RECORDING METHOD

To use this method of recording the coding format is divided into **intervals**.

In each interval box there are **two levels**: a top level and a lower level. The top level of the interval box is used to describe the **context of the interval (C)**. There are ten choices of context from three categories: general content, subject matter knowledge and subject matter motor (see below). This decision is made on the basis of what the class as a whole is doing, for example, are they involved in warm-up, a lecture on strategy, or skill practice?

The **lower** level of the interval box is used to describe the **involvement of one pupil (LI)**. Choices are from the categories described as not motor engaged and motor engaged (see below).

The **letter code** for the appropriate category is placed in the appropriate part of the interval box.

Typically, it is suggested that **three pupils** of differing skill levels are observed, **alternating observation** of them at every interval. This system provides a total picture of what the class does throughout the lesson and a finely graded picture of the involvement of several pupils.

Those interval boxes marked as motor appropriate **(MA)** are **ALT-PE** intervals. Total ALT-PE is the total for the pupil during the lesson.

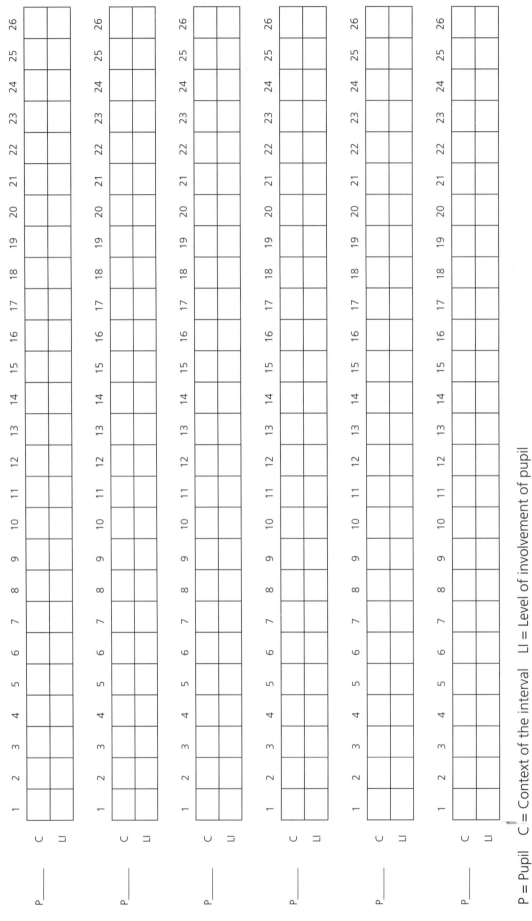

P = Pupil   C = Context of the interval   LI = Level of involvement of pupil

Context level (C)			Learner involvement level (LI)	
General content	*Subject matter knowledge*	*Subject matter motor*	*Not motor engaged*	*Motor engaged*
Transition (T)	Technique (TN)	Skill practice (P)	Interim (I)	Motor appropriate (MA)
Management (M)	Strategy (ST)	Scrimmage/routine (S)	Waiting (W)	Motor inappropriate (MI)
Break (B)	Rules (R)	Game (G)	Off-task (OF)	Supporting (MS)
Warm-up (WU)	Social behaviour (SB)	Fitness (F)	On-task (ON)	
	Background (BK)		Cognitive (C)	

Chapter 13   Teaching to enable intended learning outcomes to be achieved

SUSAN CAPEL, RICHARD BLAIR AND JULIA LONGVILLE

INTRODUCTION

The main function of teaching in schools is to achieve intended learning. Learning can be defined as a change in an individual's knowledge, skills, understanding, values, beliefs and/or attitudes brought about through particular experiences (Mazur, 1990).

Planned learning in physical education is usually specified as: longer-term outcomes (aims) specific to the subject, into which medium-term outcomes (objectives) for a unit of work fit and which, in turn, inform short-term outcomes (intended learning outcomes) for a lesson (see Chapters 4 and 5). Intended learning outcomes are the operational segments which have a specific focus in individual lessons that inform what pupils should be achieving in the lesson. Their achievement helps towards developing the unit of work objectives and the aims of physical education in the school.

Aims, objectives and intended learning outcomes cover a range of physical, affective, cognitive, personal and social outcomes, some of which are unique to physical education and some of which are shared with other curriculum subjects. The aims, objectives and intended learning outcomes must meet the diverse needs of individuals and groups of pupils within the class. To achieve this range of outcomes, what and how you teach to engage pupils in their learning needs to be planned appropriately.

The aim of this chapter is to further your understanding of the relationship between intended learning outcomes and what and how you teach a lesson. It should be read in conjunction with Chapters 2 and 5 which are also concerned with the relationships between intended learning outcomes and content and how we teach, and Chapters 6, 7, 8 and 9 which look at broader aspects of learning.

By the end of this chapter you should be able to:

- appreciate why intended learning outcomes are important;
- understand how intended learning outcomes inform the choice of content and teaching strategies to be deployed;
- be able to select appropriate teaching strategies to enable intended learning outcomes to be achieved.

WHY INTENDED LEARNING OUTCOMES ARE IMPORTANT

First, complete Activity 13.1.

Activity 13.1

What are the intended learning outcomes from this lesson?

Let's start by looking at a hypothetical lesson. Sally is teaching a lesson of outwitting opponents through invasion games and she has chosen to do this through netball to a Year 7 group. She starts her planning by deciding to focus on the chest pass. She then organises some practices to enable pupils to learn the skills, followed by a conditioned game in which pupils are required to use the chest pass just learned for all passes in the game. She finishes the lesson by asking the pupils the key teaching points of a chest pass.

What learning outcomes might Sally have in mind when planning the lesson in this way?

Are the pupils likely to achieve these outcomes within this lesson?

This way of planning lessons may be familiar to some of you. You may have participated in such lessons, both in physical education and in coaching sessions. You may also have taught such lessons. We return to this hypothetical lesson at the end of the chapter. However, we now focus on another way of planning lessons by starting with your intended learning outcomes.

Intended learning outcomes specify what pupils should be able to do, know or understand at the end of a lesson. They inform lesson planning and delivery by identifying what the pupils and the teacher need to do to create the right learning environment. This will include the teaching approaches and strategies to be adopted, the specific learning activities the pupils participate in and the individualised tasks and key teaching points to help support pupils' learning. In turn, they form the focus of the feedback given to pupils to assess what they have achieved. They are also the focus by which the success of the lesson in enabling learning can be measured. Thus, in this approach, the intended learning outcomes for each lesson are planned first and it is these that drive the selection and planning of content of how the lesson is taught.

How learning outcomes are written is important. Activity 13.2 asks you to try to write some learning outcomes.

Activity 13.2

Planning lesson learning outcomes from unit of work objectives

Identify a set of unit of work objectives (either ones written by staff in your placement school, ones you have written for a class you are teaching, or ones from other sources) which cover both objectives specific to physical education and also a broader range of affective, cognitive, personal and social objectives including, for example, those related to key skills, thinking skills, or the development of citizenship. From the list of objectives for the unit of work, devise physical education specific learning outcomes for one lesson within this unit of work. Try to include learning outcomes that focus on developing skills, improving performance, planning and applying decisions, evaluating and improving performance, helping pupils to make healthy, active lifestyle choices. Be careful not to focus solely, or indeed, too heavily, on developing skills with few or none for the others.

In addition to subject-specific learning outcomes, if physical education is to contribute to the broader goals of education, a wider range of objectives also need to be included in the planning and delivery of the lessons. Activity 13.3 asks you to identify affective, cognitive, personal and social outcomes to supplement those you have already identified in Activity 13.2.

Activity 13.3

Including broader learning outcomes in lessons

Using the same unit of work objectives you used in Activity 13.2, now identify two broader objectives and write appropriate learning outcomes to enable these to be achieved.

What we cannot stress too strongly is that in this approach, the learning outcomes must be developed first in your lesson planning. They are then used to plan the rest of your lesson.

HOW LEARNING OUTCOMES INFORM THE CHOICE OF CONTENT AND TEACHING STRATEGIES

By setting the intended learning outcomes first, you have begun planning what you hope to achieve by the end of the lesson. In order to achieve the intended learning outcomes you need to plan carefully what you will teach and how you will teach it.

You need to select the aspects of the selected activity to enable specific learning outcomes of lessons in the unit to be achieved e.g. in Activity 13.1, the activity is netball, the aspect is an attacking skill; passing and, more specifically, a chest pass. Likewise, careful consideration needs to be given to how that content is taught. It is therefore important that you select teaching approaches which enable different learning outcomes to be achieved. Examples of teaching approaches which might be used to support pupils learning are given in Table 13.1. You may want to change the terminology in the first column to that used in the curriculum in which you are working. Table 13.1 includes in the third column the focus of the feedback needed to help pupils towards achieving the intended learning. This re-emphasises the need to think through and plan every aspect of the lesson thoroughly to ensure consistency in all aspects of the lesson to support pupils in working towards the achievement of the learning outcomes. Activity 13.4 asks you to undertake the same process, but this time with a broader range of learning outcomes.

Table 13.1 Key processes and teaching approaches

Key process	Broad strategic approach	Key elements
Developing and improving physical skills	Model of the skill provided by the teacher through, for example, demonstration Opportunities for pupils to practise the skill	Tasks focused on a particular aspect of the movement Feedback focused on improving performance
Planning and applying decisions	Provision of discovery and problem-solving situations with responsibility devolved to the pupils as individuals or groups	Open tasks Open questions Feedback related to imagination and creativity
Evaluating and improving	Devolvement of responsibility to pupils to evaluate own and others' movement	Provision of resource (e.g. criteria sheet/video) with aspects of the movement to be observed Feedback on the accuracy of observation/self- and peer-assessment
Making healthy, active lifestyle choices	Information giving and discussion Providing a range of opportunities to experience different activities	Discussion, encouraging pupils to engage in dialogue and develop their communication skills
Developing physical and mental capacity	Challenges set to build physical strength and promote mental perseverance Pupils setting own goals and practising skills, routines, etc.	Tasks that allow pupils to set own goals Feedback on the choice of goals Questioning/discussion on progress, etc.

Source: Adapted from Whitehead with Blair (2010: 163).

Activity 13.4

Identifying learning outcomes and teaching strategies to enable affective, cognitive, personal and social learning outcomes to be achieved

Using Table 13.2, identify a specific learning outcome you might include for an affective, cognitive, personal and social outcome; then identify a broad strategic approach and constituent element for each outcome.

Table 13.2 Intended learning outcomes

Intended learning outcome	*Broad strategic approach*	*Constituent elements*
Affective outcome		
Intended learning outcome		
Cognitive outcome		
Intended learning outcome		
Personal outcome		
Intended learning outcome		
Social outcome		
Intended learning outcome		

SELECTING APPROPRIATE TEACHING STRATEGIES TO ENABLE SPECIFIC LEARNING OUTCOMES TO BE ACHIEVED

It is now important that you identify and select specific teaching strategies to enable the learning outcomes to be achieved. According to Whitehead with Blair (2010: 156): 'A strategy is designed to serve an intended learning outcome and should be planned after the intended learning outcomes of the lesson have been identified.'

There are many different classifications of teaching strategies, including Bennett, 1976 (see also Whitehead with Blair, 2010: 165); Cox and Dyson, 1975; Galton and Croll, 1980; Mosston and Ashworth, 2002; Oeser, 1955; The Plowden Report (Central Advisory Council for Education, 1967); the Qualifications and Curriculum Authority, 2003; and Rink, 2003. Although some of these are quite dated, they are included as it is useful to consider a range of classifications. Although Mosston and Ashworth's (2002) classification is probably the one most frequently used in physical education, we suggest that you also look at some of the other alternatives suggested here (and elsewhere). The teaching strategy you use in any one part of any lesson could be selected from any of these classifications. Indeed, you may include strategies from a mix of classifications within one lesson but also you may use several at the same time to meet the learning needs of different pupils. The strategies are likely to be different in order to achieve physical, affective, cognitive and social learning outcomes. Activities 13.5 and 13.6 are designed to help you consider which teaching strategies are appropriate to enable you to achieve specific learning outcomes.

Activity 13.5

Selecting appropriate teaching strategies to achieve specific outcomes (1)

To achieve one learning outcome you identified in Activities 13.2 and 13.3 above, identify which teaching strategies and specific activities/tasks you will use to help pupils achieve the learning outcomes.

Once you have selected the teaching strategies and activities/tasks, you also need to be alert to any adaptations you might need to make as the lesson progresses. These adaptations will be made according to whether the pupils are progressing as intended towards achieving the outcomes.

Activity 13.6

Selecting appropriate teaching strategies to achieve specific outcomes (2)

For one of the lessons you are planning to teach in the near future, identify the physical education specific and broader range of learning outcomes. Then identify the content you will teach and the teaching strategies and activities/tasks you will plan to enable pupils to achieve the learning outcomes. Then plan how you will assess progress during the lesson and what feedback you might give to help pupils achieve the intended learning. The specific learning outcomes will help you to identify what you and your pupils might assess within the lesson.

Discuss your plan with your tutor. Ask your tutor to observe the lesson and comment on how well the teaching strategies, activities/tasks, assessment and feedback enabled pupils to achieve the learning outcomes. Incorporate the feedback from your tutor into planning the next lesson and/or other lessons.

We now return to the hypothetical lesson in Activity 13.1 (see p. 159). It is likely that the range of learning outcomes achieved in this lesson is limited to those of performance, i.e. performing the chest pass. However, the format of the lesson, specifically the requirements in the conditioned game, may result in pupils being unlikely to be successful in each of their attempts to perform a chest pass as they are trying to do this when another pass would have been more appropriate. Further, pupils are not required to think about when it is appropriate to use a chest pass, therefore this limits their learning. Activity 13.7 is designed to help you rethink the hypothetical lesson by building on the content of this chapter.

Activity 13.7

Planning a lesson with a specific learning outcome

You are asked to teach netball to a Year 7 group. Two of the learning outcomes are that, by the end of this lesson, pupils will be able to:

- send the ball using a chest pass; and
- understand when to execute a chest pass in a game of netball.

Outline what teaching strategies and activities/tasks you might include in this lesson to enable these learning outcomes to be achieved. Also identify the assessment you might undertake to check achievement of the learning outcomes and the feedback you might give to enhance learning. How is this different from the hypothetical lesson above?

SUMMARY

This chapter has aimed to help you understand the relationship between intended learning outcomes and what and how you teach a lesson. If you plan lessons by starting with the activity and skills you want the pupils to learn, pupils are less likely to achieve the specific and broader learning outcomes. As a result of reading this chapter, we hope that you have understood the importance of starting planning each lesson by identifying what you want your pupils to learn through first identifying the intended learning outcomes for the lesson (these can be set by you or in conjunction with the pupils). These learning outcomes help to build towards achieving the overall outcomes of the unit of work in which the lesson fits and can be used to inform your planning for the rest of the unit of work. By using this approach pupils are more likely to achieve the intended learning outcomes, including outcomes which are not focused on performance. These include physical education specific outcomes, for example, evaluating and improving performance and broader outcomes which are shared with other curriculum subjects.

FURTHER READING

The three chapters below provide good background information to help you to focus on planning your teaching to enable specific learning outcomes to be achieved.

Capel, S. and Blair, R. (2013) Why do physical education teachers adopt a particular way of teaching?, in S. Capel and M. Whitehead (eds) *Debates in Physical Education*, London: Routledge, pp. 120–39.

Gower, C. (2010) Planning in PE, in S. Capel and M. Whitehead (eds) *Learning to Teach Physical Education in the Secondary School: A Companion to School Experience*, London: Routledge, pp. 24–45.

Murdoch, E. and Whitehead, M. (2013) What should pupils learn in physical education?, in S. Capel and M. Whitehead (eds) *Debates in Physical Education*, London: Routledge, pp. 55–73.

Note: all proformas, tables or figures you are asked to complete to help you undertake activities in this chapter are also available on the website which accompanies the book (www.routledge.com/9780415814829).

Chapter 14 Teaching to promote positive behaviour

KERRY WHITEHOUSE

INTRODUCTION

By considering and applying techniques to create an effective learning environment as detailed in Chapter 12, pupils will spend less time off-task and the lesson will be well organised. This may help but will not necessarily prevent poor behaviour from occurring. We all know that pupils are complex individuals and can disrupt lessons and demonstrate poor behaviour for a variety of reasons which may be triggered by a range of circumstances. It is therefore important that you are aware of, well practised in, and can reflect upon, teaching strategies which can promote positive behaviour within physical education lessons. Pupils who demonstrate positive behaviour within a physical education lesson not only learn more effectively, develop positive relationships with others and grow in confidence, they also promote teacher well-being, raise teacher confidence and revitalise even the most experienced of practitioners. Positive behaviour does not happen by chance; it relies upon effective and appropriate planning (see Chapter 5), good organisation and classroom management (see Chapter 12), knowing your pupils so that you can provide an inclusive schooling approach (Chapter 15) and developing emotional literacy which promotes both teacher and pupil well-being. Your ability to manage, interact and develop positive relationships with the pupils not only promotes positive behaviour but also enhances pupil learning.

One positive approach to behaviour management is called 'behaviour2learn' (http://www.behaviour2learn.co.uk) (formally known as 'behaviour for learning'; see Garner, 2005, and www.nationalarchives.gov.uk, for further information). This emphasises the crucial link between the way in which pupils learn and their social knowledge and behaviour. It recognises that behaviour in classrooms and social settings does not occur in isolation, but is the product of a variety of influences and relationships. There are a number of other well-established theoretical positions and more recent approaches which seek to address the challenges of managing behaviour within today's classrooms. These are outlined in the further reading section at the end of this chapter.

Your ability to promote positive behaviour and understand effective management builds as you gain experience, develop positive relationships with pupils and practise a variety of positive behaviour promoting strategies. It should be remembered that teacher's well-being goes hand in glove with pupils' well-being. It is therefore important to develop your own resilience to create an enjoyable and effective working life alongside a reflective approach to both the successes and areas for development that you need to pursue.

By the end of this chapter you should be able to:

- know how to establish and maintain a learning environment and lesson climate which promotes positive behaviour;
- understand the importance of school and department policies and practices for promoting positive behaviour;
- appreciate the need for rules, rewards and consequences;
- know how to develop relationships that support teaching for positive behaviour.

DEVELOPING A LEARNING ENVIRONMENT THAT PROMOTES POSITIVE BEHAVIOUR

A lesson with an effective learning environment has a positive climate (Capel and Whitehead, 2010) and helps lead to positive pupil behaviours. A positive learning environment/lesson climate refers to the mood developed within the lesson which places the pupils and their learning at the heart of lesson planning and delivery. Interactions and relationships between teacher and pupils and between pupils are positive and effective. In such an environment the teacher uses his/her voice with varying tones and volume, uses positive and appropriate language and is able to use body language to create a presence in the classroom. A positive teaching style is used in which feedback is given for appropriate work. This can motivate and enhance pupils' confidence to learn as well as their self-esteem. The lesson has a relaxed, but purposeful atmosphere. Pupils are expected to learn and to be on-task, supported by a committed and enthusiastic teacher who is confident, authoritative and clearly in control of the situation, but also caring, understanding and sensitive to the needs of individuals. You will need to learn how to develop such a learning environment during the initial stages of your teaching.

POLICIES AND PRACTICES: ESTABLISHING CLEAR STRUCTURES AND PROCESSES TO SET EXPECTATIONS

It is important to establish clear structures to your lesson and set expectations that are agreed. One widely used framework is known as the '4 R's' which is shared with pupils and embedded into classroom practice.

1 *Rights* – The right to be safe, to learn and to be treated with respect. These are mutual expectations for both teachers and pupils.
2 *Responsibilities* – Responsibility for own choices about behaviour and to act in a way which protects mutual rights.
3 *Rules* – To establish rules which protect the right to learn, teach and be safe. For example: follow instructions willingly.
4 *Routines* – Establish routines such as handling equipment, moving to and from working areas, which are understood and well practised by pupils.

Schools and physical education departments will already have established rules and routines that you will need to find out about and implement consistently. These will vary, depending on your placement school so it is important to find out departmental policy and observe how this is effectively implemented by teachers. Now complete Activity 14.1.

Activity 14.1

Rules in physical education

Find out what the rules are for your placement school physical education department. These may be generic whole school rules that have been adapted for physical education. List these in Table 14.1 and add any more from discussion with your mentor and observation of lessons.

Routines are important in promoting positive behaviour, particularly in physical education where the movement of pupils and equipment needs to be thought through carefully to prevent pupils going off-task. Movement to working areas from changing rooms may have the same routines; however, routines in lessons will vary depending upon the activity taught (e.g. gymnastics vs football), the health and safety considerations for that activity (e.g. throwing events in athletics) and the teacher leading the lesson (individual teaching style).

One key to effective management of behaviour is to ensure that pupils stay on-task and to rectify this should they stray from the task and begin to misbehave. For this, alert observation and an immediate response are needed (see Lawrence and Whitehead, 2010). A flow diagram and further information to support you with this can be found in Lawrence and Whitehead (2010). Now complete Activity 14.2.

Activity 14.2

Routines in physical education

Observe lessons in the activity areas you will be teaching and complete Table 14.2 for each lesson you observe. This will help you to build up a number of activity-specific routines that you can use within lessons and give you ideas to develop your own routines. At the end of the lesson, reflect on the time the routines take. You could ask the class teacher to undertake the same activity for a lesson you teach and discuss how the learning environment/lesson climate was helped or hindered by the routines used. This is the same form as used in Activity 12.3, but with comments to be added.

Table 14.1 Physical education department rules

1	Arrive on time to the lesson.
2	Line up outside the changing rooms.
3	Have appropriate kit and equipment for each lesson.
4	Hand in valuables.
5	Be quiet while the register is taken.
6	Make your way to the activity area quietly and sensibly.

Table 14.2 Lesson observation: lesson routines

Class .... **Activity** .... **Working space** ....

Task	Strategy used	Time strategy takes in the lesson	Comment, e.g. could the strategy be streamlined/ adapted? Did it affect the 'climate' of the lesson?
How are pupils let into the changing rooms?	Pupils enter as they arrive	10 minutes	Many pupils found it difficult to talk and change at the same time. Could they change in silence?
When and how are valuables and jewellery collected?			
When and how is the register taken?			
How does the teacher get the pupils' attention?			
Equipment/resources, e.g. Where is equipment located during the lesson? Who is responsible for getting it out/ putting it away? How is this organised?			
Organisation of activities and movement between them, e.g. how is the first activity arranged and how is the change from one activity to the next managed?			
Organisation of groupings, e.g. how are pupils assigned to groups? Do groups change during the lesson? If so how is this managed?			

SANCTIONS AND SUPPORT

Each school should have policies and practices on sanctions and support for pupils in following the rules and codes of conduct. Schools that are most successful in promoting positive behaviour have systems which are transparent and fully understood and implemented by all staff and pupils. All teachers are expected to follow this code to ensure that there is fairness and consistency in dealing with pupils. There should be a scale of consequences which is transparent and followed consistently by all members of a department and teachers within the school. You should therefore obtain a copy of the school's behaviour policy early on in your school experience. Now complete Activity 14.3.

Activity 14.3

Sanctions in physical education

Find out the sanctions for your placement school physical education department and list them in Table 14.3. Also find out how pupils can be supported if they cannot meet one of these rules for the lesson. For example: if a pupil has forgotten their physical education kit, is there kit for them to borrow? If so what is the procedure?

Table 14.3 Sanctions in physical education

Physical education department rules	Sanction/support
e.g. Pupil forgets kit	Sanction – after school detention Support – kit available for pupils to use

PROCEDURES AND PRIORITIES FOR PROMOTING POSITIVE BEHAVIOUR

Many schools use checklists as a reminder of the basic procedures and priorities for promoting positive behaviour. Here is a checklist, adapted from Taylor (2011) for physical education, which can form a starting point for you to apply rules, routines and strategies consistently to enable pupils to feel safer and happier and hence improve behaviour. You are encouraged to create your own checklist which you will adapt depending upon your school context.

BEHAVIOUR CHECKLIST FOR PHYSICAL EDUCATION TEACHERS

Policy and practice

1 Know the names and roles of any adults in class (teaching assistants, coaches, support workers) (see also Chapter 17).
2 Meet and greet pupils when they come to the changing rooms and when you meet them in the practical activity area.
3 Display rules in the class/gym/sports hall/changing rooms/physical education corridor – and ensure that the pupils and any supporting staff know what they are. Keep a copy with you to remind pupils if you are teaching outside.
4 Display the tariff of rewards in class/changing rooms/practical working area and remind pupils of this.
5 Know the system in place to follow through with all rewards.
6 Display the tariff of sanctions in class/changing rooms/practical working area and remind pupils of this.
7 Know the system in place to follow through with all sanctions.
8 Follow the school behaviour policy.

Planning and teaching

1 Know the names of pupils.
2 Have a plan for pupils who are likely to misbehave.
3 Ensure other adults in the class know the plan.
4 Understand pupils' special needs.
5 Ensure that all resources are prepared in advance.
6 Ensure that lessons are planned to challenge the most able and are differentiated to support the least able.
7 Give regular and constructive feedback.
8 Praise the behaviour you want to see more of.

DEVELOPING POSITIVE RELATIONSHIPS

Relationships play a key role in teaching to promote positive behaviour. What you say and do in a lesson, your body language, verbal communication and expectations all impact on the way pupils respond to you. It is prudent therefore to focus on the positive, not condoning the unacceptable but applying consequences which are meaningful.

It is important to focus upon developing positive relationships in the classroom with pupils and apply principles which support them in demonstrating positive behaviour. These include: making expectations explicit by giving both verbal and visual clues; giving a rationale for expectations that show expectations are for the pupils' benefit and not yours; expecting pupils to comply; being surprised rather than angry if they don't; modelling required behaviour; keeping things simple and sentences succinct (Roffey, 2011).

You cannot control other people's behaviour, only your own, yet you can influence and manage pupils' behaviour. It is important that you find the balance between controlling the class and being over-friendly and familiar with pupils (Figure 14.1). This may take time to develop. However, once a balance has been reached, you establish trust and a rapport and your influence will be significant.

It is important to remember that all behaviour serves a purpose. For pupils this may be, for example, to receive praise, gain attention or to save face in front of their friends. Here are some strategies which can help you avoid poor behaviour:

- Model the behaviour that you want in the classroom rather than react to the behaviour you are getting.
- Look to find solutions to behavioural problems (to find out more about a solution-focused approach, see Metcalf, 2003) and see this as part of being an effective teacher. Ask questions like: When is this pupil most engaged with learning? What positive qualities can teachers identify in this pupil? What helps this pupil stay calm? What helps this pupil co-operate? What would help the pupil develop positive behaviour?
- Manage your own emotions and feel positive that a solution will be found to any behavioural problems.
- Keep reminding yourself of the things that you do well, keep things in perspective and focus upon the positive.
- Effective relationships distinguish between the behaviour and the person so ensure that it is the specific behaviour that is criticised and not the person.

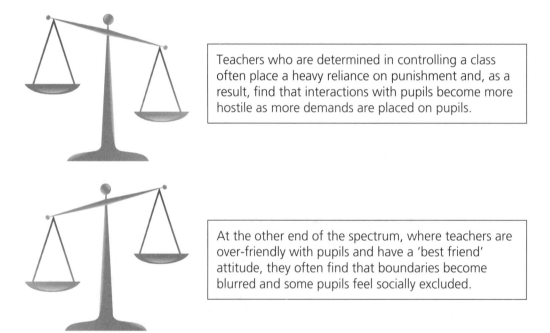

Teachers who are determined in controlling a class often place a heavy reliance on punishment and, as a result, find that interactions with pupils become more hostile as more demands are placed on pupils.

At the other end of the spectrum, where teachers are over-friendly with pupils and have a 'best friend' attitude, they often find that boundaries become blurred and some pupils feel socially excluded.

Figure 14.1 The balance of the teacher–pupil relationship

- Give pupils a second chance, allow them to consider their behaviour, learn from and modify it. This will develop relationships and also enhance self-esteem when the pupil gets it right.
- Do not make threats to pupils; this can lead to hostile relationships, damaged self-esteem and even worse behaviour. 'Jonathan, if you bounce the ball ONCE MORE, you will sit out of the lesson and lose your break time!!' It is better to make a request to the pupil and state clearly the consequences that will occur if the action is carried out. 'Jonathan, if you continue to bounce the basketball while I am talking, you are making a choice that will end up with me taking the ball away from you and you will lose five minutes of your break time.'
- It is important that you are consistent in your approach to warnings, sanctions and rewards. It is important that pupils know where they stand and that you will follow through with warnings or give the rewards you promise. Pupils need to see that you care enough to ensure this is consistent for all pupils in your class.

Now complete Activities 14.4, 14.5 and 14.6.

Activity 14.4

Strategies used in physical education to promote positive behaviour

The observation activity in Table 14.4 should be undertaken if possible on the classes of different teachers to investigate the range of rewards used, especially whether or not consistency is being applied across the department.

Activity 14.5

Observing classroom behaviour in your lesson

Video one of the lessons you teach where you have experienced problems with behaviour. Observe the video footage and reflect upon pupil behaviour using the activity template in Table 14.5. You can use some of the information given in this chapter to reflect upon your responses and the effectiveness of interventions. Your tutor could support you in the observation and strategies to inform future practice.

Activity 14.6

Reflecting on classroom behaviour

Complete the activity in Table 14.6 in line with your lesson plan (including teaching strategies, activities and the stage of the lesson). Reflect on appropriate and inappropriate behaviours related to the stage of the lesson. Identify the interventions you implemented including outcomes and/or what you could do to prevent this from happening again/ensure it remains successful.

Table 14.4 Promoting positive behaviour: rewards in physical education

Description of behaviour	Reward given	Comment
Teacher observes pupils lifting mats correctly and efficiently	Verbal praise: 'Well done, David and James, for not dragging the mats'	Positively reinforcing this expectation has a beneficial effect on the rest of the group who follow the example

Table 14.5 Observing classroom behaviours

Describe pupil behaviour	How did you respond to the behaviour? (Consider your verbal communication, body language, consequences and feedback – positive or negative)	Was your intervention effective? If so, why? If not why not?
What have you learnt from this to inform your future practice?		

Table 14.6 Pupil behaviour

(Amend this column in line with your lesson plan or part of the lesson you wish to focus upon.)						
Aspect of the lesson	**Comments on pupil behaviour**
Changing rooms	
Moving to activity area	e.g. Some pupils ran to the activity area carrying equipment and some walked. I stayed with the last pupils and so was slow getting to the group; this led to pupils messing around with the equipment. I shouted at them which led to one pupil responding disrespectfully and so being issued with a 10-minute detention. In future I will make my expectations clear with regard to equipment and movement to areas; I will walk out with pupils all at the same time to ensure they are sensible.
Sharing learning outcomes	
Warm-up	
Equipment set-up	
Teacher-led whole class	
Practise time – Activity 1	
Mini-plenary	
Transition	
Pair work – Activity 2	I gave clear instructions and demonstrations of the paired activity ensuring teaching points were clear and understood through questioning. All pupils immediately began to practise the activity as I had outlined and the majority achieved success at this. I praised pupils who were successful and gave advice and feedback on how others could improve.
Mini-plenary – questioning	
Transition	
Group work – Activity 3	
Plenary	
Putting equipment away	
Moving to changing rooms	
In changing rooms	

SUMMARY

Each teacher has their own personal approach or style for teaching to promote positive behaviour. You will need to have the knowledge of a range of generic strategies, including body language, use of voice, use of positive language and solution-focused approaches to promote positive behaviour and deal with inappropriate behaviour in line with your own individual attributes and the context in which you are teaching. You should be able to manage your own emotions and understand the effects that your verbal and non-verbal communication can have on a pupil's behaviour. It is important that you critically reflect upon lessons, your teaching and pupil responses, and be prepared to make appropriate changes. The activities in this chapter are designed to help you with this. You should understand your placement school's systems to support positive behaviour and prevent inappropriate or more challenging behaviour. These vary between schools. You should develop your own strategies and be able to modify them according to expectations of the schools in which you teach. It is essential that your practices fit consistently with school policy and that you understand that good relationships are at the heart of good behaviour. Positive, appropriate and professional relationships should be formed with pupils. Teaching to promote positive behaviour does not happen by chance; it needs to be planned, consistent, well organised and supportive of an environment where pupils feel safe, take responsibility for their learning and where positive relationships are developed.

FURTHER READING

Breckon, P., Capel, S., Whitehead, M. and Zwozdiak-Myers, P. (2010) Developing and maintaining an effective learning environment, in S. Capel and M. Whitehead (eds) *Learning to Teach in the Secondary School: A Companion to School Experience*, 3rd edn, London: Routledge, pp. 101–18.
This chapter provides a very useful overview with suggestions on how to create and maintain an effective learning environment. It contains situations and tasks to aid reflection on effective practice.

Cowley, S. (2006) *Getting the Buggers to Behave*, 3rd edn, London: Continuum.
This book gives an overview of advice on behaviour management that is practical and realistic. Basic information is discussed along with tips and suggestions that are based on technique and observations used by teachers.

Roffey, S. (2011) *Changing Behaviour in Schools: Promoting Positive Relationships and Well-being*, London: Sage.
This book provides an enlightening read; it includes well-detailed examples from 'real-life' experiences and situations. It expands upon a historical perspective that is internationally comparative and gives context to issues of behaviour. Research discussed clearly supports the progressive issues and ideas given throughout. Reflective and discussion-tasks should be beneficial in helping you gain further understanding on underlying factors to changing behaviour.

Rogers, B. (2011) *Classroom Behaviour: A Practical Guide to Effective Teaching, Behaviour Management and Colleague Support*, London: Sage.
This book looks at issues facing teachers in today's classrooms. It describes real situations and dilemmas and offers advice on dealing with challenges, building a rapport with pupils and colleagues and tapping into support mechanisms available.

Note: all proformas, tables or figures you are asked to complete to help you undertake activities in this chapter are also available on the website which accompanies the book (www.routledge.com/9780415814829).

Chapter 15 Overcoming barriers and maximising the achievement of all pupils

GILL GOLDER

INTRODUCTION

The work of a teacher in school involves meeting the needs of a wide range of pupils. It aims to remove barriers to learning by addressing specific individual needs. In order to maximise the achievement of all pupils, it is important to understand what barriers pupils may face and identify strategies and practices that work to remove the barriers to learning. Barriers may relate to, for example, special educational needs and disability, gender, ethnicity, cultural background or religion. Schools mirror society and as diversity in society has increased, so has diversity in schools. The result is that teachers need to be confident and competent to provide equality of opportunity for all pupils to enable them to meet their educational potential, by embracing the value of inclusion in education. The inclusiveness of a school is signified by the responsiveness of the school to the diversity of its community (Corbett and Slee, 2000).

By the end of this chapter you should be able to:

- understand the importance of providing an inclusive learning environment for all pupils;
- understand the importance of differentiation and adaptive practice;
- identify a range of teaching strategies that could help overcome barriers to learning;
- identify learning opportunities that can extend and challenge pupils in physical education.

INCLUSIVE EDUCATION

At the heart of the idea of inclusion lie serious issues concerning 'human rights', equality, equity and 'social justice' (Armstong et al., 2000). Sebba and Sachdev (1997) describe inclusive education as the process by which a school attempts to respond to all pupils as individuals by reconsidering and restructuring its curricular organisation and provision and allocating resources to enhance equality of opportunity. According to the Index for Inclusion (Booth et al., 2000) inclusion in education involves increasing the participation of pupils in, and reducing their exclusion from, the cultures, curricula and communities of local schools. To that end, as you work through this chapter, reflect upon the three elements of an inclusive school as identified by Booth et al. (2000), highlighted in Table 15.1.

Table 15.1 Three elements of an inclusive school

Inclusive culture	Inclusive policies	Inclusive practice
Building a community where there is collaboration, respect and partnership from all stakeholders	How the school develops as a 'school for all' through the ways it seeks to help new pupils and staff settle into the school	How a school orchestrates learning – encompassing planning, teaching strategies, setting suitable learning challenges, pupil engagement, meeting individual needs and assessment for and of learning
Establishing values that seek to remove barriers to learning and participation	How pupils manage the access to the school and the grouping strategies used	How the school mobilises resources, including the pupils themselves, staff and learning resources
All stakeholders share a common philosophy of inclusion	How the school organises support for diversity through coordination of support for all pupils and staff	
	What inclusion policies are in place to remove the barriers to learning	

Now complete Activity 15.1.

Activity 15.1

Inclusive education

In your placement school interview the following people to find out what they believe inclusive education to be:

- Head of Physical Education
- Head of Year or Key Stage
- Special Educational Needs Coordinator (SENCO).

Compare their answers

- What do they have in common?
- What is different about them?
- How do their responses relate to the notion of inclusive culture, inclusive policy and inclusive practice?

RECOGNISING DIVERSITY

Identifying pupils' support needs early is vital if you are to meet the needs of all pupils. The diversity of pupils means that barriers to learning could come in a variety of different forms. Taking account of these differences is an essential skill in teaching and is the first step in selecting appropriate teaching strategies to enable pupils to meet their potential. Activity 15.2 asks you to start to identify diversity and difference in a class that you observe and begin to identify what response teachers use to overcome the barriers that might result from this diversity, and Activity 15.3 looks at how this impacts on teaching and how differences are catered for.

Activity 15.2

Identifying difference in a class

Observe a physical education lesson with a class you have not observed or taught before. Do not talk to the teacher about the class beforehand. As you observe the lesson, write down in column 1 of Table 15.2 any pupil 'differences' you see and hear that appear to have an impact upon learning. Talk to the teacher after the lesson and see how well your record of 'differences' matches what the teacher perceives.

Activity 15.3

How do the differences impact on teaching and learning?

Observe the same class you observed in Activity 15.2. Note in column 2 of Table 15.2 the impact of the differences on pupil learning and in column 3 how the teacher caters for the difference. In column 4 record what you think you would do to cater for pupils' individual needs if you were to teach the class.

Table 15.2 Differences in a class

Pupil/pupils' difference	What is the impact on learning?	How does the teacher cater for the difference?	What would you do to cater for this need?
e.g. Pupil who is hearing impaired	Appears to disregard instruction, does not respond to questioning	Places him with a hearing partner	

EQUALITY OF OPPORTUNITY

Paying due regard to the statutory entitlement of all pupils means providing equality of opportunity for every pupil. Equality refers to the state of being equal, it is all about treating individuals equally, which is not necessarily the same as treating them the same. In some cases the need for equality may require unequal effort/time/resource to ensure that the principle of equality is achieved. Referring back to the Inclusion Index equality of opportunity is all about developing an Inclusive Culture.

Four principles for equality of opportunity were introduced in the 1992 National Curriculum (Department of Education (DoE), 1992) but are still relevant today. These principles were entitlement, accessibility, integration and integrity as outlined in Figure 15.1.

Now complete Activity 15.4.

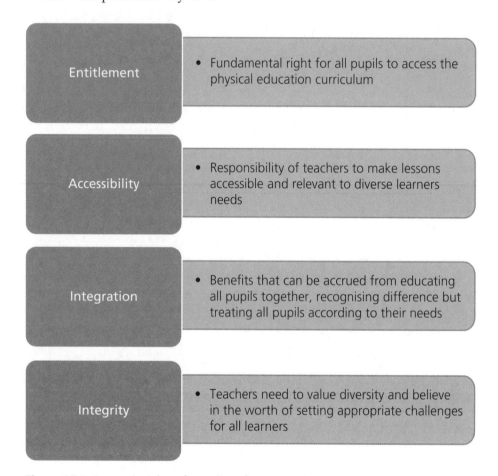

Entitlement
- Fundamental right for all pupils to access the physical education curriculum

Accessibility
- Responsibility of teachers to make lessons accessible and relevant to diverse learners needs

Integration
- Benefits that can be accrued from educating all pupils together, recognising difference but treating all pupils according to their needs

Integrity
- Teachers need to value diversity and believe in the worth of setting appropriate challenges for all learners

Figure 15.1 Four principles of equality of opportunity

Source: Adapted from Vickerman (2007)

Activity 15.4

Teaching practices to ensure equality of opportunity

Imagine you are a physical education teacher in the school described below.

> This is an average sized school with more boys than girls. It serves an inner city area with above-average pupil mobility. Over three-quarters of its pupils are from minority ethnic backgrounds, the largest groups being Black African and Black Caribbean. Just over half the pupils are eligible for free school meals and approximately half speak English as an additional language (EAL). The school has a considerably higher than average proportion of pupils with special educational needs and/or disabilities. The school is a specialist sports college.

The head of physical education recommends all staff adopt the teaching practices identified in Table 15.3 to ensure equality of opportunity. Why do you think these would enable equality of opportunity and what might it look like in physical education? Use the table to compile your ideas. Two examples are given.

Schools choose how to structure their curriculum and deploy their staff and resources, hence, physical education is delivered in a variety of different ways, for example, some schools have separate classes for boys and girls, others teach mixed ability classes, while others set their physical education classes by ability in either mixed or single gender groups. The curriculum offered in some schools could be seen to be gender-specific, e.g. 'feminine'-appropriate activities for girls such as netball and dance and 'masculine'-appropriate activities for boys such as rugby and football or the staffing could be gender biased e.g. females teaching 'feminine' activities and males teaching 'masculine' activities. There may be very valid reasons for schools adopting these structure and processes, but these may also act as barriers to learning by reducing opportunities for all. Activity 15.5 asks you to consider the notion of equality in more depth.

Activity 15.5

How accessible is the physical education curriculum?

Obtain a copy of the physical education curriculum in a mixed secondary school and answer the following questions (you may have to talk to the teacher):

1 Are all the physical education activities taught to all pupils in mixed gender or ability classes? If not, which activities are taught to different groups, e.g. gender groups, ability groups? Why is this so? Do you agree with the reasons for this?
2 Does the physical education curriculum offered differ according to any of the following? If so why – do you agree with these reasons?
   - Age
   - Ability
   - Culture/ethnicity
   - Gender

Table 15.3 Equality of opportunity

Teaching practices	Why is this important?	Provide an example of a strategy the teacher could use in physical education to help ensure equality of opportunity
Show sensitivity when asking pupils to demonstrate in mixed ability/sex classes		
Avoid gendered terms or phrases		
Encourage pupils and staff to wear suitable physical education clothing		
Involve all pupils in principal roles in lessons		
Display material must represent non-stereotypical images		
Staff act as role models		
Introduce a range of non-stereotypical activities		
Challenge forms of discriminatory behaviour	Pupils see all have a worthwhile contribution to make	Make sure all are given the opportunity to demonstrate
Share teaching of all activities among all staff	Help challenge traditional stereotypes	Females teaching rugby, males teaching dance
Allocate resources, time and facilities equally		

INCLUSIVE POLICY AND INCLUSIVE PRACTICE IN PHYSICAL EDUCATION

The statutory inclusion statement introduced in 1999, but retained in all subsequent reviews of the National Curriculum, provides a framework for teachers to use to ensure they are enabling pupils to meet their potential by providing effective learning opportunities for all pupils. Three principles for Inclusion (Department for Education and Employment/Qualifications and Curriculum Authority (DfEE/QCA), 1999: 28) are:

1 Setting suitable learning challenges.
2 Responding to pupils' diverse learning needs.
3 Overcoming potential barriers to learning and assessment for individuals and groups of pupils.

These principles are all about planning programmes of study that can be adapted or modified, e.g. by different teaching approaches or materials, in order to provide pupils with opportunities to succeed. In order for the three inclusion principles to be embedded in inclusive teaching and learning practice, physical education departments need to have policies that support staff, pupils and parents/carers. Activity 15.6 encourages you to explore the range of policies a school has to develop a 'school for all'.

Activity 15.6

School policies on inclusion and equality of opportunity

Read both your placement school's whole-school and physical education department policies that enable inclusive practice and equality of opportunity, then answer the following questions:

1 Do the policies communicate a shared common philosophy about inclusive practice. If yes, what is this common philosophy? If not, where do the differences lie?
2 Do the policies focus on any particular groups? If so, which ones and what unique provision do they cite to support these pupils?
3 Do the policies embed the four principles of equality of opportunity and/ or exemplify the three principles for inclusion? If yes, how? If no, how could they be developed to do so?
4 Do the policies have specific roles and responsibilities outlined? If yes, who has specific roles and responsibilities?
5 What would your role be as a teacher of physical education to implement these policies in practice?

Having looked at school and physical education department policies, it is possible to explore how these policies manifest themselves in practice. Figure 15.2 illustrates the three principles of inclusion and what elements of pedagogic practice a physical education teacher might change in order to overcome barriers and maximise achievement of their pupil. Use this to help you complete Activity 15.7.

The relationship between the three principles is key to establishing an inclusive learning environment which encourages all pupils to achieve. A starting point for all teachers is to know their pupils. In order to do this, you need to know who holds information about pupils. This should be evident from your research into school and department policies in Activity 15.6. The type of information you need is:

- prior attainment levels in physical education for all pupils;
- details of specific learning or individual needs;
- any individual targets pupils may have set, e.g. on individual learning plans, behaviour plans, language intervention plans, attendance records;
- learning and cognitive style preference;
- pupil background and who to contact for parental/carer support;
- it is also useful to find out more about what interests and motivates your pupils.

By knowing your pupils, you can then identify and understand their needs. Ekins (2012) suggests six groups of pupils who are more 'vulnerable to underachievement'. Generally identifying the following groups of pupils gives you a better understanding of the range of needs impacting on progress and achievement. However, individual schools may have other higher priority groups particular to the school context:

- special educational needs and disability, by level of need and area of need;
- gifted and talented pupils;
- looked after children;
- social service involved;
- English as an additional language (EAL);
- Gypsy, Roma or traveller.

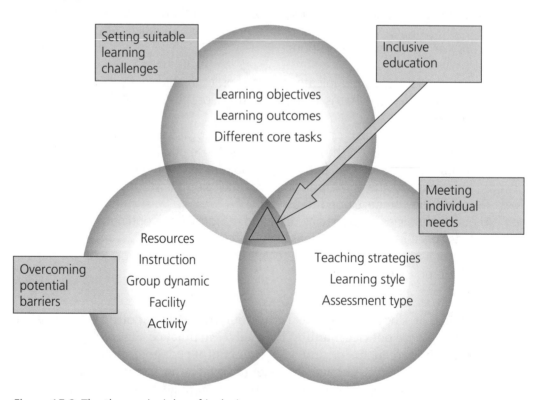

Figure 15.2 The three principles of inclusion

Activity 15.7

Observing inclusive teaching

Select a class to observe that has a diverse group of pupils in it. With the help of the teacher identify up to six pupils who have specific learning or individual needs and observe them throughout the lesson.

Using Table 15.4, identify how the teacher used the three principles of inclusion to enable each pupil to reach their potential in that lesson. Some examples have been given below.

MEETING THE NEEDS OF ALL PUPILS

Viewing teaching from a pupil's perspective is a helpful way to enable pupils to reach their full potential. A starting point is ensuring that your planning meets individual needs and you have identified barriers to learning in how you design intended learning outcomes, activities and assessments. Effective planning for all pupils should be embedded in the teacher's usual planning format not something as a bolt-on extra. It should draw upon the three circles of inclusion, including: intended learning outcomes, teaching approaches/strategies, access strategies involve collaboration and incorporate personal targets wherever possible.

Your teaching has to allow for differences in the abilities and other characteristics of pupils. This is what differentiation is all about; it is a continuous process which involves knowing your pupils' needs. Differentiation strategies should start with planning clear and shared intended learning outcomes, core tasks with reinforcement and extension activities and learning broken down into small, achievable steps. To make learning accessible, you need to create resources that enable pupils to progress. These resources might include, for example, different size/weight equipment; reading age appropriate task cards; images rather than texts; suitable information and communications technology (ICT) resources, e.g. hand-held learning or digital technologies. In teaching the lessons it is important to meet individual needs by, for example, using a wide range of teaching strategies and activities; balancing questioning techniques using a mixture of lower- and higher-order thinking skills and providing opportunities for pupils to question each other and you; adjusting the pace of learning to ensure pupils are stretched and challenged but not so fast they cannot keep up. All this requires flexibility of approach and response that provides pupils with the opportunity to consolidate learning. Now complete Activity 15.8.

Activity 15.8

Observing differentiation strategies in practice

Observe an experienced member of staff teaching a class with a range of abilities; make a note of the following:

- How did their planning account for the different pupils' needs in the class?
- How did they use different resources to make learning accessible?
- What teaching strategies did they implement to meet individual needs?

Table 15.4 Three principles of inclusion

Pupil	What was the pupil doing during the lesson?	Setting suitable intended learning outcomes	Meeting individual needs	Overcoming barriers	Who supported this?
John – talented pupil	Used to demonstrate, acted as a peer coach and language buddy	Learning outcome was leadership role not skill development	Self-directed teaching style used	Given peer coaching card to allow independence	Teacher
Jasmine – wheel chair user Muscular Dystrophy	Working with Learning Support Assistant (LSA) on modified tasks along with two other pupils	Learning outcome and core tasks changed	One-to-one support	Resources/ rules changed to enable access – size of ball and conditions on game	LSA
Jamil – EAL pupil	Completing core tasks with majority of other pupils	Same intended learning outcome as for the majority of the class	Guided discovery used with the majority of the class 'Show what you know' rather than questions used at assessment points	Worked with peer as language buddy, key words translated on a white board	John – talented pupil

Having observed the lesson what do you think you could have done differently to ensure inclusive practice?

There are a number of different ways to differentiate in physical education. The simplest form of differentiation uses the 'STEP' principle, where:

S = Space, where you reduce or increase the space in which a pupil works to make the task more challenging or easier to achieve.

T = Task, where the activity is changed to add greater complexity or simplify.

E = Equipment, where you change the type of equipment pupils use to achieve the task.

P = People, where you change how pupils work together to make the activity easier or more difficult, e.g. adding or removing active defence or changing from, for example, 3 vs 1 to 2 vs 2.

Activity 15.9 asks you to consider an alternative way to differentiate and come up with mini-lesson plans that illustrate application of the three differentiation strategies noted below.

- Differentiation by TASK where pupils are given different but related tasks according to their ability.
- Differentiation by OUTCOME where the same task set is to pupils but it is open enough to enable pupils to achieve at different levels of outcome.
- Differentiation by STIMULUS where you use different instructional methods or resources to enable pupils to prompt pupil learning.

Many issues impact upon your choice of strategy for differentiation. The *curriculum* being offered in the school has the potential to engage or disengage pupils, so finding out what activities are offered and why the department have selected these activities helps you consider what learning outcomes to plan for. The *human resources* available impacts upon your choice of strategies. Do any of your classes have additional adults in with them, e.g. LSAs, physical education technicians or Year 12 sports leaders? The way in which the *school groups* classes for teaching impacts on how you teach your pupils; physical education can be taught to single gender groups, mixed ability groups, tutor groups, setted or streamed groups. Some schools may use vertical groups that enable physical maturity rather than age to be used to group pupils. *Physical resources* may also impact upon what you do, the facilities available, including practical teaching spaces, changing spaces, notice boards, equipment and ICT resources need factoring in to your plans when trying to meet the needs of all pupils.

Activity 15.9

Differentiating teaching and learning

Using your lesson planning template, plan a teaching episode for the following three scenarios – pay particular attention to the strategy for differentiation in each.

Scenario 1: You have a mixed ability and mixed gender Year 9 class. The unit uses athletics as the activity but the outcomes are for pupils to develop and refine techniques for run, jump and throw activities, to improve personal performance and to be able to identify strengths and weaknesses in performance suggesting ways to improve. You decide to differentiate your lessons by OUTCOME.

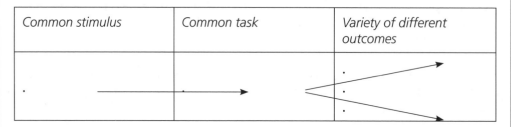

Common stimulus	Common task	Variety of different outcomes

Scenario 2: You have a mixed ability Year 7 class with 5 pupils with EAL. The unit uses aesthetics with outcomes are for pupils to develop and refine techniques, make decisions and select suitable choreographic techniques, accurately replicating movement patterns showing mental determination to perform routines in front of an audience. You decide to differentiate your lessons by STIMULUS and TASK.

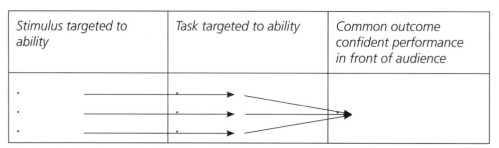

Stimulus targeted to ability	Task targeted to ability	Common outcome confident performance in front of audience

Scenario 3: You have a mixed ability and single-gender Year 10 class with 3 pupils who are identified as talented in physical education and are part of the school's Football academy. The unit uses basketball as the activity but the outcomes are for pupils to develop and refine techniques, to make decisions by planning and implementing what needs to be practised to improve personal performance and to be able to identify strengths and weaknesses in performance suggesting ways to improve. You decide to differentiate your lessons by PROGRESSIVE TASKS and GRADED OUTCOME.

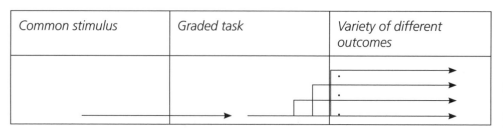

Common stimulus	Graded task	Variety of different outcomes

Figure 15.3 Lesson plan template

Flexibility in teaching strategies can be supported by using the 'inclusion Spectrum' designed by the Youth Sport Trust and the English Federation of Disability Sport (EFDS). This is an alternative approach that can be combined with the Inclusion statements for the National Curriculum and differentiation strategies to ensure maximum participation and access to physical education by all pupils. Activity 15.10 illustrates the Inclusion spectrum's five strategies of open, modified, parallel, separate and disability sports activities and asks you to consider examples of how these are implemented in practice.

Activity 15.10

The inclusion spectrum

The inclusion spectrum gives teachers the opportunity to respond to pupils' diverse learning needs by providing five different, yet complementary, ways of including all pupils in physical education. Discuss with an experienced teacher and observe practice in school to consider the following and complete Table 15.5.

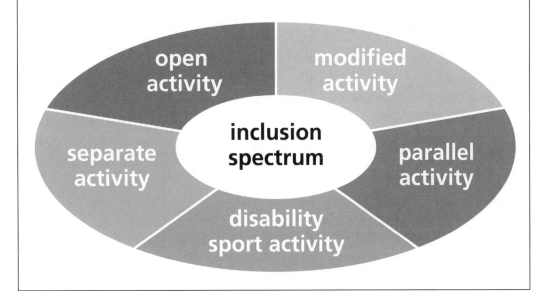

Table 15.5 The inclusion spectrum

Inclusion spectrum category	Example of how this is used in physical education	Potential benefits of this approach
Open activity In an open activity all pupils are included in the same task with minimal or no adaptation or modification		
Modified activity In a modified activity changes are made to the task so that all pupils are included and can participate at a level appropriate to their ability. Modifications can be made to equipment, space, rules, speed, interaction and/or position		
Parallel activity Everyone plays the same game but different groups play the game in different ways according to their abilities		
Disability sport activity Disability sports activities, such as seated volleyball, boccia and goalball, are developed or modified specifically with disabled people in mind. Non-disabled pupils can take part in disability sport activities		
Separate activity Occasionally, it may be appropriate for individual pupils to play separately from the rest of the class, or with their disabled peers, e.g. when preparing for a disability sport event. This is generally part of extra-curricular provisions; and does not generally happen in physical education lessons and should not happen at the expense of inclusion in the wider physical education curriculum		

EXTENDING AND CHALLENGING THE MOST TALENTED PUPILS IN PHYSICAL EDUCATION

The notion of maximising the potential of all pupils does not just apply to those pupils with specific learning needs or from groups more likely to underachieve. Underachievement can be as important for pupils who are identified as talented in physical education. The inclusion strategies and differentiation approaches outlined in this chapter can be used to equal effect to extend and challenge pupils who are more able by enriching and enhancing opportunities.

Talent education in physical education is the process of identifying, selecting, providing for and supporting the most able pupils. Bailey and Morley (2006) suggest that pupils are recognised as talented when they demonstrate high level ability within the full range of physical education contexts, or have the potential to do so and are likely to excel in one or a combination of the following five abilities:

- *Physical ability*, revealed through pupil's competence and fitness to perform a range of physical activities.
- *Social ability*, exhibited in social contexts and is the basis of leadership, teamwork and similar concepts.
- *Personal ability* underpins an individual's capacity for self-regulation, self-belief and commitment to mastery.
- *Cognitive ability*, shown in planning and compositional settings, as well as knowledge and understanding of central physical educational concepts.
- *Creative ability*, evidenced when pupils respond to challenges and tasks with fluency, originality and sensitivity to problems.

Now complete Activity 15.11.

Activity 15.11

Talented pupils

While on school placement, find out the following:

- How does your department identify pupils as talented in physical education?
- What opportunities are offered to talented pupils to extend their experiences in physical education lessons?
- How are talented pupils supported by the school through extra-curricular activity, interagency work or parent/carer involvement?

SUMMARY

This chapter has highlighted the importance of enabling all pupils to progress and achieve in physical education by reducing barriers to learning and setting challenging and engaging learning activities for the diverse range of pupils in the school. Responding to the challenges of inclusive and diverse nature of schools requires teachers to unpick the inclusive culture of the school, examine the inclusive policies in place and develop inclusive practices. Knowing your pupils is at the heart of effective teaching and learning, by doing this you can adopt flexible approaches to teaching, learning and assessment that enable pupils to maximise their potential.

FURTHER READING

Dowling, F., Fitzgerald, H. and Flintoff, A. (2012) *Equity and Difference in Physical Education, Youth Sport and Health: A Narrative Approach*, London: Routledge.
This book confronts issues of equity and difference through the innovative use of narrative method, telling stories of difference that enable the reader to engage both emotionally and cognitively with the subject. It offers detailed, practical suggestions for how narrative might be used in, or inform, teaching sessions.

Vickerman, P. (2007) *Teaching Physical Education to Children with Special Educational Needs*, London: Routledge.
This book offers practical strategies to include pupils with special educational needs fully into physical education. It explores the complexities in depth.

Note: all proformas, tables or figures you are asked to complete to help you undertake activities in this chapter are also available on the website which accompanies the book (www.routledge.com/9780415814829).

Chapter 16 Assessing pupils' learning

MARK BOWLER, SOPHY BASSETT AND
ANGELA NEWTON

INTRODUCTION

Assessing pupils' learning is an integral part of teaching and learning and should not be seen as a 'bolt-on' process. Thus, assessment must be included in the planning and delivery of all lessons and units. This chapter includes sections on developing intended learning outcomes, establishing assessment criteria and assessing learning through teacher questioning, peer and self-assessment. The chapter builds on the concepts of planning introduced in Chapters 4 and 5.

By the end of this chapter you should be able to:

- understand what is meant by assessment *for* and *of* learning;
- identify clear and differentiated learning outcomes and associated assessment criteria for lessons;
- design questions that allow you to assess levels of pupil understanding;
- develop resources that support pupils in peer and self-assessment;
- assess pupils' achievement of learning outcomes and use this information to plan for pupils' learning in subsequent lessons.

ASSESSMENT FOR LEARNING OR ASSESSMENT OF LEARNING?

Assessment can be formative or summative. Formative assessment (assessment *for* learning) focuses on strategies to develop pupil learning. Summative assessment (assessment *of* learning) is intended to identify the current level of pupil learning. As a teacher you use both formative and summative assessment strategies. The aim is to continuously challenge pupils to improve their learning. Planning assessment into lessons in a systematic way allows you to gather information which can inform the next planning cycle.

Assessment *for* learning is the process of seeking and interpreting evidence for use by learners and teachers to decide where pupils are in their learning, where they need to go and how they could get there (Assessment Reform Group, 2002). There are ten principles underpinning assessment *for* learning. These identify that assessment should:

1   Be considered as part of your planning.
2   Focus on pupil learning.

3   Be a central part of your practice as a teacher.
4   Be regarded as a key professional skill for teachers.
5   Be sensitive and constructive to take account of the emotional impact on pupils.
6   Foster motivation in pupils.
7   Promote understanding of the criteria for assessment and pupil commitment to the goals they need to attain.
8   Provide pupils with guidance about how to improve.
9   Enable pupils to reflect and self-assess so that they can become independent learners.
10 Recognise a full range of educational achievement for all pupils.

(adapted from Assessment Reform Group, 2002)

Assessment *of* learning provides a summary of pupil learning at the end of a lesson, unit, year or key stage. A very important aspect of assessment in schools is the formative use of summative data. 'Teachers can use information gained through summative assessment formatively, in order to draw pupils into the assessment process, help pupils understand ... improve motivation ... develop independence, enhance target setting ... increase pupils' understanding and raise ... standards' (Department for Education and Skills, 2004: 2).

PLANNING LEARNING OUTCOMES

It is crucial that teachers plan learning outcomes that are *clear, concise* and *easily assessed*. Outcomes should express pupils' anticipated learning and can identify what they will 'know', 'understand' and 'be able to' do (see also Chapters 4 and 5 on planning). Joanne is a newly qualified teacher (NQT). Here are Joanne's learning outcomes for a first tennis lesson with a Year 8 class.

By the end of the lesson, pupils will:

1   Know how to place ground strokes deep into the court.
2   Understand why it is important to place the ball deep to the back of the court.
3   Be able to play ground strokes with consistent depth.
4   Be able to provide feedback to a partner on the depth and consistency of their ground strokes.

Learning outcomes can be differentiated by stating what different groups of pupils will be able to achieve during a lesson. Differentiated learning outcomes can be written in terms of 'All' (every pupil), 'Most' (the middle ability range) and 'Some' (the most and/or least able). For example, the learning outcomes below highlight how learning outcome 3 above has been sub-divided to differentiate for most pupils (learning outcome 3a) and the higher ability (learning outcome 3b). Learning outcomes 4 provides another example of how to differentiate for all (learning outcome 4a) and higher ability (learning outcome 4b) pupils.

By the end of the lesson, pupils will:

1   Know how to place ground strokes deep into the court (ALL).
2   Understand why it is important to place the ball deep to the back of the court (ALL).
3a Be able to play ground strokes with depth in a practice situation (MOST).

3b Be able to play ground strokes with depth and consistency in a competitive situation (SOME).

4a Be able to identify strengths and weaknesses of a partner's ground strokes using a peer assessment resource (ALL).

4b Be able to provide detailed feedback to a partner on how to improve their ground strokes (SOME).

Now complete Activity 16.1.

Activity 16.1

Reviewing learning outcomes

Look at a specific series of lesson plans for one unit you have taught. Review the learning outcomes in each lesson and answer the following questions:

1 Were your learning outcomes clear and concise and thus easily assessed? If you answer no, rewrite the learning outcomes.

2 Were your learning outcomes differentiated? If you answer no, rewrite the learning outcomes for ALL/MOST/SOME pupils.

3 At the start of every lesson did you explain your learning outcomes to the class (see below)? If you answer no, or you were inconsistent in doing this, what strategies could you use to improve your practice?

4 At the end of the lesson did you review the learning outcomes with all of the pupils? Did this process involve identifying the extent to which they achieved each outcome? What strategies did you employ to make a judgement on their level of achievement of each outcome?

STRATEGIES AND CRITERIA FOR ASSESSMENT

It is important that both the teacher and pupils are aware of the learning outcomes for the lesson. These should be shared with pupils at the beginning of every lesson. Many schools use the acronym WALT (we are learning today) when introducing learning outcomes. Differentiated learning outcomes can be regarded as one form of assessment criteria. However, for a more detailed assessment of pupils' learning, you should write additional assessment criteria for each of the differentiated learning outcomes. These criteria are brief and explicit and are often used as teaching/learning points. Many schools use the acronym WILF (what I'm looking for) when introducing these criteria. It is also important to identify how you assess each of the learning outcomes. Assessment strategies might include questioning, observation, peer and self-assessment. Table 16.1 demonstrates how you can map the learning outcomes, the assessment strategy and assessment criteria.

Table 16.1 Mapping learning outcomes, assessment strategy and assessment criteria

Learning outcome	Assessment strategy	Assessment criteria
1 Know how to place ground strokes deep into the court (ALL)	Questioning	Pupils describe how to place ground strokes deep into the court: Early movement to the ball Early racket preparation Balanced stance Contact ball at waist height slightly in front of body Swing from low to high Transfer weight forward Keep head still Return to ready position
2 Understand why it is important to place the ball deep to the back of the court (ALL)	Questioning	Pupils describe the benefits of playing deep to the back of the court: Gives player more time to recover from their shot and prepare for their next Makes their opponent's return more difficult Gives them time to come into the net
3a Be able to play ground strokes with depth in a practice situation (MOST)	Pupils self-assess how many shots bounce in the target zone	Ground stroke bounces into target zone between service and baseline
3b Be able to play ground strokes with depth and consistency in a competitive situation (SOME)	Observation	Placement of ground stroke shows consistent depth and accuracy to outwit opponent
4a Be able to identify strengths and weaknesses of a partner's ground strokes using a peer assessment resource (ALL)	Observation Listening to pupil feedback	Stand in the most appropriate position Provide clear feedback using appropriate terminology Identify two strengths and one weakness ('two stars and a wish')
4b Be able to provide detailed feedback to a partner on how to improve their ground strokes (SOME)	Observation Listening to pupil feedback	Stand in the most appropriate position Provide clear feedback using appropriate terminology Identify strengths and weaknesses Provide corrective feedback to improve partner's weaknesses

Now complete Activity 16.2.

Planning learning outcomes, assessment strategies and assessment criteria

Plan a lesson identifying a maximum of four differentiated learning outcomes that include 'know', 'understand' and 'be able to do'. Using Table 16.2, map appropriate assessment strategies and assessment criteria for each learning outcome.

THE EFFECTIVE USE OF QUESTIONING

Table 16.1 showed some assessment criteria that would be assessed through teacher questioning. In order to assess learning outcomes for knowledge and understanding, you should plan specific questions which allow pupils to demonstrate their learning. These may be asked at points during the lesson to assess progress against the learning outcomes, or at the end of a lesson, during the plenary.

Once you have identified appropriate questions which allow pupils to demonstrate their learning, you must also consider how you will present the question to the pupils and/or how they will be required to respond. Remember that the strategy should help you to determine whether all pupils know or understand the answer(s) to your question. Table 16.3 highlights a range of effective questioning strategies to consider. (Further guidance can be found in Newton and Bowler, 2010, and Department for Education and Skills, 2004.)

Table 16.2 Planning learning outcomes, assessment strategy and assessment criteria

Learning outcome	Assessment strategy	Assessment criteria

Table 16.3 Effective questioning strategies

Questioning strategies	Description	Advantage
1 'No hands up' policy	Teacher selects pupils at random to answer questions	This strategy encourages all pupils to think of an answer and prevents the same pupils answering all questions
2 Differentiated questioning	Teacher targets specific questions to pupils of different abilities (closed/ open questions for lower/ higher order thinking skills)	This strategy ensures that higher ability pupils are stretched and that lower ability pupils can still demonstrate their learning
3 Adequate thinking time	Teacher gives pupils time to consider their answers before requesting a response	This strategy gives pupils time to consider a more in-depth answer to the question, as well as reinforcing the expectation that all pupils may be required to give an answer (if paired with 'no hands up')
4 Think-pair-share	Teacher asks a question for all pupils to consider, discuss with a partner and share with the class	This strategy gives pupils the opportunity to rehearse answers and provides pupils with the opportunity to learn from a more informed peer
5 Traffic lights	Teacher asks a question and pupils demonstrate their confidence in answering (red = not confident, amber = quite confident, green = very confident)	This strategy helps the teacher to judge how well pupils feel they have met the intended learning outcomes
6 Pupil-designed questions	Pupils create their own questions and model answers	This strategy ensures that pupils can prioritise key learning topics and provide appropriate answers
7 Probing	Teacher provides additional 'probing' questions to clarify and extend pupil responses	This strategy supports pupils in demonstrating clearer or more in-depth understanding
8 WOWO (write on, wipe off) boards	Pupils write their answers down on a WOWO board	This strategy allows pupils to respond in a less intimidating environment than one which requires an oral response. WOWO boards can also support the development of literacy skills

Now complete Activity 16.3.

Activity 16.3

Designing questions and questioning strategies to assess learning outcomes

Using Table 16.4, record the 'know' and 'understand' learning outcomes you identified in Activity 16.2. Identify specific questions that could enable pupils to demonstrate the assessment criteria you have designed and decide what would be the best questioning strategy for each question.

PEER AND SELF-ASSESSMENT

Peer and self-assessment will play an integral part in assessment for learning. To facilitate effective peer and self-assessment you should plan opportunities in lessons and provide resources and appropriate guidance (such as the peer assessment resource in learning outcome 4a on p. 200). In practical physical education, it is recommended that you teach pupils to assess each other before they assess themselves. This is because of the difficulties (without the use of technology) in observing certain elements of their own performance.

Before pupils begin to peer assess, you should ensure that they are aware of some of the potential benefits. These include:

1   Receiving more feedback than the teacher alone can provide.
2   Developing their understanding of the assessment criteria, which may have a positive impact on their future performance.
3   Developing their observation skills.
4   Providing opportunities for social interaction.
5   Developing their speaking and listening skills.
6   Developing their ability to work and assess independently of the teacher.

Similarly, when planning for self-assessment, pupils should be made aware of some of the potential benefits. These include:

1   Developing their ability to reflect on their learning.
2   Developing their understanding of the assessment criteria, which may have a positive impact on their future performance.
3   Understanding their own strengths and areas for development.
4   Understanding what they could do to improve and how this could be achieved.
5   Developing their ability to work and assess independently of the teacher.

When introducing peer assessment to pupils, you should ensure they have a clear understanding of the criteria for assessment and where best to position themselves as the assessor. Pupils should be reminded to focus on each assessment criterion in turn, providing constructive feedback to the performer on their level of success only after observing for a suitable length of time. Effective feedback is based upon strengths and areas for development ('two stars and a wish') in relation to the criteria. Sufficient time must be planned so that pupils have the opportunity to perform and assess. Pupils should ideally then be given time to practise following feedback.

Table 16.4 Questions and questioning strategy to assess learning outcomes

Learning outcome	Questions	Questioning strategy

Once pupils have experienced peer assessment, you may choose to extend their ability to assess their own performance (self-assessment), for the benefits listed on p. 204. As with peer assessment, pupils should be reminded to focus on each criterion in turn. When assessing their own performance pupils can assess either during the performance or at the end, depending on the type of activity. The nature of self-assessment means that it can be less reliable and should be monitored carefully by the teacher.

An effective strategy for supporting peer and self-assessment is to create resources with clear and unambiguous assessment criteria. The assessment criteria are usually devised from your teaching/learning points. In creating an effective resource for assessment purposes, consider the following points:

1   Use of language: should be appropriate for the pupils' age and development.
2   Textual presentation: fonts should be easily readable such as Comic Sans MS; font size should be no smaller than 14; dark text should be printed on a light (not white) background; avoid green and red/pink as these are difficult to read for colour-blind individuals.
3   Use of appropriate images to support the criteria: images should be technically accurate and suitable for the level of expectation; images should represent the diverse nature of society.
4   Layout and amount of text: text and images should be well spaced and complement each other.
5   Annotation: space for pupils to record the extent to which assessment criteria have been met.
6   Differentiation: through a range of resources for different abilities, or adding differentiated criteria onto one resource.

Now complete Activity 16.4.

Activity 16.4

Designing peer and self-assessment resources

Using some of the assessment criteria you identified in the previous tasks, create a resource that enables pupils to effectively assess their own or others' performance. You should consider how you can effectively implement the strategies suggested in this section.

If you elected to produce a peer assessment resource, consider how this might require modification for self-assessment purposes. Similarly, if you elected to produce a self-assessment resource, how might this be modified for peer work?

SELF-ASSESSMENT AND THE USE OF INFORMATION AND COMMUNICATIONS TECHNOLOGY (ICT)

To enhance the process of self-assessment, it is recommended that pupils are able to see their own performance. This is particularly applicable when the assessment criteria are based on the 'process' of a performance, rather than the 'outcome'. There are numerous software packages, recording and playback devices that support movement analysis and assessment. This technology allows pupils to view their performance more than once and in slow motion, providing a clear visual image from which to self assess. Although the use of information and communications technology (ICT) can more readily be used for self-assessment, it can also be applied to peer assessment. For more information on the use of ICT in physical education, see Chapter 8, and also Stidder and Capel (2010). Now complete Activity 16.5.

Activity 16.5

Using ICT in peer and self-assessment

Using a form of ICT that you have available to you, trial its use with pupils during a lesson where you have planned to use peer or self-assessment. What were the advantages and disadvantages of using ICT to support formative assessment? Consider how you might overcome any disadvantages in your future use of ICT.
   Trial the use of other forms of ICT in the peer and self-assessment process. Evaluate the effectiveness of different types of ICT in aiding pupils to peer and/ or self assess effectively.

TARGET SETTING

An important consideration in making the most effective use of formative assessments is target setting. This is crucial for ensuring that pupils know where they are in their learning, where they need to go and how they could get there (Assessment Reform Group, 2002). Targets can be set by the teacher, by peers (peer assessment) or by themselves (self-assessment). As pupils become familiar with using and understanding assessment criteria, they can be encouraged to set personal targets for themselves or others, based on criteria that are not being met consistently. They will need help from the teacher in the early stages of this process but if provided with sufficient time to practice, they will develop independence. A useful strategy to support the target setting process is to use the acronym SMART (**s**pecific, **m**easurable, **a**chievable, realistic, **t**imed).
   Activity 16.6 asks you to set SMART targets.

Activity 16.6

Setting SMART targets

Over a series of lessons with one class, set a small sample of pupils a SMART target to develop an area for improvement. During the peer and/or self-assessment process set a specific task for pupils where they must set a SMART target for themselves or others. Can you see any benefits or limitations of pupils setting their own targets?

JUDGING THE QUALITY OF LEARNING IN YOUR LESSONS

You should record pupil progress against your identified differentiated learning outcomes (all/most/some) as well as identifying what to teach in the following lesson in order challenge all pupils. The following questions may guide you in the assessment process:

- What proportion of pupils achieved the outcome?

- What evidence do you have of pupil achievement?
- If all pupils achieved a particular learning outcome, was it appropriate for their ability level?
- If some pupils did not achieve a particular learning outcome, why were they unsuccessful?

The answers to the questions above should assist you in answering the following question, when you evaluate your lesson:

- What points must you consider when planning your next lesson in order to progress pupil learning?

Below are the lesson learning outcomes from Table 16.1 (provided here as a reminder).

Lesson learning outcomes:

By the end of the lesson, pupils will:
1   Know how to place ground strokes deep into the court (ALL).
2   Understand why it is important to place the ball deep to the back of the court (ALL).
3a Be able to play ground strokes with depth in a practice situation (MOST).
3b Be able to play ground strokes with depth and consistency in a competitive situation (SOME).
4a Be able to identify strengths and weaknesses of a partner's ground strokes using a peer assessment resource (ALL).
4b Be able to provide detailed feedback to a partner on how to improve their ground strokes (SOME).

Here is an example evaluation of the lesson learning outcomes.

ASSESSMENT OF PUPIL LEARNING

Learning outcomes 1 and 2 were met by all pupils. This was evidenced through pupil responses to teacher questioning. However, for some pupils, the use of think-pair-share was required to demonstrate the expected understanding. Learning outcomes 1 and 2 were appropriate for most pupils, but it was evident that MB, AN and SB already had an awareness of ground strokes and could have been challenged further about the use of spin.

Learning outcome 3a was achieved by most (approx 80%) pupils, as expected. Most pupils identified through self-assessment that they were able to hit the ball into the target zones consistently from a partner feed. More pupils may have achieved this outcome if the feed had been more sympathetic.

Learning outcome 3b was only achieved by 3 pupils (MB, AN and SB). During the lesson I observed a lack of consistency in the competitive situation with many pupils making unforced errors, particularly on the backhand side.

Learning outcome 4a was achieved by all pupils but PB and GM were not always accurate in their identification of their partner's strengths. The achievement of learning outcome 4b was observed in MB, AN and SB, but particularly SB, who provided detailed guidance to her partner on how to adjust racket head angle to improve depth of shot.

Now complete Activity 16.7.

Activity 16.7

Assessing against lesson learning outcomes

For one lesson you have planned and are teaching, carry out an assessment of pupil learning against the differentiated learning outcomes and assessment criteria you have written. Judge the quality of the learning in this lesson using the suggested questions on pp. 207–8. Share your judgements with the class teacher and discuss similarities and differences in your reflections.

RECORDING PUPILS' LEARNING

Regularly assessing pupils provides a detailed record of pupil learning across a unit of work (assessment *of* learning). In addition, using assessment to inform the next lesson provides the means to use this information formatively (assessment *for* learning). This particularly relates to the final question: *what points must you consider when planning your next lesson in order to progress pupil learning?*

You may be required to record evidence of pupil attainment for your department, school or provider of accredited courses. Forms of evidence might be provided through practical performance, written work or pupil presentations. You might also be required to provide recorded evidence of pupil attainment through video, still images or verbal recordings.

Now complete Activity 16.8.

Activity 16.8

Tracking pupils' progress

In your placement school investigate the departmental requirements for recording pupil learning across units of work. Make sure that you understand the expectations for assessing against National Curriculum requirements, core physical education as well as those for accredited courses in your school. How does this differ and why?

SUMMARY

This chapter enables you to understand how to assess pupils' learning, including managing the interrelationship between summative (assessment *of* learning) and formative assessment (assessment for learning), particularly when planning and evaluating the quality of learning in lessons. Consequently you should realise that the information gained from assessing pupils' learning is used *systematically* to inform the planning and delivery of future lessons and also pupils' learning. Assessment for learning also requires pupils to share the responsibility for lesson delivery and appraisal of their work through peer and self-assessment.

FURTHER READING

DfES (Department for Education and Skills) (2004) Pedagogy and Practice: Teaching and Learning in the Secondary School, Unit 12 Assessment for Learning, London: DfES. Available online at: http://www.teachfind.com/national-strategies/pedagogy-and-practice-study-guides-unit-12-ndash-assessment-learning (accessed 26 June 2012).

Mosston, M. and Ashworth, S. (2008) Teaching Physical Education (First Online Edition). Available at: http://www.spectrumofteachingstyles.org/ebook (accessed 28 June 2012). Chapter 8 (reciprocal teaching style) and Chapter 9 (self-check teaching style) provide very useful strategies to consider when planning for peer and self-assessment. Although reciprocal teaching is not exactly the same as peer assessment, there are a number of important similarities.

Newton, A. and Bowler, M. (2010) Assessment for and of learning, in S. Capel and M. Whitehead (eds) *Learning to Teach Physical Education in the Secondary School: A Companion to School Experience*, 3rd edn, London: Routledge, pp. 119–33.
This highlights the need both for assessment *for* and *of* learning to be fully integrated into everyday teaching; not included as a 'bolt-on' extra. The chapter specifically focuses on assessment *for* learning strategies such as shared intended learning outcomes, questioning, feedback and peer- and self-assessment, as these enhance pupil learning and improve your teaching.

Note: all proformas, tables or figures you are asked to complete to help you undertake activities in this chapter are also available on the website which accompanies the book (www.routledge.com/9780415814829).

Chapter 17 Working with others

RICHARD BLAIR

INTRODUCTION

In your role as a physical education teacher in the second decade of the twenty-first century it is important that you appreciate the range of 'others' with whom you can collaborate to support learning and raise the educational standards in pupils' physical and broader education. As Whitehead and Pack (2010: 252) remind us, 'it would be true to say that, unlike 20 years ago, physical education departments can no longer be self-sufficient entities'. It is therefore important that as a student teacher or newly qualified teacher you start to develop an understanding regarding who you may have to work with, and what policy and practice you will need to follow in order that there is a common philosophical view regarding the deployment of adults other than teachers (AOTTS) in the department and school in which you are working. This chapter asks you to consider your role in working with other adults who may or may not have qualified teacher status (QTS) but who contribute to the physical and broader education of the pupils in your school. The chapter presents a specific focus on the contemporary issues of working with AOTTS who lead learning in both curricular physical education lessons and extra-curricular school sport (Blair and Capel, 2008, 2011, 2013; Griggs, 2007, 2008, 2010).

By the end of this chapter you should be able to:

- understand what your role is in working with 'others' who:
  - have QTS but are not specialist physical education teachers. For example, a teacher who holds a coaching qualification or the school special educational needs coordinator (SENCO);
  - do not have QTS but contribute either to the physical education of pupils, for example, sports coaches, choreographers, sports development officers, or contribute to the overall health and safety of the pupils in your school and specifically within physical education, such as, onsite – the school caretaker, and offsite – a specialist instructor at an outdoor adventure centre.
- articulate your philosophy (what you believe, what you value) and how you feel about the use of AOTTS who lead learning in physical education lessons;
- articulate how AOTTS (particularly coaches or instructors) contribute to the overall raising of educational standards in physical education and broader education of the pupils in your school.

WORKING WITH COLLEAGUES

Working with teaching colleagues with specific expertise in an activity

This section looks at your responsibility as a physical education specialist who has the opportunity to support one or more of your classes with an experience of being taught by a teacher who has specific expertise in, for example, athletics, but is not a specialist physical education teacher. This may be in the form of a one-off lesson on jumping or a series of between three to six lessons on different aspects of athletic activity.

The distinct advantage of working with another teacher is that they will be aware of the broader National Curriculum (NC) and the overall curriculum aims of promoting:

- successful learners who enjoy learning, make progress and achieve;
- confident individuals who are able to live, safe, healthy and fulfilled lives;
- responsible citizens who make a positive contribution to society.

(DfE, 2012a)

They will also be aware of the latest educational initiatives or trends emanating from central government, for example, behaviour for learning, assessment for learning, etc.

On the other hand, they will be less familiar with the National Curriculum Physical Education (NCPE). However, due to their understanding of the NC, as well as their own specific curriculum area, they should be able to access and understand the NCPE with support from members of the physical education department, including you. They will require details of the class they have agreed to teach. It would be particularly helpful if they already teach at least some of the pupils in their own subject but, regardless, they need an understanding of how these pupils work and attain in physical education lessons. They will also need a detailed hand-over, with information from previous units of work, lesson plans and the formative assessments made of the pupils and class up to this point in time. They will also need to be made aware of any physical education specific policy or routines regarding, for example, behaviour or the transport of equipment, etc. Now complete Activity 17.1.

Activity 17.1

Continuity in pupil learning

How does your physical education department ensure continuity of pupil learning when a new teacher or coach takes over a class? Think specifically about how you would hand over to a teaching colleague who has sport-specific expertise but is not a physical education specialist.

Ask members of your physical education department how they feel about a non-specialist with QTS teaching physical education classes. Note similarities and differences between the answers, for example, you may consider answers in relation to the different ages of the staff members.

Working with school colleagues without QTS who support learning in physical education through curricular and extra-curricular provision

This section discusses how you might consider working with school support staff who may contribute to or support pupil learning. These may include:

- learning support assistant (LSA);
- the school caretaker;
- the school secretary and administrators;
- the school cleaners.

Working with an LSA should, in theory, present very similar issues to that of working with a school colleague with QTS. As a member of school staff they will be aware of the NC and the latest initiatives or educational trends and may already be working with some of the pupils in your class. The central difference between the two is that, as they do not have QTS, the LSA is more likely to be engaged in supporting an individual pupil or small group of pupils within your lesson. In order that they can support individual pupils in physical education, it is important that they are explicitly aware of and ideally have had the opportunity, before the unit begins, to read and ask questions about:

- medium-term planning;
- your short-term planning: ideally 48 hours before each lesson, the LSA should have the intended learning outcomes for the lesson;
- resources for the unit or lesson: you may need to support the LSA in learning how to work the equipment, including, for example, a flip camera or a piece of specialised physical education specific software for video analysis;
- the formative assessment you have made about the classes and individual pupils to date;
- if possible, the Individual Education Plan (IEP) for the identified pupil or group of pupils.

The same points apply if the LSA has specialist knowledge of a specific area of activity and therefore takes on the role of overall class learning. However, in such situations you also need to refer to working with staff without QTS below for additional information regarding them meeting the definition of specified work. Activity 17.2 focuses on how you might work with an LSA in different but specific contexts.

Activity 17.2

Working with an LSA

Consider how you would work with and support an LSA in the following contexts:

- The LSA is a qualified athletics coach and has agreed to deliver three lessons to a year group of your choice.
- You have a talented gymnast in one of your Year 7 classes and you have asked the LSA to work with her.
- You have a pupil who uses a walking frame.
- The LSA is a qualified basketball coach and has been running one of the school teams for the last two years. He approaches you to ask your advice on how best to present his ideas on running an inter-school competition with five local schools.

The school caretaker is a valuable ally for any physical education department and it is important that they are kept informed regarding the plans and requirements of the department. Whitehead and Pack (2010) provide an excellent example of how the school caretaker can support the successful running of the physical education department in the context of an after-school fixture being played away from school. The caretaker could feasibly be the only member of staff still on site when you arrive back at school and could act as a valuable support at the end of a long day, depending on the school context in which you work. Additionally, it is good practice to be able to contact the caretaker in case of a delayed return to school or a more serious matter regarding you, the pupils or indeed the mini-bus or other mode of transport.

Weekly, even daily, contact with school administrative staff is now common practice within all schools. Any letter sent home to parents regarding all aspects of work within the physical education department goes through the school administrators. You also need to liaise with them and provide information regarding extra-curricular provision, including what is on and where it is located (especially if your placement is in a large school), and who attends clubs or session. You will provide administrative staff with details of all school fixtures, including a team list with details of all pupils due to attend the event. As you become established in a school, you will increase your work with the administrative staff, so it is good to develop a strong relationship as early as you can.

Although working with school cleaners may be more of a role for your head of department, there could be occasions where you are required to interact with them. Due to the physical nature of the subject, things get dirty. Muddy rugby boots, rubbish left in the sports hall from the public badminton session the night before, etc. all contribute to a less than supportive learning environment if not cleaned daily. Unclean working and changing areas are an unnecessary hurdle that could act as a blocking mechanism for some pupils not engaging in physical education lessons. One of your professional attributes is to develop your ability to communicate as a professional teacher. Activity 17.3 asks you to practise your communication skills.

Communicating as a teacher

Consider how you might deal with and communicate the problems/issues presented in the following scenarios. Consider who you might need to communicate with:

- You are at a local squash club with a group of Year 11 pupils. Two of the pupils are playing a competitive game when one pupil misjudges his position in relation to his opponent and is hit on the head with his opponent's racket.
- You are at an away fixture with the Year 7 netball team. You get back to the mini-bus after the game but the bus will not start.
- You are teaching athletics to Year 9 on the public track next to, but attached to, your school site. As your lesson progresses, you notice a group of school-aged youths running around and sitting in the main stand. The group of youths are getting louder and start directing their comments at the pupils in your class.

Working with staff without QTS who contribute to learning in physical education curricular and extra-curricular time

North (2009) reports that there are 100,000 sports coaches working in schools, with 90,000 working exclusively in this context. Sportscoach UK (2004) report there were around 514,000 people operating as school sports coaches, with a large percentage of these being unpaid. These include around: 70,000 specialist physical education teachers; acting in the role of a sports coach, 250,000 non-specialist teachers; 67,000 AOTTS; and 85,000 external coaches. Further, Sportscoach UK (2007) suggests that the most frequent coaching environment for a full-time coach is a school. In addition, there are others working in schools such as choreographers, swimming teachers, OAA personnel, etc.

Your perspective regarding the deployment of a specialist coach or choreographer to lead learning in physical education classes will be connected to your philosophical position in relation to your values and beliefs regarding how you feel physical education should be taught. For example, if you value the teaching of physical education as the development of physical and technical skills which are most likely (but not exclusively) to be sport-specific, there would be a greater chance that you would favour employing a sports coach with specific knowledge due to the coaches' emphasis on the development of a specific sport skill and fitness. On the other hand, if you value a holistic approach to physical education in which domains of learning, e.g., cognitive, psychomotor and affective (Bloom *et al.*, 1956) are equally valued, you would in theory be less in favour of deploying a sports coach with sport-specific knowledge as you believe that physical education contributes to policy agendas beyond sport, including health, education and social. Now complete Activity 17.4.

Activity 17.4

Deploying staff without QTS in physical education lessons

- Consider how you view the teaching of physical education. Do you lean towards prioritising objective (technical and physical development) or more subjective (overall and holistic) development?
- What are your views on the deployment of staff with specialist knowledge but without QTS in curricula physical education lessons? For example, do you believe their deployment should be restricted to working in extra-curricular school sport or should they also work in curriculum time?

Blair and Capel (2013) provide an alternative viewpoint. They argue there is a place for sports coaches, choreographers or instructors in curriculum time lessons – highlighting the valuable opportunity adults with specialist knowledge and engagement may provide for pupils to be motivated and inspired, in particular, pupils who may be excluded from optional activities for a range of social or economic reasons (Pickup, 2012). However, Blair and Capel (2013) are clear about the knowledge, skill and understanding that these AOTTS must demonstrate in order that they can be deployed in such a role of responsibility. Now complete Activity 17.5.

Activity 17.5

Read and reflect

Read the chapter by Blair and Capel (2013) Who should teach physical education in curriculum time and extra-curricular time? In S. Capel and M. Whitehead (eds) *Debates in Physical Education*, London: Routledge. How does this chapter influence your views on employing AOTTS in curriculum and extra-curricular time?

As outlined in Blair and Capel (2013), in the view of the authors, it is of vital importance that if AOTTS, including sports coaches and choreographers, are engaged to work in curriculum time, there is a fully comprehensive induction process and you are satisfied that they have the knowledge, skill and understanding to meet the required standards and the definition of specified work, defined by the British Association of Advisers and Lecturers in Physical Education (BAALPE, 2005: 4) with regard to:

- planning and preparing lessons and courses for pupils;
- delivering lessons to pupils – including distance learning or computer-aided techniques;
- assessing the development, progress and attainment of pupils;
- reporting on the development, progress and attainment of pupils.

If staff meet the definition of specified work, there is the potential for pupils to be engaged in detailed and inspiring learning opportunities that make explicit connections to the outside community and therefore for extended opportunities to be fostered for pupils to participate in physical activities which allow a variety of agendas (e.g. sport, health, education and social) to be addressed. Blair and

Capel (2013) extend this point to coaches working in extra-curricular school sport and highlight that, in some cases, depending on the focus of the extra-curricular context, coaches may be better placed than a teacher to work with, for example, a competitive sports team. In theory, the coach has a more detailed specialist set of knowledge in order to prepare a team for competition. However, it may not be appropriate in other contexts; it is important to match the AOTT to the context.

SUMMARY

It is clear that as a physical education teacher working in the twenty-first century, there is the opportunity to engage with other adults to increase the educational opportunities for all pupils. This chapter has focused on the importance of engaging with non-specialist teachers with activity expertise and AOTTS in order that you can deliver the best possible learning environment for physical education. The chapter asks you to consider going beyond your existing curriculum to consider how you collaborate with a range of other teachers and AOTTS to create motivating and inspiring learning environments that support higher quality physical education.

FURTHER READING

Blair, R. and Capel, S. (2013) Who should teach physical education in curriculum time and extra-curricular time? In S. Capel and M. Whitehead (eds) *Debates in Physical Education*, London: Routledge, pp. 171–87.
This chapter takes a critical look at who should be teaching physical education in both curricular and extra-curricular settings and asks question regarding the knowledge of both teachers and coaches.

Griggs, G. (2008) Outsiders inside: The use of sports coaches in primary schools, *Primary Physical Education Matters*, 3, 1: 33–7.

Griggs, G. (2010) For sale: primary physical education, £20 per hour or nearest offer, *Education 3–13*, 38, 1: 30–46.
Both articles by Griggs raise questions regarding the appropriateness of coaches working in primary schools delivering physical education lessons.

Whitehead, M. and Pack, K. (2010) Working with others to achieve the aims of PE, in S. Capel and M. Whitehead (eds) *Learning to Teach Physical Education in the Secondary School: A Companion to School Experience*, 3rd edn, London: Routledge, pp. 252–64.
This chapter looks at working with a range of different colleagues with the specific focus on achieving the aims of physical education. The chapter looks at how working with others can support both curricular and extra-curricular contexts.

Note: all proformas, tables or figures you are asked to complete to help you undertake activities in this chapter are also available on the website which accompanies the book (www.routledge.com/9780415814829).

Chapter 18 Viewing physical education from a different perspective

An alternative approach to planning for learning

JACKIE ARTHUR AND GILL GOLDER

INTRODUCTION

This chapter seeks to encourage you to view physical education from a different perspective. Fundamental movement skills, social skills and cognitive skills are used as a means to provide the backbone that underpins learning. The chapter explores how you could use these skills as a common thread to structure medium-term planning that links learning through diverse activities, thus enabling continuity and progression.

The chapter also looks at including a diverse range of content and learning through different environments. The move towards more diverse content and alternative approaches to teaching and learning in physical education has come from a range of external pressures and influences. In England, the review of the National Curriculum in 2008 and again in 2010 promoted greater flexibility for schools to decide what could be taught. The Office for Standards in Education (Ofsted, 2009: 7) further recommended that schools should 'broaden provision further to incorporate non-traditional activities so that young people in hard-to-reach groups are motivated to participate'. However, justifying the inclusion of diverse activities from a learning perspective is key; the introduction of diverse activities just as tasters of something new can hinder rather than help progression. There are a number of justifications for including a diverse range of activities in physical education. First, the need to reach hard to reach pupils aligns itself well with the focus on health, empowering learning to make healthy lifestyle choices, with support and guidance from teachers and others, to enable pupils to more confidently manage lifestyles choices. Second, the *Learning Outside the Classroom* manifesto (Department for Education and Skills (DFES), 2006: 3) suggested that learning outside traditional classroom environments enables far deeper learning experiences. 'It provides a context for learning in many areas: general and subject based knowledge; thinking and problem-solving skills; life skills such as co-operation and interpersonal communication.' Third, there is the influence of the 2012 London Olympics' legacy. The legacy plan has four areas of focus, the most significant to physical education being that of participation. 'Harnessing the United Kingdom's passion for sport to increase grass roots participation, particularly by young people – and to encourage the whole population to be more physically active' (DCMS, 2010: 3). Fourth, as an inclusive component of the whole curriculum, physical education should aim to enthuse those pupils who have not necessarily been selected to play for the school, or who have been challenged by their environment. All pupils are entitled to a broad and engaging curriculum which enables them to realise their individual physical, cognitive and social potential. (Generally, a well-established curriculum is available for pupils who are inspired to be in a school team, taking part in the many competitions, festivals, leagues and tournaments that link our schools.)

This chapter aims to challenge your thinking about the starting point for planning and help you to develop the confidence to enable you to shape the learning experiences of your pupils, according to individual capacity and environmental opportunities.

With these influences impacting upon physical education, by the end of this chapter you should be able to:

- understand how fundamental movement skills can enhance learning in physical education;
- appreciate the importance of developing pupils socially and cognitively through physical education;
- understand the rationale for including diverse activities in the physical education curriculum;
- gain an awareness of the impact and opportunities available when learning through different environments.

FUNDAMENTAL MOVEMENT SKILLS AS THE STARTING POINT FOR LEARNING IN PHYSICAL EDUCATION

If we are to encourage young people to engage in healthy, lifelong participation in physical activity and sport and enable talented pupils to fulfil their potential, it is imperative that a firm foundation of core, transferrable skills are built in physical education. Recognising how core locomotor, manipulative and stability building blocks are developed by all pupils in physical education is the hallmark of a successful teacher. For Lubans *et al.* (2008), the mastery of fundamental movement skills is thought to provide the foundation for an active lifestyle. It has also been purported as contributing to a pupil's physical, cognitive and social development.

May (2011) states that development and learning progresses at different rates from child to child. These rates are also uneven in one child in both timing and magnitude. Although human growth and development take place anyway, without training, it is important to shape that development to enhance the development of movement skills. A teacher's confidence to recognise, through assessment, developmental level rather than chronological age enables the individual development needs of each pupil to be considered, rather than a 'one-size-fits-all' model.

Fundamental movement skills can be categorised into three aspects: body management skills; locomotor skills; and object control (see Table 18.1).

Table 18.1 Three categories of fundamental movement skills

Body management skills	Locomotor skills	Object control skills
1. Rolling	1. Crawling	1. Throwing
2. Stopping	2. Running	2. Catching
3. Bending	3. Galloping	3. Striking
4. Twisting	4. Walking	4. Bouncing
5. Landing	5. Hopping	5. Dribbling
6. Stretching	6. Skipping	6. Kicking
7. Climbing	7. Dodging	
8. Static and dynamic balancing		
9. Turning		

Source: Western Australia Education Department (2004).

According to Okely and Booth (2004), fundamental movement skills form the foundation for many of the specific motor skills employed in popular sports and leisure activities. The Western Australia Education Department (2004) suggest that physical development and movement are about experiencing and developing a range of fundamental movement skills that improve co-ordination, locomotion, control, balance and manipulation. Now complete Activity 18.1.

Activity 18.1

Observation and reflection on prior experiences

1   Explore the range of diverse activities currently offered at Key Stage (KS) 3 (ages 11–14 years) in your placement school. In columns 1, 2 and 3 of Table 18.2, record which fundamental movement skills are being developed in each activity, what teachers are teaching and what pupils are learning.
2   Consider how this could be a progression from KS2 (ages 7–11 years), making a note of your reflections in column 4.

Table 18.2 Pupils' prior experiences

Which fundamental movement skill is being developed?	What are teachers teaching?	What are pupils learning?	How does this link to prior learning?

DEVELOPMENT OF SOCIAL AND COGNITIVE LEARNING IN PHYSICAL EDUCATION

In Chapters 6, 7 and 9 you were introduced to the broader dimensions of the curriculum. Social and cognitive development could be argued to be central threads that hold learning together. Much of the theory behind the importance of social development in education comes from Vygotsky's (1978) social constructivism learning theory in which learning is a social act occurring through collaboration, social interaction and learning from more knowledgeable others. Squires (2002) defines social-emotional competence as cooperative and pro-social behaviour, initiation and maintenance of peer friendships and adult relationships, management of aggression and conflict, development of a sense of mastery and self-worth and emotional regulation and reactivity. How we develop these skills in physical education is through creating supportive learning environments. These can enable pupils to practise communication skills, teamwork, collaboration and leadership, learn how to cope with success, failure and develop empathy for other pupils. Pupils will also be enabled to explore creative solutions to problems set, abide by fair play codes of conduct, become self-motivating and take part in a mixture of individual and group challenges and activities they develop greater self-efficacy and improved interaction skills with other pupils and adults.

The work of Jean Piaget has been influential to thinking on cognitive development. According to Burton (2009), central to his theory are concepts of *assimilation* which involve taking in and adapting experience or objects to existing strategies or concepts and *accommodation* which involves modifying and adjusting strategies and concepts. By offering a broad range of activities in a variety of environments, pupils have to assimilate and accommodate ideas, concepts and strategies all the time. They use cognitive skills of problems-solving, decision-making, transfer of knowledge, synthesis and reflection to make sense of learning and progress knowledge, skills and understanding. According to Shayer (2003), to enable this, teachers need to create learning experiences that increase the proportion of pupils attaining higher thinking skills (knowledge, comprehension, application, analysis, evaluation, synthesis). (See also Chapter 11 on applying theories of learning.)

Social skills and cognitive skills can be categorised in a variety of different ways. For the purpose of this chapter we have characterised social skills as either intrapersonal or interpersonal and cognitive skills as relating to visual and audio processing, logic and reasoning or attention and memory. Table 18.2 suggests skills that fit this categorisation and Activity 18.2 asks you to consider what social and cognitive skills look like in physical education.

Activity 18.2

Developing social and cognitive skills in physical education

Discuss with another student teacher or your tutor what social and cognitive skills look like in physical education. What mechanisms have you seen experienced teachers use to develop social and cognitive skills. (You might like to refer here to activities undertaken in Chapter 6.)

What triggers might you look for in pupils that are not progressing or engaging with others, with the environment or the task?

You might want to use Table 18.3 as prompts for your discussion.

Table 18.3 Social skills and cognitive skills

Social skills	Intra-personal	Inter-personal
	self-awareness	empathy
	trust	communication: verbal/non-verbal
	confidence	observation
	self-esteem	listening
	motivation	leadership
	independence	trust
	fun	fun
	fair play	team allegiance
	self-management	competition
Cognitive skills	*Audio and visual processing*	*Logic and reasoning*
	perception of stimuli	problem solving
	sequencing	decision-making
	understanding of environment	evaluating and synthesising
		negotiating
		refining technique
		higher-order thinking skills
	Memory and attention	
	mental determination	
	focus	
	challenge	
	risk management/awareness	
	transfer of knowledge	
	confronting fear	
	engagement beyond the curriculum	

Having considered fundamental movement skills, social skills and cognitive skills we are now in a position to see how these are taught across the physical education curriculum. Now complete Activity 18.3.

Activity 18.3

Mapping physical social and cognitive skills

Focusing on Year 7 in your placement school, find out what pupils are taught across the year, writing the objectives of each unit of work in the first column and the activity area in the third column of Table 18.4.

Then using the key in the table, map this with what you see to be the objectives in terms of physical, social and cognitive skills that run from the start to the end of Year 7. Then, using the final column, suggest possible alternative activities that would retain these learning objectives.

LEARNING THROUGH DIFFERENT ENVIRONMENTS IN PHYSICAL EDUCATION

Physical education is unique as a subject in that pupils learn in different environments, e.g. gymnasium, sports hall, field, swimming pool, fitness suite, climbing wall and ski slope etc. These provide opportunity for diversity and flexibility in teaching approaches to enhance pupils learning.

As suggested by the *Learning Outside the Curriculum* manifesto (DfES, 2006) learning in different environments provides the opportunity for pupils to develop transferable skills, knowledge and understanding. How pupils learn in new and different environments helps to explain the value of using different environments to enable pupils to develop physically, cognitively and socially. One model that explores the idea of learning and environment is the 'Cycle of development' (Clarke and Dawson, 1998). This identifies significant stages in social and emotional development which can be summarised by the process that occurs when we enter a new situation and gradually become familiar with that environment (Barrow and Newton, 2004).

Figure 18.1 illustrates six stages of development that learners encounter when entering a new environment. The first stage is arriving in the new environment (becoming); the second stage is marked by an initial sense of confusion (being); followed by the third stage where learners begin to explore surroundings while being watched over. This is much to do with how safe and secure the learners feel (doing); the fourth stage (thinking) involves recognising the need to do things differently in the new environment while being encouraged by teachers; this leads to the fifth stage (identify and power) where learners develop a new identity accepting the environment and their place in it; the final stage (skills and structure) is where learners develop skills and competencies they need to survive and thrive in the environment (Barrow and Newton, 2004).

Table 18.4 Mapping physical and cognitive skills

Unit of work objectives	Common threads Physical (P)/ Social (S)/ Cognitive (C)	Current Year 7 curriculum activity	Alternative activities

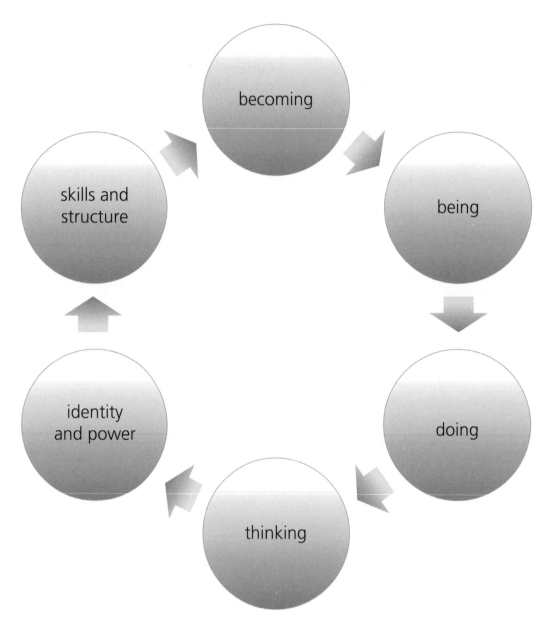

Figure 18.1 Cycle of development

Source: Adapted from Barrow and Newton (2004).

Figure 18.2 (pp. 227–34) presents three case studies of units of work exemplifying how learning can be enhanced in a range of different activities using different environments.

CASE STUDY 1: LEARNING THROUGH WATER

The school:

1,300-pupil Academy (ages 11–18 years). Rural/Urban location. Six members in the physical education department. Seven of the 9 feeder primary schools deliver swimming as part of their KS2 programme of learning.

Lesson length: 90 minutes; 14-week unit of work	Sports centre, 25 metre swimming pool in the town (8 minutes walk) Free-flowing river beside the school Beach 40 minutes away

Fundamental movement, social and cognitive skills to be developed

Aquatics can support the development of fundamental movement, social and cognitive skills that occur throughout childhood and adolescence.

Fundamental Movement skills	Social skills	Cognitive skills
Locomotor **(L)** Manipulative **(M)** Stability **(S)** Movement concepts **(MC)** Physiological components **(PC)**	Intra-personal **(Intra)** Inter-personal **(Inter)**	Audio and visual processing **(AVP)** Logic and Reasoning **(LR)** Attention and memory **(AM)**

Aims

To provide a curriculum which develops pupil learning in a progressive order to engage, up-skill and develop pupils' trust in the environment.

Synchronised swimming (pool) 3 lessons		
Fundamental movement skills	Social skills	Cognitive skills
(L): Agility **(M):** Co-ordination **(S):** Gliding, Buoyancy	**(Intra & Inter):** Fun, Trust **(Inter):** Verbal communication Listening	**(AVP):** Understanding of water Sequencing

Sub-aqua (pool) 3 lessons		
Fundamental movement skills	Social skills	Cognitive skills
(S): Buoyancy, Balance **(M):** Co-ordination **(MC):** Kinaesthetic awareness	**(Intra & Inter):** Fun, Trust **(Inter):** Non-verbal communication, Observation	**(AVP):** Understanding of water **(LR):** Challenge **(MA):** Engagement beyond curriculum (4 local clubs)

River swim 3 lessons

Fundamental movement skills	Social skills	Cognitive skills
(L): Agility **(M):** Co-ordination **(S):** Gliding, Buoyancy (with and without wet suit)	**(Intra & Inter):** Fun, Trust **(Inter):** Verbal and non-verbal communication, Listening, Observation	**(AVP):** Understanding of moving water **(LR):** Challenge, Negotiating hazards, Decision-making

Sea swim 3 lessons

Fundamental movement skills	Social skills	Cognitive skills
(L): Agility **(M):** Co-ordination **(S):** Gliding, Buoyancy (with and without wet suit), Balance **(MC):** Kinaesthetic awareness	**(Intra & Inter):** Fun, Trust **(Inter):** Verbal and non-verbal communication, Observation, Listening, Teamwork	**(AVP):** Understanding of moving water **(LR):** Challenge, Negotiating hazards, Refining technique, Decision-making **(MA):** Confronting fear

Surfing 2 lessons

Fundamental movement skills	Social skills	Cognitive skills
(L): Agility **(M):** Co-ordination **(S):** Buoyancy (with wet suit), Balance **(MC):** Kinaesthetic awareness	**(Intra & Inter):** Fun, Trust **(Inter):** Verbal and non-verbal communication, Observation Listening, Teamwork	**(AVP):** Understanding of moving water **(LR):** Challenge, Negotiating hazards, Refining technique, Decision-making

Objectives. Pupils will:

- Show progression in awareness, confidence, trust, competence, self-esteem through the use of different environments. By progressing from inside to outside environments, from static water to moving to tidal pupils will develop awareness of the power of the various environments. Respect for these environments will develop symbiotically.
- Develop skills to meet the changing environments and capacity for decision-making will be a key feature of learning.
- Have awareness of the surrounding environment to enable pupils to seek out clubs/activity groups or inspire family networks to use the environment in different ways, e.g. coasteering.

Implications for teaching

• Confidence in understanding of fundamental movement skills and movement analysis • Subject knowledge competencies • Knowledge of surrounding environment • Access to and relationship with local, regional and national agencies	• Risk assessment • Cost • Transport • Time allocation • Experts in the field • Empathy with challenge these learning environments bring at individual level • Departmental/whole school support and collaboration

CASE STUDY 2: LEARNING THROUGH THE ALTERNATIVE GAMES

The school:

1,000-pupil Community College (ages 11–18 years). Inner City location. Five members in the physical education department. Physical education taught in mixed gender tutor groups throughout KS3.

Lesson length: 60 minutes, 13-week units of work School has use of Community Sports Centre opposite the school (4 court sports hall, multi-use games area, 25 metre swimming pool, aerobic studio)	On-site concrete playground, gymnasium, outdoor climbing wall Community Park with football pitch, 5 minutes walk

Fundamental movement, social and cognitive skills to be developed

Alternative games can support fundamental movement, social, cognitive and emotional development providing personal challenge and opportunities for team cohesion.

Fundamental movement skills	Social skills	Cognitive skills
Locomotor **(L)** Manipulative **(M)** Stability **(S)** Movement concepts **(MC)** Physiological components **(PC)**	Intra-personal **(Intra)** Inter-personal **(Inter)**	Audio and visual processing **(AVP)** Logic and Reasoning **(LR)** Attention and memory **(AM)**

Aims

To provide a curriculum which challenges pupils to develop as independent learners and transfer common principles underpinning games activities using the Sport Education Model.

Introduction to Sport Education using korfball (hard court area) 3 lessons

Fundamental movement skills	Social skills	Cognitive skills
(L): Agility **(M):** Co-ordination **(S):** Balance **(MC):** Reaction time	**(Intra):** Fair play **(Inter):** Team allegiance, Verbal communication, use of 'Tactics Huts', Listening **(Intra & Inter):** Trust	**(AM):** Transfer of principles of attacking space and defence from basketball **(LR):** Negotiating roles, Evaluating tactical success

Ultimate (community park) 3 lessons

Fundamental movement skills	Social skills	Cognitive skills
(MC): Kinaesthetic awareness **(S):** Balance **(M):** Co-ordination, Control, Handling	**(Intra):** Fair play, Self-management **(Inter):** Team allegiance, Listening, Observation, Leadership **(Intra & Inter):** Trust	**(AM):** Transfer the principles of footwork and selection of type of pass to outwit opponents from netball **(AVP):** Understanding environment (wind and air flow) **(LR):** Decision-making, Self-refereeing

Tchoukball (Sports hall) 3 lessons

Fundamental movement skills	Social	Cognitive
(L): Agility **(M):** Co-ordination **(MC):** Reaction time	**(Intra):** Fair play **(Inter):** Team allegiance, Verbal and non-verbal communication, Observation **(Intra & Inter):** Trust, Fun	**(AM):** Transfer the principles exploiting space from badminton and short tennis **(LR):** Negotiating roles (add new team roles e.g. commentator, statistician, analyst and evaluation)

Water polo (swimming pool) 3 lessons

Fundamental movement skills	Social	Cognitive
(L): Agility **(M):** Co-ordination **(S):** Buoyancy (with aids if needed) **(PC):** Endurance, Strength **(MC):** Kinaesthetic awareness	**(Intra):** Fair play, Self-management **(Inter):** Team allegiance, Listening, Observation, Leadership, Verbal and non-verbal communication, Teamwork **(Intra & Inter):** Trust	**(AVP):** Understanding environment of water **(AM):** Transfer the principles of supporting the player in possession of the ball from football **(LR):** Refining technique, Decision-making

Festival Week - 4 activities against other Year 9 classes. All pupils perform in at least one competitive activity and negotiate roles for each activity (all venues)		
Fundamental movement skills	*Social*	*Cognitive*
(L): Agility **(M):** Co-ordination, Control, Handling **(S):** Buoyancy (with aids if needed, Balance **(PC):** Endurance, Strength **(MC):** Kinaesthetic awareness, Reaction time	**(Intra):** Fair play, Self-management **(Inter):** Team allegiance, Listening, Observation, Leadership, Verbal and non-verbal communication Teamwork, Competition **(Intra & Inter):** Trust, Fun	**(LR):** Decision-making, Negotiating roles **(AM):** Transferring learning: Reporting on festival (Literacy, Numeracy and ICT cross-curricular project)

Objectives. Pupils will:

- Have knowledge and understanding of different roles and responsibilities and leadership skills, confidence, communication, teamwork and team allegiance through the use of different environments and activities.
- Have skills that will gradually evolve to meet the changing environments and activities and capacity for decision-making and application of techniques, tactics and principles underpinning games will be a key feature of learning.
- Be aware of alternative activities and roles in and through physical education which enable pupils to identify their own strengths and interests and make informed choices about how they use their leisure time.

Implications for teaching

- Confidence in understanding of transferable principles across games activities - Subject knowledge competencies in 4 alternative games - Knowledge of surrounding environment - Development of resources to empower pupils to take on new roles	- Risk assessment - Cost (festival) - Time allocation (3 lessons per activity) - Empathy with challenge that these learning environments and activities bring at an individual level - Inter subject collaboration for Festival Week Project - Staff training on Sport Education model

CASE STUDY 3: LEARNING THROUGH THE URBAN ENVIRONMENT

The school:

800–1,000-pupil City Community College (ages 11–18 years). Urban location, surrounded by ring road (high rise building, concrete courtyards, terrace and maisonette dwellings). Four full-time members of staff and one at 0.6 in the physical education department. Seven Feeder Primary schools deliver KS2 programme of learning.

Lesson length: 90 minutes Unit of work over 10.5 hours; 7 lessons per unit	Sports hall (utilised for school exams), small gymnasium (wooden floor). Skateboard and BMX bike park, fenced basketball court, area sports centre with pool and purpose-built diving pit

Fundamental movement, social and cognitive skills to be developed

Adventure/challenge can support the development of fundamental movement, social and cognitive skills that occur throughout childhood and adolescence.

Fundamental movement skills	Social skills	Cognitive skills
Locomotor **(L)** Manipulative **(M)** Stability **(S)** Movement concepts **(MC)** Physiological components **(PC)**	Intra-personal **(Intra)** Inter-personal **(Inter)**	Audio and visual processing **(AVP)** Logic and Reasoning **(LR)** Attention and memory **(AM)**

Aims

To provide a curriculum which develops the following activities in a progressive order to engage, up-skill and develop trust in the environment.

Free running (gym > outside yard) 2 lessons		
Fundamental movement skills	Social	Cognitive
(L): Travelling/agility **(M):** Co-ordination **(S):** Static and dynamic balance **(MC):** Body awareness/space awareness/qualities/relationships **(PC):** Cardio-vascular/Strength/Endurance/Flexibility	**(Intra):** Confidence, self-esteem, Motivation, Independence **(Intra & Inter):** Trust, Fun **(Inter):** Observation, Non-verbal communication	**(LR):** Problem solving, Decision-making, Evaluating and synthesising, Negotiating **(AVP):** Sequencing **(AM):** Risk awareness

Street surfing (sports hall and outside basketball court) 1 lesson		
Fundamental movement skills	*Social*	*Cognitive*
(L): Travelling/agility **(M):** Control/co-ordination **(S):** Static and dynamic balance **(MC):** Body awareness/space awareness/qualities/relationship **(PC):** Cardio-vascular/Strength/Endurance/Flexibility	**(Intra):** Motivation, Self-esteem **(Inter):** Non-verbal communication, Observation **(Intra & Inter):** Fun, Trust	**(LR):** Problem solving, Negotiating, Refine technique **(AM):** Mental determination, Engagement beyond curriculum

BMX (school outdoor courts, BMX park) 2 lessons		
Fundamental movement skills	*Social*	*Cognitive*
(L): Agility **(M):** Handling/control/co-ordination **(S):** Static and dynamic balance **(MC):** Body awareness/space awareness/qualities/relationship **(PC):** Cardio-vascular/Strength/Endurance/Flexibility	**(Intra):** Confidence, Independence, Motivation **(Inter):** Non-verbal communication, Observation **(Intra & Inter):** Trust, Fun	**(LR):** Negotiating hazards, Decision-making, Evaluating and synthesising, Refine technique **(AM):** Engagement beyond curriculum, challenge, Risk management

Diving (sports hall, trampoline/diving pit [city pool]) 2 lessons		
Fundamental movement skills	*Social*	*Cognitive*
(L): Travelling/agility **(M):** Co-ordination **(S):** Static and dynamic balance **(MC):** Body awareness/space awareness/qualities/relationship **(PC):** Cardio-vascular/Strength/Endurance/Flexibility	**(Intra):** Confidence, self-esteem **(Inter):** Non-verbal communication, Observation **(Intra & Inter):** Trust, Fun	**(LR):** Refine technique, Decision-making **(AVP):** Understanding environment **(AM):** Challenge, Mental determination

Objectives. Pupils will:

- Show progression in awareness, confidence, trust, competence, self-esteem through engagement with different environments.
- Appreciate different environments from inside to outside environments, from non-specific to purpose-built facilities.
- Gradually develop skills, as the level of challenge progresses and their capacity develops, to enable them to meet the demands of the changing environments. Capacity for risk assessment and decision-making will be a key feature of learning.
- Have increased awareness of the surrounding environment which encourages them to seek/form social groups.
- Develop awareness of transferable skills between environments.

Implications for teaching

• Confidence in understanding of fundamental movement skills and movement analysis • Subject knowledge competencies • Awareness of potential of surrounding environment • Access to and relationship with local groups or clubs • REAL understanding of pupil skill potential relevant to immediate location	• Risk assessment • Cost • Time allocation • Enthusiasm to tackle new style activity • Empathy with challenge these learning environments bring at individual level • Departmental/whole school support and collaboration

Figure 18.2 Case studies

Now complete Activity 18.4.

Activity 18.4

Creating your own case study

Write a unit of work plan using one of the environments in Figure 18.2 or a different environment you have either experienced at school or which you are going to use on your school placement. In writing this unit of work, make sure you consider the following features:

- intended outcomes of learning include objectives for fundamental movement skills, social and cognitive learning;
- implications for pedagogy (a) teaching: what teaching strategies would be most suitable, what underpinning knowledge would be needed, what resources would be needed; (b) learning: how would pupils learn best, what core tasks might be used, how pupils might be grouped; and (c) assessment: what assessment for learning strategies would work best, how pupils might demonstrate progress made, how you might make informed decisions and targets that would progress pupils further;
- implications for engaging with outside providers/other professionals.

Now try writing the first lesson plan for this unit, identifying the starting point for the pupils' learning journey through the unit.

SUMMARY

As stated at the start of this chapter, the intention has been to encourage you to think about the physical education curriculum from a different perspective. As teachers, we need to develop a curriculum that engages and inspires a diverse range of pupils, providing them with knowledge, skills and understanding appropriate to fulfil their potential within society.

The recognition that all skill sets are founded upon a secure base of fundamental movement skills helps teachers design programmes that enable pupils to approach physically challenging situations with ever increasing levels of confidence. At the same time we share the responsibility with other subjects of the school curriculum in developing pupils socially and cognitively. We can genuinely prepare and engage pupils with the world they live in, enabling them to evaluate the level of challenge presented to them, negotiate the barriers presented and demonstrate the trust required to learn and succeed.

Our culture can destroy curiosity in the most curious of creatures (MacLean, 1990), therefore there remains a need to engage pupils in experiential learning activities that encourage them to reflect. In this way, they are learning and thinking which, according to Hannaford (2005), occurs when we engage with the world.

Beams, Higgins and Nicol (2012: 52–3) encourage teachers to remember:

> There is a world outside the classroom where curiosity and curriculum combine to offer powerful stimuli for learning. Integrating outdoor learning and indoor teaching places the focus on arousing children's curiosity about landscapes and communities within the scope of their everyday lives.

We hope the chapter has enabled you to reflect on what you teach and prompted you to consider alternative approaches to planning a curriculum based upon aspects of pupils' development.

FURTHER READING

Beams, S., Higgins, P. and Nicol, R. (2012) *Learning Outside the Classroom: Theories and Guidelines for Practice*, London: Routledge.
The principles and guidelines in this book are intended to be adapted by teachers to suit the needs of their pupils in ways that draw upon opportunities offered by the local landscape and its natural and built heritage. This is not a book of prescriptive activities that can be read and used uncritically. The idea of adaptation for personal relevance is central. By referring to the useful principles and practices in this book, as teachers you can incorporate more meaningful outdoor learning opportunities into your daily teaching activities

Haskins, D. (2010) *Coaching the Whole Child: Positive Development through Sport*, Leeds: National Coaching Foundation.
This book explores the 5C's of coaching and how they can be used to enhance the development of young participants by offering them exciting, challenging and well-structured environments in which to learn.

Kirk, D. (2011) *Physical Education Futures*, London: Routledge.
In this book Kirk argues that multi-activity, sport-based forms of physical education which have been dominant in schools since the mid-twentieth century, have been highly

resistant to change. The practice of physical education has focused on the transmission of de-contextualised sport techniques to large classes of pupils who possess a range of interests and abilities, where learning rarely moves beyond introductory levels. He argues that we need a different model for physical education in the future.

Note: all proformas, tables or figures you are asked to complete to help you undertake activities in this chapter are also available on the website which accompanies the book (www.routledge.com/9780415814829).

Part IV

Your own professional learning

Chapter 19 The reflective practitioner

PAULA ZWOZDIAK-MYERS

INTRODUCTION

One very important aspect of teaching and learning about teaching involves the process of reflection and this chapter aims to develop your understanding of, and capacity for, reflection.

By the end of this chapter you should be able to:

- understand how reflection might be conceptualised;
- know where in teaching reflection should take place;
- engage in reflective practice;
- consider why reflecting on your practice is important.

UNDERSTAND HOW REFLECTION MIGHT BE CONCEPTUALISED

Reflection has been described by Loughran (1996: 14) as 'the deliberate and purposeful act of thinking which centres on ways of responding to problem situations in teaching and learning'. This view of the way teachers think about their practice involves a number of steps or phases in thinking which, when organised and linked, lead to a consequence in action.

Dewey (1933) identified five phases or states of thinking: suggestions, problem, hypothesis, reasoning and testing. Each phase is contextualised by past and future actions and experiences and some might be expanded or overlap, depending on the nature of the problem. Although these phases need not necessarily link in any particular order, when pieced together, they form a process of *reflective thinking* that involves: '(i) a state of doubt, hesitation, perplexity, mental difficulty, in which thinking originates, and (ii) an act of searching, hunting, inquiring, to find material that will resolve the doubt, settle and dispose of the perplexity' (Dewey, 1933: 12).

Boud *et al.* (1985: 19) consider reflection to be an activity in which people 'recapture their experience, think about it, mull it over and evaluate it'. They include the dimension of feelings and emotions in their interpretation of reflection and reconfigure Dewey's five phases into three: (1) returning to experience; (2) attending to (or connecting with) feelings; and (3) evaluating experience.

The importance of reflecting on what you are doing, as part of the learning process, has been emphasised by many educational theorists. Schön (1983) built on and extended Dewey's work on the properties of reflection and suggested that the capacity to reflect on action so as to engage in a process of continuous learning is one of the defining characteristics of professional practice. A new wave of research and learning about reflection emerged in the mid-1980s in response to Schön's concept of reflection as 'knowledge gained from the practitioner's own experience' through 'reconstructing experience'. It therefore takes place in the 'crucible of action' (Grimmett and Erickson, 1988: 13).

Schön distinguished between two fundamental processes: reflection *in* action and reflection *on* action:

1 *Reflection in action* (while doing something) is understood through such phrases as thinking on your feet and keeping your wits about you which suggest that 'not only can we think about doing but that we can think about doing something whilst doing it. Some of the most interesting examples of this process occur in the midst of performance' (Schön, 1983: 54).

2 *Reflection on action* (after you have done something), similar to Dewey's notion of reflection, is the basis of much literature that is related to reflective teaching and reflective teacher education. Within his model of 'pedagogical reasoning and action', Shulman (1987) explains this form of reflection in terms of what a teacher does when she looks back at the teaching and learning that have occurred and reconstructs, re-enacts and/or recaptures the events, emotions and accomplishments. It incorporates processes through which a teacher learns from experience and uses particular kinds of analytical knowledge to reflect on her work. Central to this process should be a review of the teaching in comparison with the ends that were sought. The insights gained about aspects of teaching and learning about teaching are subsequently used to inform future practice.

Now complete Activity 19.1.

Activity 19.1

How reflection might be conceptualised

Read Chapter 3 in Zwozdiak-Myers (2012: 33–47) to further elaborate the contributions of Dewey (1933), Boud *et al.* (1985) and Schön (1983) in addition to those of other key theorists on 'how reflection might be conceptualised'.

WHERE IN TEACHING REFLECTION SHOULD TAKE PLACE

Situations where reflection, in teaching and learning about teaching, should occur to inform your practice include:

- reflection in action;
- reflection on action; and
- reflection on your teaching as a whole.

Reflection in action

Reflection in action takes place within the context of an ongoing lesson and involves monitoring the class by observing pupils as they work, on given tasks in a specific situation and environment, to judge whether the intended learning outcomes are being achieved. Having observed pupil response, you must then decide what action needs to be taken to maximise the learning opportunities in the lesson. Some of these actions will be minor modifications to your plan whereas others might require a more substantial review. In both instances, you must respond to the class to guide the work towards their learning the intended learning outcomes.

Due to the transient nature of the teaching-learning context, when situations arise that could either inhibit or promote pupils' knowledge and understanding of concepts and skills you should, whenever possible, respond to them as soon as they occur. This relates directly to the development of your observation skills and ability to 'read the class' along with your ability to draw from a repertoire of relevant past experiences and of your personal frame of reference. Activity 19.2a asks you to think about reflection in action.

Activity 19.2a

Reflection in action

Complete the worksheet (Table 19.1 on p. 242) by identifying what action(s) you might take during the lesson as a consequence of observing the following pupil response. Add some examples from your own experience.

Reflection on action

Reflection on action is usually undertaken once you have taught a lesson or series of lessons (end of unit of work). This enables you to judge, for example, what was happening with a particular group of pupils in a particular teaching situation and to explore how and why you acted as you did.

Post lesson

This reflection involves looking back at what happened during a lesson, considering why things (e.g. the poor level of behaviour) occurred. Such questions should be responded to on your lesson evaluation as soon as possible after the lesson. Although the focus for this reflection may be on the teaching, you should begin the process by identifying what proportion of pupils achieved each of the lesson learning outcomes. Based upon this evidence, you must consider your influence on this learning or lack of learning and question the outcome. For example, if all pupils achieved a particular learning outcome you might question whether it was appropriate for their level of ability or, if some did not achieve a particular learning outcome you should question why they did not succeed. You should also evaluate the overall quality of the lesson including the introduction, transitions between lesson episodes and plenary.

Responses to *why* (the questions raised) are vital aspects of your reflection and self-appraisal since they guide your thinking on *how* to plan the next lesson to ensure that pupils achieve the next set of learning outcomes. Successful approaches that you have identified should be revisited and less successful aspects changed. These aspects, both successful and less successful, may become your teacher performance targets when teaching your next lesson.

Table 19.1 Reflection in action

Pupil response	Action(s) you might take	Why is this action being taken?
• Some group work is of very high quality • Confused by task • Inattentive • Pairs working through progressions at different rates • One pupil being physically bullied • Chatty group is off-task • Some individuals appear disinterested • Pupils for whom English is an Additional Language (EAL) do not respond appropriately to a given task	• Extension tasks are set	• To ensure that all pupils are working at their own ability level

Post unit of work

A similar process to that described above should be undertaken at the end of each unit of work, when you evaluate how far you have achieved the unit outcomes. This reflection should provide insight of both your pupils' future developmental needs and your personal development in terms of the knowledge, skills and understanding required to effectively accommodate these. This reflection could influence how you teach the class in question in their next unit of work and/or how you teach this same unit to another class. Activity 19.2b asks you to think about reflection on action.

Activity 19.2b

Reflection on action

In relation to selected aspects of your teaching, identify possible reasons why opportunities for pupil learning might be maximised or inhibited. Use Table 19.2 and draw on personal experience where possible. How can you transform the inhibited learning opportunities into maximised ones?

Reflection on the development of your teaching as a whole

During each school experience you receive a considerable amount of verbal, visual and written feedback that focuses on different aspects of your development as a teacher. For example, you receive valuable feedback from your pupils during a question/answer session to ascertain whether they have understood a particular concept or skill and you receive focused lesson observation critiques from your tutor. You are also required to evaluate each of your lessons/units of work and to undertake a range of school-based tasks.

From this emerging 'evidence' base you must consider the effectiveness of your teaching in the interests of all your pupils' learning. This can be quite a challenging exercise to engage in during the early stages of your school experience. For example, at the beginning it may have been pointed out to you that you were disorganised in your classroom management and organisation, or that you did not use demonstration to introduce new concepts and skills to best advantage. It is in the interests of all your pupils for you to work on improving these particular aspects of your teaching.

Reflection on the development of your teaching as a whole means that you take into account the 'whole picture': you analyse the effectiveness of a lesson or series of lessons in order to evaluate 'what was learned, by whom, and how more effective learning might take place in the future' (Moore, 2000: 129). This involves a systematic analysis of your current practice by careful evaluation of your own 'classroom performance, planning and assessment, in conjunction with evaluations of students' behaviour and achievement' (Moore, 2000: 129). This also requires an understanding of relevant educational theory and research, for example, theories of cognitive development and pupils' dominant learning styles, when coming to understand issues that are not only concerned with the 'what' and 'when' of education but moreover, embrace the questions of 'how' and 'why'.

Table 19.2 Reflection on action

Aspect of teaching	Maximised pupil learning opportunities	Inhibited pupil learning opportunities
Planning, expectations and targets	e.g. conditioned game for more able • • •	e.g. unrealistic targets for many pupils • • •
Class management and organisation	e.g. matched ability groups • • •	e.g. poor behaviour ignored • • •
Strategy/tasks	e.g. focused questions • • •	e.g. limited feedback • • •
Content knowledge	e.g. new concepts build on prior knowledge/ skills • • •	e.g. inaccurate technique demonstrated • • •

The times when you might be asked to reflect on your teaching as a whole include:

- Regular debriefing sessions with your tutor when weekly targets should be set in consultation with your tutor and your reflection of achievements of these should provide the content of your weekly evaluation.
- At the end of each school experience, you should identify targets for your next school placement with your tutor.
- Regular points during your degree course with your personal tutor to identify targets for your continuing professional development.

For each occasion, you should generate a list of targets or next steps – each of which is the outcome of reflecting on the development of your teaching as a whole. The focus for these targets will be directly linked to specific assessment criteria that are used to identify effective teaching and the standards you need to achieve to qualify as a teacher. Your programme of study will be designed and delivered in such a way as to allow you to meet these standards systematically and progressively until the completion of your initial teacher education. Activity 19.2c enables you to reflect on your teaching as a whole.

Activity 19.2c

Reflection on your teaching as a whole

In relation to each of the Teachers' Standards for England (Department for Education (DfE), 2012) presented in Table 19.3 (www.education.gov.uk/publications) (or the relevant standards for your course), identify problems you have encountered and resolved as well as problems you have encountered but not as yet resolved.

ENGAGE IN REFLECTIVE PRACTICE

Informed by your readings of 'how reflection might be conceptualised' along with an increased awareness of 'where in teaching reflection should take place' you have come, in part, to realise how to 'engage in reflective practice'. This process begins after you have taught your very first lesson and seek to answer the question 'Did it go well?'

Reflective practice is, however, a complex, multifaceted phenomenon which has been defined as: 'a disposition to enquiry incorporating the process through which student, early career and experienced teachers structure or restructure actions, beliefs, knowledge and theories that inform teaching for the purpose of professional development' (Zwozdiak-Myers, 2012: 5). Two very broad, interrelated strands – a *disposition to enquiry* and a *process* – are embedded within this definition.

Reflective practice as a disposition to enquiry has at its roots the early work of Dewey (1933), specifically in relation to the reflective attitudes of *open-mindedness*, *responsibility* and *wholeheartedness*, which he considers to be both prerequisite and integral to reflective action. The second strand, which captures reflective practice as a process, incorporates numerous concepts advanced by theorists over past decades, particularly in relation to the nature of reflective activity and its translation into professional practice. The author has designed two discrete, yet interrelated frameworks to capture the complex nature of reflective practice. Now complete Activities 19.3a, 19.3b and 19.3c.

Table 19.3 Reflection on your teaching as a whole

Aspect of teaching	Problem	Resolved	Not yet resolved
1 Set high expectations which inspire, motivate and challenge pupils	e.g. learning outcomes not appropriate for all pupils	e.g. worked with tutor to identify specific learning outcomes that stretch and challenge the full range of pupils within the class	
2 Promote good progress and outcomes by pupils			
3 Demonstrate good subject and curriculum knowledge			
4 Plan and teach well structured lessons			
5 Adapt teaching to respond to the strengths and needs of all pupils			
6 Make accurate and productive use of assessment			
7 Manage behaviour effectively to ensure a good and safe learning environment			
8 Fulfil wider professional responsibilities			

Then answer the following questions:

- What alternative strategies are there to the resolved problems? What possible solutions are there to the problems yet to be resolved?
- How did you arrive at these solutions?
- What knowledge, skills and understanding did you need?
- What thinking and decision-making processes did you go through?

Activity 19.3a

Key characteristics of reflective practice

Read Chapters 1 and 2 of Zwozdiak-Myers (2012: 3–29) to gain an understanding of how:

- reflective practice can be captured, framed and defined
- qualitative distinctions in reflective practice can be recognised.

Make notes on the different kinds of questions teachers should ask in order to engage in descriptive, comparative and critical reflective conversations.

Activity 19.3b

Engaging in reflective practice

In relation to the problems you identified in Activity 19.2c concerning aspects of teaching which have as yet to be resolved, use Table 19.4 to consider and record:

- strategies you might use to improve these aspects of your teaching;
- how and when you could try these out in practice;
- what criteria you would use to judge how well the strategies worked;
- where you can expect to find evidence to support your judgments.

Activity 19.3c

Descriptive, comparative and critical reflective conversations

Select a strategy you have tried out in relation to one of the problems identified in Activity 19.3b and think about what questions you might ask yourself in order to engage in descriptive, comparative and critical reflective conversations, using the template in Table 19.5.

Table 19.4 Engaging in reflective practice

Aspect of teaching	Strategies	How	When	Criteria	Evidence

Try these out and appraise their impact to inform your own future practice.

Table 19.5 Questions that might be asked

Aspect of teaching yet to be resolved:
Strategy selected to resolve the problem:
Questions

UNDERSTAND WHY REFLECTING ON YOUR PRACTICE IS IMPORTANT

The purpose, rationale and justification for all of this reflection is to improve the effectiveness of your teaching in order to maximise the learning opportunities that you provide for pupils.

All three situations where reflection, in teaching and learning about teaching, should occur – in action, on action and on your teaching as a whole – must be developed since they are an integral part of a teacher's way of life and should continue to be a part of your practice throughout your teaching career. Activity 19.4 helps you to appreciate why reflecting on your practice is important.

Activity 19.4

Why reflecting on your practice is important

Look back over your evaluations for three lessons that you have taught recently. In relation to aspects of teaching that need further development, in Table 19.6 record what you plan to do, how you plan to do it and why this is important.

- Identify five consequences that should emerge from systematically reflecting on aspects of your teaching and learning about teaching.
- Identify five consequences that might emerge from failing to systematically reflect on aspects of your teaching and learning about teaching.
- Compare both sets of consequences to enable you to make change where appropriate.

Table 19.6 Planning for the development of aspects of your teaching

What you plan to do	How you plan to do it	Why this is important
Lesson 1 1 2 3		
Lesson 2 1 2 3		
Lesson 3 1 2 3		

SUMMARY

This chapter has provided you with the basis for developing your skills of reflection and an understanding of the complex nature of reflective practice. In order to help you further, Chapter 4 looks at action research. This encourages teachers to assume the role of teacher as researcher and engage in the process of systematic critical reflection about their own current practice so as to move in an informed and principled way towards developing the art of self-study and mastery of their chosen craft.

FURTHER READING

Kelchtermans, G. (2009) Who I am in how I teach is the message: self-understanding, vulnerability and reflection, *Teachers and Teaching: Theory and Practice,* 15 (2): 257–72.
Inspired by research into teacher thinking and the narrative biographical approach to teaching and teacher development, the author argues that the person of the teacher is an essential element in what constitutes professional teaching; and the 'scholarship of teachers' is fundamentally characterised by personal commitment and vulnerability, which have consequences for the kind of reflective attitudes and skills professional teachers should master.

Stooksberry, L., Schussler, D. and Bercaw, L. (2009) Conceptualising dispositions: intellectual, cultural and moral domains of teaching, *Teachers and Teaching: Theory and Practice,* 15(6): 719–36.
The authors provide a heuristic that organises dispositions around three domains of teaching: intellectual, cultural and moral. They equate dispositions with the teacher's internal filter, shaped by prior experience, beliefs, culture, values and cognitive abilities and which affect ideas about the nature of pupils, teaching and learning.

Zwozdiak-Myers, P. (2012) *The Teacher's Reflective Practice Handbook: Becoming an Extended Professional Through Capturing Evidence-Informed Practice,* London: Routledge.
This accessible guide supports the facilitation of reflective practice through self- and peer assessment, problem-based learning and professional development planning. It presents an innovative multi-dimensional framework that is underpinned by concepts and theories advanced by eminent scholars, researchers and practitioners and which enables you to build a meaningful, personally relevant portfolio of evidence-informed practice.

Note: all proformas, tables or figures you are asked to complete to help you undertake activities in this chapter are also available on the website which accompanies the book (www.routledge.com/9780415814829).

Chapter 20 Action research

PAULA ZWOZDIAK-MYERS

INTRODUCTION

This chapter is designed to develop your understanding of the principles of action research and to recognise its potential within the teaching-learning context. By the end of this chapter you should be able to:

- understand characteristic features of action research;
- identify a focus for action research;
- engage in the action research process; and
- assess the validity of action research.

UNDERSTAND CHARACTERISTIC FEATURES OF ACTION RESEARCH

There are a number of research strategies and procedures you can draw upon to systematically evaluate your own teaching in order to become more informed critics of your own practice. Action research is commonly used for this purpose, and building on Lewin's (1946) legacy of the action research spiral a number of models (e.g.. Ebbutt, 1985; Elliott, 1991; Kemmis, 1988; McKernan, 1996) have been developed, each providing a highly structured approach to this research paradigm. Carr and Kemmis (1986: 162) define action research as a form of: 'self-reflective enquiry undertaken by participants in social situations in order to improve the rationality and justice of their own practices, their understanding of these practices, and the situations in which the practices are carried out'.

Action research for improving practice, thinking and creating more meaningful work environments seeks to take the value-laden, socially constructed nature of practice as its starting point. When you, as teachers, identify action for improvement this can usefully be viewed as both a dialogical and reflective process. The commitment to learn from, and improve, practice are characteristic features of action research as is the concern to generate and produce new knowledge. Reflecting on practice is a core component of action research and an important vehicle through which you can gain greater insight, understanding and awareness of your professional growth and development as a teacher; identify possible avenues for alternative practice; gain a greater sense of autonomy over your own work; and, internalise the processes associated with the art of self-study. It also enhances pupils learning; the ultimate goal.

Central to the concept of *teacher as researcher* is the 'systematic reflection on one's classroom experience, to understand it and to create meaning out of that understanding' (Hopkins, 2002: 5). Now complete Activity 20.1a.

Activity 20.1a

Characteristic features of action research

Read Chapter 4 'Action research and classroom research by teachers' in Hopkins (2002: 42–54). Make notes on the six principles he suggests should be followed by teachers when undertaking classroom research; state the extent to which you feel that you understand how to proceed in relation to each principle. Discuss any concerns you may have with your tutor.

To further pursue this line of enquiry you might explore the similarities and differences between the models of action research advanced by Ebbutt (1985), Elliott (1991), Kemmis (1988) and McKernan (1996).

Ethical considerations

Ethical issues arise in research undertaken with human participants, and in particular with pupils in schools, when the conduct of the researcher involves the interests and rights of others. By its very nature, research in education involves studying people's activities in one way or another. Research involving interviews or observations for example, may impinge on the confidentiality, privacy, convenience, comfort or safety of others. Such issues constitute ethical problems. Therefore, *before* undertaking any form of research with pupils and adults in school there are a number of ethical issues that must be addressed. Activity 20.1b highlights the kind of ethical considerations that should be important to you.

Activity 20.1b

Ethical considerations

Access a copy of the Ethical Guidelines for Educational Research developed by the British Educational Research Association (BERA, 2011) from www.bera.ac.uk. Record below the ethical issues that need to be addressed *before* you undertake any form of research with pupils and adults in school e.g.

- voluntary informed consent
  right to withdraw

  _____

  _____

  Find out what documentation you need to complete within your own institution for gaining ethical approval before you undertake any form of research with pupils and adults in school. Record these below:

  _____

  _____

IDENTIFY A FOCUS FOR ACTION RESEARCH

Action research characteristically begins by selecting a topic for investigation in relation to, for example, an aspect of teaching that needs developing; solving a particular issue or problem to promote pupil learning; achieving a particular goal; enabling pupils to achieve a specific learning outcome; exploring an area of personal interest; or, evaluating the impact of a particular strategy or new initiative. The rationale and justification behind selecting a particular research topic need to be context-specific, appropriate and manageable within a given time frame.

In broad terms, the aim of action research within the school context is to improve the quality of the teaching and learning opportunities you provide for the pupils you teach by identifying, investigating and reflecting upon a specific aspect of your teaching. Your particular goal or focus for undertaking a study might, for example, be to examine:

- how grouping pupils according to ability, size of group and friendship affects individual performance and on-task behaviour;
- which teaching strategies are most important in promoting independent, self-directed pupil learning;
- how to develop your use and range of questioning techniques to challenge the more able pupils; or
- how to develop your use of demonstration or your use of praise to enhance pupil learning.

Once you have identified the goal or focus for your investigation, you need to analyse and justify why you have chosen to investigate that particular area and begin to read relevant literature, e.g. policy documents, books and research articles. Your justification is developed from thinking about and reflecting on an aspect of your practice that you have identified as an area for further development.

Reviewing the literature

A search and review of relevant literature (see Activity 20.2a) is undertaken to give insight into the current body of knowledge that exists with regard to a research issue and enables you to situate your study within the wider context of theory and practice. It should include definitions of key concepts and terms, theoretical underpinnings of focal areas, and demonstrate an understanding of findings from related research studies. For instance, in relation to the first example given above, you need to clarify, on the one hand, what you mean/understand by 'performance' and 'on-task behaviour' as well as group structure and group dynamics; and, on the other, you need to search the literature to find out what research tells us about pupil performance and on-task behaviour.

As you review studies undertaken by other researchers, it is important to make notes on such factors as the research methods employed, what data was gathered and how that data was analysed, as this kind of information can guide the decisions you make in relation to your own research. Table 20.1 presents a summary template of the kind of information you can extract from each literary source for the purpose of comparing, contrasting and evaluating literature relevant to your study. This critical and analytical study of relevant literature is a vitally important aspect of action research and one that should be undertaken to guide the formulation of your research question and subsequent plan of action.

Table 20.1 Summary template for literature review

Author(s)	Title	Source
Key words:		
Aims/purpose:		
Context:		
Research participants:		
Methodology:		
Analysis:		
Key findings:		
Conclusions:		
Recommendations for further studies:		
Quotes:		
Relevance to research question:		
Evidence base:		
Date reviewed:		

Source: Adapted from Zwozdiak-Myers (2012: 57).

Activity 20.2a is designed to help you conduct a literature search and review and Activity 20.2b to help you with selecting appropriate teaching strategies.

Activity 20.2a

Literature search and review

1   Select an area which needs development in relation to an aspect of your teaching or of pupil learning,
2   Conduct a literature search (library and/or web-based) on your chosen topic or area of study.
3   Produce an annotated bibliography based upon your literature search. This is characterised by accurately referencing the sources you have read/searched, detail of context, theory, methods and findings, along with short notes of possible use for your study that respond to relevant questions identified in Table 20.1. Page numbers(s) are needed for all quotes.
4   Write a literature review that brings together the relevant literature and compares, contrasts and discusses that which has a bearing on your topic and relates to your particular goal or focus. (Be mindful not to generate a series of book reviews.) The review of literature should refer to previous research on the topic/concept in relation to established views of: (1) value of the topic; (2) definition of the concept; (iii) how this relates to research on teaching or on pupils learning. You need to discuss this critically and draw out that which is of value to your action research investigation.
5   Informed by your review of literature, identify a specific focus for your action research investigation and frame this in a research question.

Note: If you are unclear about conducting a literature search or writing a literature review, you can also refer to Chapters 5 and 6 in Bell (2010) for further guidance.

Activity 20.2b

Select appropriate teaching strategies

1   Having decided upon an aspect of your teaching/pupils' learning that you would like to investigate you need to select appropriate teaching strategies to promote its development. For example, you might want to develop your ability to motivate pupils. Appropriate teaching strategies may include, e.g. providing a task-orientated environment; treating each pupil as an individual; providing constructive feedback to pupils; rewarding appropriate behaviour; rewarding effort as well as success; planning tasks that are challenging but achievable with effort; differentiating work according to individual needs.
2   In relation to a real or an imaginary situation, select and justify three teaching strategies that you want to try to develop in order to address your own research question.

ENGAGE IN THE ACTION RESEARCH PROCESS

Plan of action

Having determined that you are going to use an action research approach for your investigation to make an improvement in a particular teaching-learning situation, you need to make decisions about what forms of data are appropriate to your investigation and how you plan to go about collecting this data. Such decisions are made in light of your research question, informed by your critical review of relevant literature, your understanding of the cyclical nature of the action research process and the specific research context. For example, you need to devise a *plan of action* that considers:

- the way you are going to work with pupils to try to improve teaching and learning (see Activity 20.2b);
- the methods you are going to use to collect evidence about the extent of improvement in teaching and learning;
- the nature of the data you are going to collect;
- how you are going to analyse and interpret the evidence;
- the way in which you are going to use the results to modify your course of action in terms of teaching and learning.

From the outset you must monitor the way you carry out your investigation with the selected group(s) of pupils to provide a record of *ongoing research*. This is achieved by systematically collecting data/information for the purpose of evaluation and analysis. The data might, for example, be drawn from:

- field notes;
- observation schedules;
- pupil questionnaires and/or diaries;
- structured, semi-structured or focus group interviews;
- videotape recordings.

This information provides the basis for a lesson-by-lesson account of your action research experience. Now complete Activity 20.3a.

Activity 20.3a

Classroom research techniques

Conduct a literature search to identify the characteristics, possible advantages, disadvantages and uses of the classroom research techniques featured in the worksheet in Table 20.2.

Table 20.2 Classroom research techniques

Technique	Characteristics	Advantages	Disadvantages	Uses
Pupil diary	Pupils asked to make entries about specific things at various times	Captures pupils' perceptions in their own words	Quality of entries relies on pupils' writing skills	In studies related to self-esteem, enjoyment or understanding
Audiotape recording				
Documentary analysis				
Interviews: • structured • semi-structured • unstructured • focus group				
Observation schedules				
Reflective journal				
Questionnaires: • closed questions • open questions • multiple choice questions • rank order questions				
Videotape recording				

Source: Adapted from Hopkins (2002: 127).

Data collection is crucial. The nature of the data and the collection techniques you select should be described and justified, along with some indication of their strengths and limitations, and a detailed account of how you are going to apply them within the context of your study, e.g. how questionnaires have been constructed or a description of the pilot run for an observation schedule (an observation can be undertaken by you, your mentor or another student teacher). The data needs to be accurate (you must record what you intend to record) so that it can be analysed and interpreted in order to give the best possible reasons for explaining behaviours or events that occur.

Conceptual clarity (using precise terminology) is important as is validity (being able to show that the questionnaire or observation schedule is getting the information you say that it is). The questions you ask, how you frame them and the language you use must be appropriate (see Activity 20.3b).

Activity 20.3b

Wording questions

When designing questions for interview or questionnaire purposes, what you ask and how you word, phrase and sequence the questions you ask are important. In the following examples, identify which questions might be leading, have a double meaning or are restrictive in nature. Rewrite them to ensure that each has a clear focus, is unambiguous and is not leading.

- Do you think that PE teachers privilege elite performers over those less gifted, able and talented?
- What are the advantages and disadvantages of working in mixed ability, friendship or mixed gender groups for your gymnastics lessons?
- Do you enjoy dance more than basketball and are you pleased with your duet choreography?
- Are female PE teachers more compassionate and caring than male PE teachers?
- Do you feel that teachers fail to listen to pupils' opinions and views?

The way pupils respond to questions will be influenced by the options you provide (open, closed, multiple-choice or rank order questions), how they understand and perceive the questions and the particular climate/context when filling them in. Now complete Activity 20.3c to check your knowledge and understanding of questionnaires and interviews.

Activity 20.3c

Questionnaires and interviews

Read the following: Chapter 9 in Robson (2002) and Chapters 8 and 9 in Bell (2010). Make notes on:

- designing and administering questionnaires;
- planning and conducting interviews.

Similarly, an observation schedule (see Activity 20.3d) designed to record pupils' on-task and off-task behaviour must clearly state what is meant by on-task and off-task behaviour within the given context (what specific behaviour or non-verbal communication signify the behaviour?). The validity of recordings made on this schedule are dependent upon your or your observer's ability to perceive pupil behaviour in relation to criteria that you have identified (see the Academic Learning Time (ALT-PE) observation sheets in the Appendix in Chapter 11 (Siedentop *et al.*, 1982), which look at on-task and off-task behaviour).

Activity 20.3d

Focused observation schedules

The aim of the two prepared observation schedules, in Figures 20.1 and 20.2, is to guide your thinking about what to observe, who to observe, how to observe, when to observe and why. These can be used as a springboard to inform the development of observation schedules relevant to your personal area/s of research.

See also observation schedule for Academic Learning Time-Physical Education (ALT-PE) (Siedentop *et al.*, 1982) in Chapter 11. Further observation schedules are available on the www.routledge.com/9780415814829.

Account of experience

For your action research investigation you should collect two kinds of data:

1 Data to monitor what you, as the teacher, do in each lesson and to evaluate how successful you are at putting your plans into practice.
2 Data to demonstrate the effectiveness of your innovation as a whole, for example, whether pupils' motivation increases in response to your modified teaching strategies.

Data collected from these sources can be *quantitative* (numerical) or *qualitative* (generally written narrative) and should enable you to describe and reflect on each lesson in relation to:

- key events or critical incidents;
- teacher, pupil and/or observer behaviour;
- problems encountered;
- necessary adjustments to your plan of action and/or refinements to data collection techniques.

In light of your response to the above issues, you should plan what to do next and the data you need to collect. You must record this process with clarity and consistency throughout your investigation, indicating the basis upon which changes were made to the strategy and used to modify and develop your teaching and pupil learning from lesson to lesson through formative evaluation. Your results and discussions provide opportunities for reflection and the cross-referencing of findings. What is important in this record of ongoing research is the clear explanation of a development based upon sound evidence and the quality of conclusions you have drawn.

Name of teacher/student teacher observed: .... **Date:** ....

Name of observer: ....

Note as many questions as you can. Try to reproduce exactly what is said.

	Question	Who answers?				Comment here if question is extensive or unexpected
		Teacher	No answer	Pupils	Many pupils	
1						
2						
3						
4						
5						
6						
7						
8						
9						
10						

At end of observation, fill in:

Number of **open** questions .... Number of **recall** questions ....

Number of **pupil** questions .... Number of questions **requiring thinking** ....

Number of **question sequences** (guided discovery) ....

Figure 20.1 Focused observation schedule 1: questioning

Name of teacher/student teacher observed: .... Date: ....

Name of observer: ....

Concentrate on ONE pupil throughout the lesson and complete the record for that one pupil only during each teacher episode. The teacher should not know which pupil you have chosen.

Record of praise and criticism:

Name of pupil ....

	Instances of:		Given to:			Comments e.g. for good work or effort or improvement or behaviour or other reason
	PRAISE	**CRITICISM**	**Individual**	**Group**	**Class**	
1						
2						
3						
4						
5						
6						
7						

Task appropriateness for this SAME pupil.

	Task	**Too easy**	**Reasonable challenge**	**Too difficult**	**Comments**
1					
2					
3					
4					
5					
6					
7					

Other comments:

Figure 20.2 Focused observation schedule 2: motivation

Collation and analysis of data

Once you have completed your action research investigation, you need to present, interpret and analyse your findings. You should collate your raw data and organise your research evidence into categories that are appropriate to your study. For example, in the case of a study which has used focused observation schedule 2 on Motivation (Activity 20.3d), you should begin to categorise findings in relation to: instances of individual praise; instances of group praise; instances of class praise; and so forth. Findings can be presented in the form of summaries of your data rather than the raw data itself, along with tables, graphs and transcripts of significant conversations and/or records of illuminating incidents. Having established appropriate categories, you can examine the findings and look for evidence of similarities and differences, groupings, patterns, trends and events/incidents that are of particular significance to your research question and focus. You should be able to survey all the data you have collected over the research period to interpret, analyse and critically reflect on your overall findings.

ASSESS THE VALIDITY OF ACTION RESEARCH

The validity and usefulness of your findings for teaching should be judged realistically and be considered in the light of prior reading and relevant research. You need to recognise that your findings have arisen from a specific context, one that involves you as the researcher focusing on a particular aspect of your teaching and/or pupil learning, with a particular group of pupils in a particular environment and at a particular moment in time. Care needs to be exercised to avoid making claims or generalisations based upon limited data that have emerged from a small-scale investigation.

Triangulation is often used in action research as one of several techniques designed to measure the 'trustworthiness' or validity of a category or hypothesis. It is characterised by collecting data about a particular teaching-learning situation from three quite different perspectives: usually those of the pupils, an observer and the teacher/researcher. In this way, different sources of data can be cross-referenced to validate whether something has occurred. For example, if you claim that your study has promoted inclusion, you should also ask: 'Does the pupil's account fit with observer and teacher data?', 'Does the pupil feel included?', 'On what observations and data are you claiming that she is included and that your strategy has worked?'

Activity 20.4 highlights broad questions that Elliott (2006) has devised explicitly for the purpose of assessing the process, democratic, catalytic and outcome validity of action research. You should search this source further to gain an understanding of specific criteria aligned to each of these questions and which you can apply when judging the validity of your own research study.

Activity 20.4

Assessing the validity of action research

- Process validity: Are appropriate methods used to answer the research question?
- Democratic validity: Are the researchers and researched engaged and included in the enquiry?
- Catalytic validity: Is the research transformative?
- Outcome validity: Has the process led to a resolution and/or reframing of the problem?

In drawing conclusions, you might suggest changes that, if you were to undertake your study again, you could make to improve some aspect of the research. Also, you might consider whether your findings have relevance to other teaching and learning situations. Perceived limitations of your study should be identified and you might recommend possible avenues to explore for future research and developments.

SUMMARY

When you engage in action research you can gain a better understanding of your practice and of ways to improve it. This not only involves a high degree of reflexivity and sensitivity to the role of teacher as researcher but also encourages exploratory engagement with a wide range of existing knowledge drawn from the social sciences and education. As a consequence, powerful learning can take place through combining research with reflection on practice.

By working through this chapter you will have gained an understanding of the characteristic features of action research and know: how to identify a focus for action research; how to engage in the action research process; and, how to assess the validity of action research. This should enable you to conduct your own action research study to support your development into becoming a reflective practitioner and therefore a more effective teacher.

FURTHER READING

Bell, J. (2010) *Doing your Research Project: A Guide for First-Time Researchers in Education, Health and Social Science*, 5th edn, Maidenhead: Open University Press.
This book is designed for people undertaking small-scale research projects and is usefully organised in three sections: Part I – Preparing the ground; Part II – Selecting methods of data collection; Part III – Interpreting the evidence and reporting the findings.

Eraut, M. (2007) Learning from other people in the workplace, *Oxford Review of Education*, 33(4): 403–22.
The author presents an epistemology of practice, which treats socio-cultural and individual theories of learning as complementary rather than competing. He explores a range of ways through which people can learn in the workplace (e.g. asking questions, listening and observing, giving and receiving feedback) and provides a useful typology of early career learning.

Hopkins, D. (2002) *A Teacher's Guide to Classroom Research*, 3rd edn, Buckingham: Open University Press.
This book is a good starting point for anyone wishing to research aspects of personal practice. It contains practical ideas and examples of a variety of data collection techniques to improve classroom practice and guidance on each aspect of the research process.

Wilson, E. (2012) *School-based Research: A Guide for Education Students*, London: Sage.
An invaluable text and contemporary resource with comprehensive sections that feature: using existing research to understand and plan your classroom-based research; carrying out and reporting on classroom-based research; methodologies and paradigms.

Note: all proformas, tables or figures you are asked to complete to help you undertake activities in this chapter are also available on the website which accompanies the book (www.routledge.com/9780415814829).

References

afPE (Association for Physical Education) (2012) *Safe Practice in Physical Education and Sport*, Leeds: Coachwise Ltd.

Armstrong, F., Armstrong, D. and Barton, L. (2000) *Inclusive Education: Policy, Contexts and Comparative Perspective*. London: David Fulton.

Assessment Reform Group (2002) *Assessment for Learning: 10 Principles*, Cambridge: University of Cambridge, Assessment Reform Group.

BAALPE (British Association for Advisors and Lecturers in Physical Education) (2005) *Workforce Reform: Essential Safe Practice in Physical Education and School Sport*, Leeds: Coachwise Business Solutions.

Bailey, R., Armour, K., Kirk, D., Jess, M., Pickup, I. and Sandford, R. (2009) The educational benefits claimed for physical education and school sport: an academic review, *Research Papers in Education*, 24, 1: 1–27.

Bailey, R. and Morley, D. (2006) *Physical Education Quality Standards for Development*, Loughborough: Youth Sport Trust.

Bandura, A. (1989) Social cognitive theory, in R. Vasta (ed.) *Annals of Child Development*, volume 6: *Six Theories of Child Development*, Greenwood, CT: Jai Press, pp.1–60.

Barrow, G. and Newton, T. (2004) *Walking the Talk: How Transactional Analysis Is Improving Behaviour and Raising Self-Esteem*, London: David Fulton.

Beams, S., Higgins, P. and Nicol, R. (2012) *Learning Outside the Classroom: Theories and Guidelines for Practice*, London: Routledge.

Beedy, J.P. (1997) *Sports Plus: Positive Learning Using Sports*, Hamilton: Project Adventure.

Bell, J. (2010) *Doing Your Research Project: A Guide for First Time Researchers in Education and Social Science*, 5th edn, Maidenhead: Open University Press.

BERA (British Educational Research Association) (2011) *Ethical Guidelines for Educational Research*, Southwell: BERA. Available at: http://www.bera.ac.uk (accessed 14 December 2012).

Blair, R. and Capel, S. (2008) Intended or unintended? Issues arising from the implementation of the UK Government's 2003 Schools Workforce Remodelling Act, *Perspectives in Education*, 26, 2: 105–21.

Blair, R. and Capel, S. (2011) Primary physical education, coaches and continuing professional development, *Sport, Education and Society*, 16, 4: 485–506.

Blair, R. and Capel, S. (2013) Who should teach physical education in curriculum time and extra-curricular time? in S. Capel and M. Whitehead (eds) *Debates in Physical Education*, London: Routledge, pp. 171–87.

Bloom, B.S., Engelhart, M.D., Furst, E.J., Hill, W.H. and Krathwohl, D.R. (1956) *Taxonomy of Educational Objectives Handbook 1: The Cognitive Domain*, New York: David McKay Co Inc.

Booth, T., Ainscow, M., Black-Hawkins, K., Vaughan, M. and Shaw, L. (2000) *Index for Inclusion: Developing, Learning and Participation in Schools*, Bristol: Centre for Studies in Inclusive Education.

Boud, D., Keogh, R. and Walker, D. (eds) (1985) *Reflection: Turning Experience into Learning*, London: Kogan Page.

Breckon, P., Capel, S., Whitehead, M. and Zwozdiak-Myers, P. (2010) Developing and maintaining an effective learning environment, in S. Capel and M. Whitehead (eds) *Learning to Teach in the Secondary School: A Companion to School Experience*, 3rd edn, Routledge, London, pp. 101–18.

Bruner, J. (1983) *Child's Talk: Learning to Use the Language*, Oxford: Oxford University Press.

Burton, D. (2009) Ways pupils learn, in S. Capel, M. Leask and T. Turner (eds) *Learning to Teach in Secondary School: A Companion to School Experience*, 5th edn, London: Routledge, pp. 251–66.

Cale, L. and Harris, J. (2013) Physical education and health: considerations and issues, in S. Capel and M. Whitehead (eds) *Debates in Physical Education*, London: Routledge, pp. 74–88.

Capel, S. (2005) Teachers, teaching and pedagogy in physical education, in K. Green and K. Hardman (eds) *Physical Education: Essential Issues*, London: Sage Publications, pp.111–27.

Capel, S. (2007) Moving beyond physical education subject knowledge to develop knowledgeable teachers of the subject, *Curriculum Journal*, 18, 4: 493–507.

Capel, S. (2010) Starting out as a PE teacher, in S. Capel and M. Whitehead (eds) *Learning to Teach Physical Education in the Secondary School: A Companion to School Experience*, 3rd edn, London: Routledge, pp. 1–12.

Capel, S. and Blair, R. (2013) Why do physical education teachers adopt a particular way of teaching? in S. Capel and M. Whitehead (eds) *Debates in Physical Education*, London: Routledge, pp. 120–39.

Capel, S., Leask, M. and Turner, T. (eds) (2009) *Learning to Teach in the Secondary School: A Companion to School Experience*, 5th edn, London: Routledge.

Capel, S. and Whitehead, M. (eds) (2010) *Learning to Teach Physical Education in the Secondary School: A Companion to School Experience*, 3rd edn, Routledge: London.

Carr, W. and Kemmis, S. (1986) *Becoming Critical: Education, Knowledge and Action Research*, Lewes: Falmer Press.

Central Advisory Council for Education (1967) *Children and their Primary Schools: A Report of the Central Advisory Council for Education (England)* (The Plowden Report), London: Her Majesty's Stationery Office.

Chappell, A. and Katene, W. (2010) Teaching safely and safety in physical education, in S. Capel, and M. Whitehead (2010) *Learning to Teach Physical Education in the Secondary School: A Companion to School Experience*, 3rd edn, London: RoutledgeFalmer, pp. 134–53.

Clarke, J.I. and Dawson, C. (1998) *Growing Up Again: Parenting Ourselves, Parenting Our Children*, 2nd edn, Central City, MI: Hazelden.

Cockburn, A.D. and Handscomb, G. (eds) (2012) *Teaching Children 3 to 11*, 3rd edn. London: Paul Chapman Publishing.

Cohen, L., Manion, L. and Morrison, K. (2010) *A Guide to Teaching Practice*, 5th edn, London: Routledge.

Corbett, J. and Slee, R. (2000) An international conversation on inclusive education, in F. Armstrong, D. Armstrong and L. Barton (eds) *Inclusive Education: Policy, Contexts and Comparative Perspectives*, London: David Fulton, pp. 133–46.

Cowley, S. (2006) *Getting the Buggers to Behave*, 3rd edn, London: Continuum International Publishing Group.

Cox, C.B. and Dyson, R.E. (eds) (1975) *Black Paper 1975: The Fight for Education*, London: Dent.

DCMS (Department for Culture Media and Sport) (2010) *Plans for the Legacy from the 2012 Olympic and Paralympic Games*, Nottingham: Department for Culture Media and Sport.

DCSF (Department for Children, Schools and Families) (2010) *Functional Skills Support Programme: Developing Functional Skills in Physical Education*, Available at: http://dera. ioe.ac.uk (accessed 14 December 2012).

DES (Department of Education and Science) (1987) *The Curriculum from 5 to 16: Curriculum Matters 2*, London: HMSO.

DES (Department of Education and Science) (1988) *The Education Reform Act*, London: HMSO.

DES (Department of Education and Science) (1992) *Physical Education in the National Curriculum*, London: HMSO.

DES/WO (Department of Education and Science and the Welsh Office) (1991) *Physical Education for Ages 5–16*, Proposals of the Secretary of State for Education and Science and the Secretary of State for Wales, London: DES/Welsh Office.

Dewey, J. (1933) *How We Think*, New York: Heath and Co.

DfE (Department for Education) (2010) *Social and Emotional Aspects of Learning (SEAL) Programme in Secondary Schools: National Evaluation*, Available at: www.education.gov.uk (accessed 14 December 2012).

DfE (Department for Education) (2012a) *Aims, Values and Purposes: Aims*, London, Department for Education Schools. Available at: http://www.education.gov.uk/ schools/teachingandlearning/curriculum/b00199676/aims-values-and-purposes/ aims (accessed 29 July 2013).

DfE (Department for Education) (2012b) *Teachers' Standards*, London: DfE. Available at: www.education.gov.uk/publications (accessed 14 December 2012).

DfEE/QCA (Department for Education and Employment/Qualifications and Curriculum Authority) (1999) *Physical Education: The National Curriculum for England*, London: HMSO.

DfES (Department for Education and Skills) (2004) *Pedagogy and Practice: Teaching and Learning in the Secondary School, Unit 12 Assessment for Learning*, London: DfES. Available at: http://www.teachfind.com/national-strategies/pedagogy-and-practice-study-guides-unit-12-ndash-assessment-learning (accessed 26 June 2012).

DfES (Department of Education and Skills) (2005) *What are Key Skills?* Available at: http:// web archivenationalarchives.gov.uk (accessed 20 July 2012).

DfES (Department for Education and Skills) (2006) *Learning Outside the Classroom: Manifesto*, Nottingham: Department for Education and Skills.

Donovan, G., McNamara, J. and Gianoli, P. (1988) *Exercise Danger*, Floreat Park: Wellness Australia.

Dowling, F., Fitzgerald, H. and Flintoff A. (2012) *Equity and Difference in Physical Education, Youth Sport and Health: A Narrative Approach*, London: Routledge.

Dyson, B. and Casey, A. (2012) *Cooperative Learning in Physical Education: A Research-Based Approach*, London: Routledge.

Ebbutt, D. (1985) Educational action research: some general concerns and specific quibbles, in R. Burgess (ed.) *Issues in Educational Research*, Lewes: Falmer Press.

Ekins, A. (2012) *The Changing Face of Educational Needs: Impact and Implications for SENCOs and their Schools*, London: Routledge.

Elbourn, J. (2008) *Aerobics and Circuits for Secondary Schools*, Leeds: Coachwise Ltd.

Elliott, J. (1991) *Action Research for Educational Change*, Milton Keynes: Open University Press.

Elliott, J. (2006) *Reflecting Where the Action Is*, London: Routledge.

Ellis, V. (2011) *Learning and Teaching in Secondary Schools (Achieving QTS)*, 4th edn, Exeter: Learning Matters.

Eraut, M. (2007) Learning from other people in the workplace, *Oxford Review of Education*, 33, 4: 403–22.

Eyre, D. and Marjoram, T. (1990) *Enriching and Extending the National Curriculum*, London: Kogan Page.

Fautley, M. and Savage, J. (2010) Developing your classroom practice, in M. Fautley and J. Savage, *Secondary Education: Reflective Reader*, Exeter: Learning Matters, pp. 47–66.

Fautley, M. and Savage, J. (2011) *Cross Curricular Teaching and Learning in the Secondary School: The Arts*, London: Routledge.

Galton, M. and Croll, P. (1980) *Inside the Primary Classroom*, London: Routledge & Kegan Paul.

Gardner, H. (1993) *Frames of Mind: Multiple Intelligences*, London: Fontana.

Gower, C. (2010) Planning in PE, in S. Capel and M. Whitehead (eds) *Learning to Teach Physical Education in the Secondary School: A Companion to School Experience*, 3rd edn, London: Routledge, pp. 24–45.

Green, A. and Leask, M. (2013) Becoming a teacher, in S. Capel, M. Leask and T. Turner (eds) *Learning to Teach in the Secondary School: A Companion to School Experience*, 6th edn, London: Routledge, pp. 9–21.

Griggs, G. (2007) Physical education: primary matters, secondary importance, *Education 3–13*, 35, 1: 59–69.

Griggs, G. (2008) Outsiders inside: the use of sports coaches in primary schools. *Primary Physical Education Matters*, 3, 1: 33–7.

Griggs, G. (2010) For sale – primary physical education, £20 per hour or nearest offer, *Education 3-13*, 38, 1: 30–46.

Grimmett, P. and Erickson, G. (1988) *Reflection in Teacher Education*, New York: Teachers College Press.

Harris, J. and Elbourn, J. (2002) *Warming Up and Cooling Down*, Leeds: Human Kinetics.

Haskins, D. (2010) *Coaching the Whole Child: Positive Development through Sport*, Leeds: National Coaching Foundation.

Holmes, B., Tagney, B., Fitzgibbon, A. and Mehan, S. (2001) *Communal Constructivism: Students Constructing Learning For as Well as With Others*, Dublin: Centre for Research in IT in Education, Trinity College, Dublin. Paper presented at the SITE Conference, 2001. Cited in S. Capel, M. Leask and T. Turner (2005) *Learning to Teach in the Secondary School: A Companion to School Experience*, 4th edn, London: Routledge.

Hopkins, D. (2002) *A Teacher's Guide to Classroom Research*, 3rd edn, Maidenhead: Open University Press.

Hopper, B., Grey, J. and Maude, P. (2003) *Teaching Physical Education in the Primary School*, London: RoutledgeFalmer.

Hopson, M.H., Simms, R.L. and Knezek, G. (2002). Using a technology-enriched environment to improve higher-order thinking skills, *Journal of Research on Technology in Education*, 34, 2: 109–20.

Hoyle, E. and John, P.D. (1995) *Professional Knowledge and Professional Practice*, London: Cassell.

Hramaik, A. and Hudson, T. (2011) *Understanding Teaching and Learning in Secondary Schools*, Harlow: Pearson Education Ltd.

HSE (Health and Safety Executive) (1999) *Five Steps to Risk Assessment*, Sudbury: Health and Safety Executive.

Kelchtermans, G. (2009) Who I am in how I teach is the message: self-understanding, vulnerability and reflection, *Teachers and Teaching: Theory and Practice*, 15, 2: 257–72.

Kellam, K. and Whewell, E. (2009) Linked learning and its place within the teaching of physical education in the primary school, *Physical Education Matters*, 4, 2: 24–8.

Kemmis, S. (1988) Action research in retrospect and prospect, in Deakin University, *The Action Research Reader*, Victoria: Deakin University Press.

Kinchin, G., Penney, D. and Clarke, G. (2001) Try sport education? *British Journal of Teaching Physical Education*, 32, 2: 41–4.

Kirk, D. (2011) *Physical Education Futures*, London: Routledge.

Kolb, D.A. (1976) *The Learning Style Inventory: Technical Manual*, Boston: McBer.

Kolb, D.A. (1984) *Experiential Learning: Experience as the Source of Learning and Development*, Englewood Cliffs, NJ: Prentice-Hall.

Kolb, D.A. and Fry, R. (1975) Toward an applied theory of experiential learning, in C. Cooper (ed.) *Theories of Group Process*, London: John Wiley.

Krathwohl, D.R., Bloom, B.S., and Masia, B.B. (1964) *Taxonomy of Educational Objectives; The Classification of Educational Goals Handbook II: The Affective Domain*, New York: Longman, Green.

Laker, A. (2001) *Developing Personal, Social and Moral Education through Physical Education*, London: RoutledgeFalmer.

Lave, J. and Wenger, E. (1991) *Situated Learning: Legitimate Peripheral Participation*, Cambridge: Cambridge University Press.

Lawrence, J. (2012) Approaches to teaching physical education, in J. Lawrence, *Teaching Primary Physical Education*, London: Sage, pp. 25–38.

Lawrence, J. and Whitehead, M. (2010) Lesson organisation and management, in S. Capel and M. Whitehead (eds) *Learning to Teach in the Secondary School: A Companion to School Experience*, 3rd edn, London: Routledge, pp. 80–100.

Lawson, H. (1986) Occupational socialization and the design of teacher education programs, *Journal of Teaching in Physical Education*, 5, 1: 107–16.

Leask, M. and Younie, S. (2001) Communal Constructivist Theory: information and communications technology pedagogy and internationalisation of the curriculum, *Journal of Information Technology Teacher Education*, 10, 1–2.

Lewin, K. (1946) Action research and minority problems, *Journal of Social Issues*, 2: 34–46.

Loughran, J. (1996) *Developing Reflective Practice: Learning about Teaching and Learning through Modelling*, London: Falmer Press.

Lowrie, T. (2011) 'If this was real': tensions between using genuine artefacts and collaborative learning in mathematics tasks, *Research in Mathematics Education*, 13, 1: March.

Lubans, D. and Morgan, P. (2008) Evaluation of an extra-curricular school sport programme promoting lifestyle and lifetime activity for adolescents, *Journal of Sports Science*, 26: 519–29.

Malie, S. and Akir, O. (2012) Bridging the gaps between learning and teaching through recognition of students' learning approaches: a case study, *Research in Education*, 87, 1: 75–94.

Mazur, J. (1990) *Learning and Behaviour*, 2nd edn, Englewood Cliffs, NJ: Prentice Hall.

McKernan, J. (1996) *Curriculum Action Research*, 2nd edn, London: Kogan Page.

Metcalf, L. (2003) *Teaching Toward Solutions*, Cardiff: Crownhouse Publishing Ltd.

Moore, A. (2000) *Teaching and Learning: Pedagogy, Curriculum and Culture*, London: RoutledgeFalmer.

Mosston, M. and Ashworth, S. (2002) *Teaching Physical Education*, 5th edn, San Francisco: Benjamin Cummings.

Mosston, M. and Ashworth, S. (2008) *Teaching Physical Education* (First Online Edn). Available at: http://www.spectrumofteachingstyles.org/ebook (accessed 28 June 2012).

Murdoch, E. (2004) NCPE 2000: Where are we so far?, in S. Capel (ed.) *Learning to Teach Physical Education in the Secondary School: A Companion to School Experience*, 2nd edn, London: RoutledgeFalmer, pp. 280–300.

Murdoch, E. and Whitehead, M. (2013) What should pupils learn in physical education? in S. Capel and M. Whitehead (eds) *Debates in Physical Education*, London: Routledge, pp. 55–73.

Newton, A. and Bowler, M. (2010) Assessment for and of learning, in S. Capel and M. Whitehead (eds) *Learning to Teach Physical Education in the Secondary School: A Companion to School Experience* 3rd edn, London: Routledge, pp. 119–33.

Norris, C.M. (1999) *The Complete Guide to Stretching*, London: A and C. Black.

North, J. (2009) *The Coaching Workforce 2009–2016*, Leeds: Sportscoach UK.

Oeser, O.A. (ed.) (1955) *Teacher, Pupil and Task*, New York: Harper and Row.

Ofsted (Office for Standards in Education) (2002) *Good Teaching, Effective Departments: Findings from an HMI Survey of Subject Teaching in Secondary Schools 2000/01*, Ref. HMI 337, London: Ofsted.

Ofsted (Office for Standards in Education) (2003) *Secondary Initial Teacher Training: Secondary Physical Education Subject Inspection Reports, 1999-2003*, London: Ofsted.

Ofsted (Office for Standards in Education) (2009) *Physical Education in Schools 2005/08: Working towards 2012 and Beyond*, London: Ofsted.

Ofsted (Office for Standards in Education) (2010) *Safe Use of New Technologies*, London: Ofsted.

Okely, A. and Booth, M. (2004) Mastery of fundamental movement skills among children in New South Wales: prevalence and socio-demographic distribution, *Journal of Science and Medicine in Sport*, 7, 3: 358–72.

Pickup, I. (2012) The importance of primary physical education, in G. Griggs (ed.) *An Introduction to Primary Physical Education*, London: Routledge.

QCA (Qualifications and Curriculum Authority) (2003) *The Key Stage 3 National Strategy: Key Messages Pedagogy and Practice*, London: QCA.

QCA (Qualifications and Curriculum Authority) (2007a) *The National Curriculum for Physical Education*, London: QCA. Available at: http://www.education.gov.uk/schools/teachingandlearning/curriculum/secondary/b00198952/pe (accessed 2 July 2012).

QCA (Qualifications and Curriculum Authority) (2007b) *Physical Education Programme of Study for Key Stage 3 and Attainment Target*, London: QCA.

Raymond, C. (ed.) (1999) *Safety Across the Curriculum*, London: RoutledgeFalmer.

Rink, J.E. (2009) Investigating the assumptions of pedagogy, in R. Bailey and D. Kirk (eds) *The Routledge Physical Education Reader*, London: Routledge.

Robson, C. (2002) *Real World Research. A Resource for Social Scientists and Practitioner-Researchers*, 2nd edn, Oxford: Blackwell.

Roffey, S. (2011) *Changing Behaviour in Schools Promoting Positive Relationships and Well Being*, London: Sage.

Rogers, B. (2011). *Classroom Behaviour: A Practical Guide to Effective Teaching, Behaviour Management and Colleague Support*, London: Sage Publications.

Rose, C. (1985) *Accelerated Learning*, Aylesbury: Accelerated Learning Systems Ltd.

Schön, D. (1983) *The Reflective Practitioner: How Professionals Think in Action*, New York: Basic Books.

Sebba, J. and Sachdev, D. (1997) *What Works in Inclusive Education?* Ilford: Barnardos.

Severs, J., Whitlam, P. and Woodhouse, J. (2003) *Safety and Risk in Primary School Physical Education: A Guide for Teachers*, London: Routledge.

Shayer, M. (2003) Not just Piaget; not just Vygotsky, and certainly not Vygotsky as an alternative to Piaget, *Learning and Instruction*, 13: 465–85.

Shulman, L. (1987) Knowledge and teaching: foundations of the new reform, *Harvard Educational Review*, 57: 1–22.

Siedentop, D., Tousignant, M. and Parker, M. (1982) *Academic Learning Time: Physical Education Coaching Manual*, Columbus, OH: School of Health, Physical Education and Recreation

Siraj-Blatchford, J. and Siraj-Blatchford, I. (eds) (1998) *Educating the Whole Class: Cross Curricular Skills, Themes and Dimensions*, Buckingham: Open University Press.

Sportscoach UK (2004) *Sport Coaching in the UK; Final Report*, Leeds: Sportscoach UK.

Squires, J. (2002) *The Importance of Early Identification of Social and Emotional Difficulties in Preschool Children*, Center for International Rehabilitation.

Stenhouse, L. (1975) *An Introduction to Curriculum Research and Development*, London: Heinemann.

Stidder, G. and Capel, S. (2010) Using Information and Communications Technology to support learning and teaching in PE, in S. Capel and M. Whitehead (eds) *Learning to Teach Physical Education in the Secondary School: A Companion to School Experience*, 3rd edn, London: Routledge, pp. 183–96.

Stidder, G. and Hayes, S. (2011) Thematic learning and teaching through physical education, in G. Stidder and S. Hayes (eds) *The Really Useful Physical Education Book*, London: Routledge.

Stooksberry, L., Schussler, D. and Bercaw, L. (2009) Conceptualising dispositions: intellectual, cultural and moral domains of teaching, *Teachers and Teaching: Theory and Practice*, 15, 6: 719–36.

Taylor, C. (2011) *Getting the Simple Things Right: Charlie Taylor's Behaviour Checklists*. Available at: http://www.education.gov.uk (accessed 14 December 2012).

Verma, G. and Pumfrey, P. (1993) *Cross Curricular Contexts, Themes and Dimensions in Secondary Schools*, London: Falmer Press.

Vickerman, P. (2007) *Teaching Physical Education to Children with Special Educational Needs*, London: Routledge.

Vygotsky, L.S. (1978) *Mind in Society: The Development of Higher Psychological Processes*, Cambridge, MA: Harvard University Press.

Wertheimer, M. (2000) *Encyclopedia of Psychology* (Volume 8), Washington, DC: American Psychological Association.

Western Australia Education Department (2004) *Fundamental Movement Skills*, available at: http://www.det.wa.edu.au (accessed 22 October 2012).

Whitehead, M. (2000) Aims as an issue in physical education, in S. Capel and S. Piotrowski (eds) *Issues in Physical Education*, London: RoutledgeFalmer, pp. 7–21.

Whitehead, M. (2010a) Aims of PE, in S. Capel and M. Whitehead (eds) *Learning to Teach Physical Education in the Secondary School: A Companion to School Experience*, 3rd edn, London: Routledge, pp. 13–23.

Whitehead, M. (ed.) (2010b) *Physical Literacy: Throughout the Lifecourse.* London: Routledge. Available at: www.physical-literacy.org.uk (accessed 14 December 2012).

Whitehead, M. (2013) What is the education in physical education?, in S. Capel and M. Whitehead (eds) *Debates in Physical Education*, London: Routledge, pp. 22–36.

Whitehead, M. with Blair, R. (2010) Designing teaching approaches to achieve learning outcomes, in *Learning to Teach Physical Education in the Secondary School: A Companion to School Experience*, 3rd edn, London: Routledge, pp.154–68.

Whitehead, M., Capel, S., Wild, A. and Everley, S. (2010) National Curriculum 2007, in S. Capel and M. Whitehead (eds) *Learning to Teach Physical Education in the Secondary School: A Companion to School Experience*, 3rd edn, London: Routledge, pp. 197–216.

Whitehead, M. and Pack, K. (2010) Working with others to achieve the aims of PE, in S. Capel and M. Whitehead (eds) *Learning to Teach Physical Education in the Secondary School: A Companion to School Experience*, 3rd edn, London, Routledge, pp. 252–64.

Whitehead, M. and Woodhouse, J. (2010) Wider role of a PE teacher, in S. Capel and M. Whitehead (eds) *Learning to Teach Physical Education in the Secondary School: A Companion to School Experience*, 3rd edn, London: Routledge, pp. 217–33.

Whitlam, P. (2003) Risk management principles, in J. Severs, P. Whitlam, and J. Woodhouse (eds) *Safety and Risk in Primary School Physical Education: A Guide for Teachers*, London: Routledge.

Whitlam, P. (2005) *Case Law in Physical Education and School Sport*, Leeds: Coachwise Ltd.

Wilson, E. (2012) *School-based Research: A Guide for Education Students*, 2nd edn, London: Sage.

Zwozdiak-Myers, P. (2012) *The Teacher's Reflective Practice Handbook: Becoming an Extended Professional Through Capturing Evidence-Informed Practice*, London: Routledge.

Index

'A' (Advanced) Level examination 87
ability of pupils 27, 45, 54, 136, 189, 191, 195, 198, 206, 208, 236, 241, 243
academic learning time 153, 168
Academic Learning Time-Physical Education (ALT-PE) 146, 154–7, 261
accelerated learning 46
accessing the physical education curriculum 185–6
accidents 117–8, 124
accountability of teachers 101, 118
action research 1, 253–66
activities (in physical education) 1, 10–11, 16, 21–5, 27–8, 35–8, 41–3, 62, 72–5, 83, 91, 151, 168, 180–96, 207–8, 219; alternative 223–4, 228, 231; cooperative 36, 38, 87; extension 100, 189, 242; non-traditional 218; whole class 54, 58
activity: by pupils 73; time 58
adults other than teachers (AOTTS) 191, 211, 215–7
affective: domain 150, 215; outcomes 158–60, 162–3
afPE see Association for Physical Education
aims: curriculum 212; of physical education 1, 7–9, 11–13, 15–19, 26, 33–4, 91, 158, 227, 229, 232; of the school 33
ALT-PE see Academic Learning Time-Physical Education (ALT-PE)
AOTTS see adults other than teachers (AOTTS)
application of number 69–72, 74, 78; see also numeracy
apps (downloadable applications) 87–8
area of activity (in physical education) 34, 37, 39, 57, 80, 83–4, 105, 213
assessment 1, 15, 43–4, 46, 50, 153, 164, 189, 197–210, 219; criteria 197–202, 204, 206;

-driven curriculum 61; for learning (afl) 135, 144, 152, 197, 204, 209–10, 212, 234; formative 2, 50, 52, 58, 83–4, 197–8, 207, 209, 2011–13; ICT for 206–7; methods of 144; of learning (aol) 46, 197–8, 209; of lesson see evaluation; peer 197, 199, 204, 206–7, 209; resources for 197, 204, 206; self- 197, 199, 204, 206–7, 209; strategies 197, 199–201; summative 2, 50, 197–8, 209
Assessment Reform Group (ARG) 197–8, 207
Association for Physical Education (afPE) 102, 104–5, 109, 112, 115–6, 118, 122, 124, 136
attainment 42, 61, 83; levels of 61
attention: gaining pupils' 106, 170, 174
attitudes: of pupils to physical education 27; of teachers 20, 26; pupils' changing 158

BAALPE see British Association of Advisers and Lecturers in Physical Education (BAALPE)
background: of teacher 21
Bandura, A. 145
barriers to learning 160–96
behaviour 1, 133, 152, 166–79, 246; 2learn 166; for learning 166, 212; management 145; poor 166, 174, 244; positive pupil 1, 166–79
behaviourism (learning theory) 129–30, 132–3; see also learning theories
beliefs of teachers 20–1, 26, 28, 34, 158, 245
BERA see British Educational Research Association (BERA)
blogging sites 86
Bloom, B.S. (Taxonomy) 135, 150, 215
body language (of teacher) 165, 171, 176–7